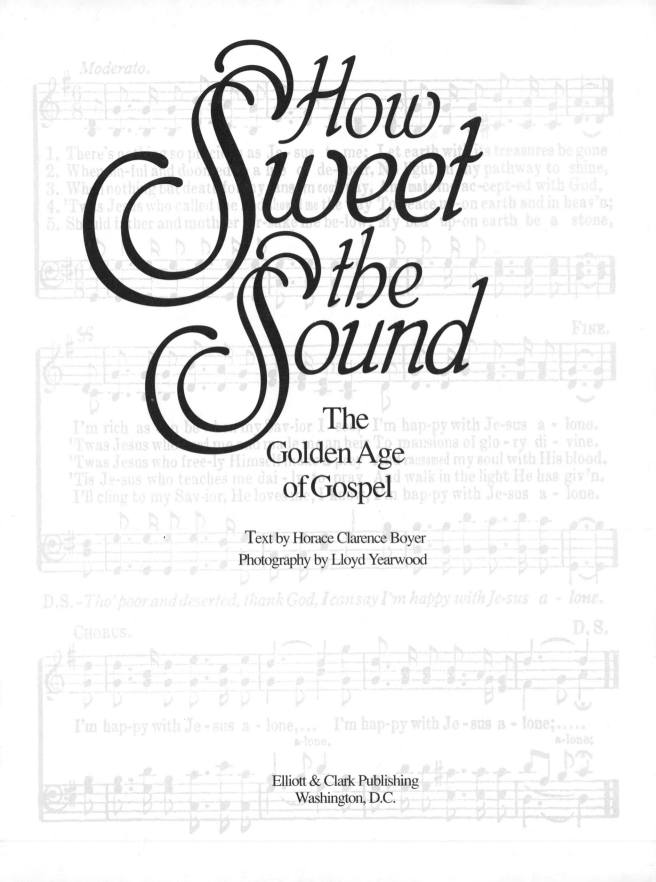

How Sweet the Sound

The Golden Age of Gospel

Text by Horace Clarence Boyer
Photography by Lloyd Yearwood

Elliott & Clark Publishing
Washington, D.C.

To my dear wife of thirty years, Gloria.
With heartfelt thanks to Eugene Smith and
my brother, James B. Boyer
—H.C.B.

Dedicated to my father Livingston Yearwood and
his deep concern for righteous living.
—L.Y.

Designed by Gibson Parsons Design
Edited by Maureen Graney
Printed in Hong Kong through Mandarin Offset

Any inquiries should be directed to:
Elliott & Clark Publishing, P.O. Box 21038, Washington, DC 20009-0538
Telephone (202) 387-9805

Table of Contents

AFRICAN AMERICAN SACRED FOLK MUSIC: 1755-1945 5

Early Sacred Singing 6
The Azusa Street Revival and the Birth of Pentecostalism 12
Pentecostal Ministers and Singers 18
Pentecostal Music Outside the Pentecostal Church 26
The Emergence of the Jubilee Quartet: The Jefferson County School 29
The Jubilee Quartet Movement Spreads 34
Church Singing Accompanied by Piano, Guitar, and Other Instruments 36
Gospel Pearls 41
Gospel Music on the Eve of the Golden Age 46

MOVE ON UP A LITTLE HIGHER: 1945-55 49

The Legacy of World War II: Radio and Recordings 51
Gospel on the Highways and Byways 54
Gospel in Chicago 57
Gospel in Philadelphia 103
Gospel in Detroit 123
Gospel in St. Louis 134
Gospel in Tennessee 138
Gospel in New York 152
Gospel Spreads across the Nation 169
The Gospel Choir 181
The Gospel Band 184

AND THE WALLS CAME TUMBLING DOWN: 1955-65 187

Gospel and the Traditions of African American Folk Music 193
The New and Newly Revised Gospel Quartets 195
The California School of Gospel 205
Piano-Accompanied Groups 212
Other Singers 240
Family Groups 241
The Second Gospel Triumvirate 247
Gospel on Broadway 250
Gospel Abroad 253
Deserters and Joiners 254

CONCLUSION: I LOOKED DOWN THE LINE AND I WONDERED: 1965 AND BEYOND 257

Bibliography 260
Index 264

The stars of the Ward Singers,
Clara Ward and Marion Williams

African American Sacred Folk Music: 1755–1945

In 1969 Edwin Hawkins, an Oakland, California, based pianist and choir director of the Church of God in Christ, reworked the nineteenth-century white Baptist hymn "O Happy Day" by Philip Doddridge (1702–51) and Edward Rimbault (1816–76). By placing the hymn in a bouncy tempo, emphasizing its inherent rhythmic possibilities with a drum set and congo drums, featuring the solo voice of a golden toned alto backed by a youthful-sounding energetic choir, and supporting the entire ensemble with piano accompaniment in a style that combined the harmonic variety of a Duke Ellington and the soulful accentuation of a Ray Charles, Hawkins (b. 1943) moved gospel into a new category. When the song was released on Buddah Records it quickly became number one on the Top Forty music chart, and gospel music, for more than sixty years the principal sacred music of many African American churches, became part of American popular music. Hawkins had synthesized not only what earlier great gospel musicians had developed but the entire sacred singing tradition of African Americans since they adopted Christianity, without which there would not be gospel music.

EARLY SACRED SINGING

While a small number of slaves worshipped with their masters or attended services especially arranged for them as early as the seventeenth century, a larger number of slaves were converted to Christianity during the Great Awakening, the first great religious movement in the United States. The Great Awakening began as early as 1734 in New England (although reports of evangelical preaching in New Jersey surfaced in the 1720s). The leader of the New England movement, Jonathan Edwards (1703–58), was a forceful preacher who espoused logic, humility, and absolute dependence on God and divine grace, which alone could save a person. The fervent zeal Edwards demanded of his followers required a much livelier music than the slow, languorous long-meter hymns that were traditional. The music produced by the Great Awakening was the hymns that used text by such hymnists as Isaac Watts (1674–1748), whose significant publications include *Hymns and Spiritual Songs* (1707) and *The Psalms of David, Imitated in the Language of the New Testament and Apply'd to the Christian State and Worship* (1717); John Wesley (1703–91), who with his brother Charles (1707–88), founded the Methodist church in 1729 and who published *Collection of Psalms and Hymns* (1737) and *Hymns and Sacred Poems* (1739); and George Whitefield (1714–70), who published *A Collection of Hymns for Social Worship* (1753; 1765).

None were more eloquent in their hymns than Watts, who, for his 1707 publication of *Hymns and Spiritual Songs,* wrote:

> *Come, Holy Spirit, heavenly dove,*
> *With all Thy quickening powers;*
> *Kindle a flame of sacred love*
> *In these cold hearts of ours.*

Although mostly a New England and eastern religious movement, the fervor of the Great Awakening overtook the entire United States and had a profound effect on southern states, where attending church, reading the Bible, singing hymns, and a comportment of piety became the mark of a Christian. Slaves were permitted to attend these services with their masters, although they were seated in separate sections. Some slave owners arranged special services for their slaves during which the white minister who preached to slave owners in the morning would preach to the slaves in the afternoon. Although the slaves sang like their masters when they attended services with them, reports of slaves singing sacred music independently began to surface in the 1750s. One of the earliest reports was based on letters sent in 1755 to church members in London by the Reverend Samuel Davies (1723–61), in which he comments on the singing of slaves in Virginia:

> *The books were all very acceptable, but none more so than the Psalms and Hymns, which enable them [the slaves] to gratify their peculiar taste for psalmody. Sundry of them have lodged all night in my kitchen, and sometimes when I have awaked about two or three-o'clock in the morning, a torrent of sacred harmony has poured into my chamber and carried my mind away to heaven. In this seraphic exercise some of them spend almost the whole night.*

The slaves were likely singing from one of the books of the Reverend Dr. Watts or from Wesley's 1737 hymn book. The style of singing would have been "lining out," a practice established in the United States in the 1640s. Adopted from the Church of England, this practice featured a song leader (precentor), minister, or church clerk singing (or reciting) each line of the hymn, immediately followed by the singing of the line by the congregation:

> *Leader: Praise God, from whom all blessings flow;*
> **Congregation: Praise God, from whom all blessings flow;**
> *Leader: Praise Him all creatures here below;*
> **Congregation: Praise Him all creatures here below;**
> *Leader: Praise Him above ye heavenly host;*
> **Congregation: Praise Him above ye heavenly host;**
> *Leader: Praise Father, Son, and Holy Ghost.*
> **Congregation: Praise Father, Son, and Holy Ghost.**

Among the slaves, lining out was called "raising" a hymn. The hymn would be raised by a minister ("exhorter" in slave language) or a devout male member of the community (who would later be called a deacon in the Baptist church or a steward in the Methodist church). Instead of singing the lines of the hymns as they were written or reciting them in an oratorical manner, the leader would chant the lines, often chanting two lines at a time to a tune unrelated to the tune the congregation would sing. The congregation then sang the lines, decorating them with bends, slurs, slides, and held tones. The congregation would match or surpass the leader in ornamentation, although such songs were sung in a harmony composed of parallel intervals. This ancient style of harmony was reminiscent of that practiced in Western Europe during the ninth century.

The African American Methodist church replaced these hymns with standard Protestant hymns. However, raising hymns continued in the African American Baptist church, and the song type and genre are known today as Baptist lining hymns.

Around the turn of the nineteenth century, a new type of song entered the repertoire of African American sacred music. This new music was inspired by the second great religious movement in the United States. Variously called the Second Great Awakening, the Camp Meeting Revival, and the Revival Movement, this movement began in 1800 in Logan County, Kentucky. (However, reports show that its earliest activities date back to 1780.) According to Richard M'Near who chronicled the 1800 and 1801 services in the *Kentucky Revival* (1808):

A gospel concert flyer

> *Neither was there any distinction as to age, sex, color, or anything of temporary nature; old and young, male and female, black and white, has equal opportunity to minister the light which they received in whatever way the spirit directed.*

These nineteenth-century services, according to M'Near, encouraged singing, shouting, and leaping for joy. The music that promoted such behavior was the newer hymns with a certain "lilt and rhythm" and shaped-note melodies. Among the most popular of the revival hymnals were *Repository of Sacred, Part Second* (1813) by John Wyeth (1770–1858), *Village Hymns for Social Worship* (1824) by Asahel Nettleton (1783–1844), and *Spiritual Songs for Social Worship* (1831; 1833) by Lowell Mason (1792–1872) and Thomas Hastings (1787–1872).

According to John Fanning Watson, who published *Methodist Error or Friendly Christian Advice to Those Methodists Who Indulge in Extravagant Religious Emotions and Bodily Exercises* (1819), slaves would gather in their quarters at these meetings and:

> *sing for hours together, short scraps of disjointed affirmations, pledges, or prayers, lengthened out with long repetition choruses.*

Often unified by the inclusion of the word "hallelujah," these songs became known as camp meeting spirituals. William Frances Allen and colleagues recorded the following camp meeting spiritual in the 1867 publication *Slave Songs of the United States*:

> *What ship is that you're enlisted upon?*
> *O glory hallelujah!*
> *Tis the old ship of Zion, hallelujah!*
> *Tis the old ship of Zion, hallelujah!*

These songs were obviously set to a marching or sprightly tempo because Watson noted that:

> *With every word so sung, they have a sinking of one or other leg of the body alternately; producing an audible sound of the feet at every step, and as manifest as the steps of actual negro [sic] dancing in Virginia, etc.*

This stamping was called "shouting," a term used exclusively for this holy dancing, whether singly or with a group. In most instances such dancing was performed in a circle and has come to be known as the "ring shout." It is worth noting that the slaves did not shout with their voices but rather with their feet, reserving the voice for hollering or yelling. While African Americans may certainly have accompanied their sacred singing with body rhythm before the observation of the shout, singing in the African American church would henceforth include rocking or moving in time to the singing. The group shout did not continue long after the turn of the twentieth century, although according to James Weldon Johnson in the preface to his 1925 edition of *American Negro spirituals*, secret shout services were still being held in the first decade of this century.

The Camp Meeting Revival may have inspired other musical creations among the slaves, because shortly after the opening of this movement, a different type of spiritual surfaced in the slave community. Unlike the camp meeting spiritual with its emphasis on scriptural passages and praising God, the new music took on an extremely personal character. These religious folksongs, called Negro spirituals, not only spoke of the slaves' relationship to God but also gave special attention to their position on earth and the difficult fate that had befallen them. The songs combined a recognition of the power of God and thanks for life, health, and strength, but more important they expressed the slaves' feelings about oppression, discrimination, and the struggle to survive. As such, references to sorrows, woes, hard trials, and the rewards they expected to receive in the next world were common themes. This is nowhere more poignantly expressed than in:

> *Nobody knows the trouble I see,*
> *Nobody knows my sorrow;*
> *Nobody knows the trouble I see,*
> *Glory, hallelujah.*

When life was extremely difficult for slaves they used these songs to inspire inner courage, for they had decided that freedom would come one day, either through emancipation or death:

> *Steal away, steal away,*
> *Steal away to Jesus;*
> *Steal away, steal away home,*
> *I ain't got long to stay here.*

So convinced were the slaves that they would be rewarded eventually for their trials on earth that they imagined what heaven would be like:

> *Plenty good room, plenty good room*
> *Good room in my father's kingdom;*
> *Plenty good room, plenty good room*
> *Just choose your seat and sit down.*

Feeling that they had no black heroes in the Bible and obviously unaware of other contemporary people who might be experiencing a similar slavery, the slaves adopted Old Testament heroes and celebrated them in song, often replacing the Israelites with themselves. Moses became the abolitionist and Pharaoh became the slave owner in:

> *Go down, Moses, way down in Egypt's land,*
> *Tell old Pharaoh to let my people go.*

"Joshua Fit [Fought] the Battle of Jericho," "Ezekiel Saw the Wheel," "Rock My Soul in the Bosom of Abraham," and "We Are Climbing Jacob's Ladder" are but a few of such songs. These heroes were often used to make direct supplication to God:

> *Didn't my Lord deliver Daniel?*
> *Deliver Daniel, deliver Daniel?*
> *Didn't my Lord deliver Daniel?*
> *Then why not deliver poor me?*

When slaves finally had a strong feeling that earthly freedom would eventually be theirs, especially around the middle of the nineteenth century, songs of celebration expressed their anticipation:

> *In that great gettin' up morning,*
> *Fare ye well, fare ye well;*
> *In that great gettin' up morning,*
> *Fare ye well, fare ye well.*

It was not the sophistication of the text nor the brilliance of the melody and harmony of these songs, most often consisting of a verse and chorus, that so inspired the slaves and caused wonderment among white listeners. Rather it was the release and satisfaction that the songs brought to the singer. Melodies had only a few tones, often as few as five, and were laden with blue (or flatted) notes that would later serve as one of the principal elements of the blues. Harmonies were those of Protestant hymns, but rhythms were the intricate patterns remembered from Africa. Singers made no pretense of placing the voice "in the head," as was the practice of European singing masters, but chose the voice of those "crying in the wilderness." While there were songs in which text was sung by everyone at the same time, the most characteristic practice was to divide the song into a part for the leader and a part for the other singers:

> *Leader: Have you got good religion?*
> ***Others: Certainly, Lord,***
> *Leader: Have you got good religion?*
> ***Others: Certainly, Lord,***

> *Leader: Have you got good religion?*
>
> ***Others: Certainly, Lord, certainly, certainly, certainly, Lord.***

The part taken by the leader was later named the "call," while that taken by the other singers was labeled the "response."

While it is known that these songs were used in work, religious meetings, and times of leisure as well as for teaching young and old the stories of the Bible and the values of the slave community, it is unknown exactly how and when they were composed. William Frances Allen, in *Slave Songs of the United States* (1867), reported the often quoted account given by a former slave:

> *My master call me up, and order me a short peck of corn and a hundred lash. My friends see it, and is sorry for me. When dey come to de praise-meeting dat night dey sing about it. Some's very good singers and know how; and dey work it in—work it in, you know, till they get it right; and dat's de way.*

Eileen Southern, author of *Black American Music: A History* (1983), supports the belief that many of these songs might have been composed first by congregations in northern African American churches. These congregations used the *sense* of some of the Protestant hymns and reworked the text to fit their needs but supplied original melody and harmony. In either case, the Negro spiritual not only shaped the composition and singing style of African American sacred music, but also became the first music considered "American" by people outside the United States.

THE AZUSA STREET REVIVAL
AND THE BIRTH OF PENTECOSTALISM

There was no great religious movement at the beginning of the twentieth century on the eastern seaboard, but California witnessed a series of religious meetings unlike any ever held before in the United States. This movement was called the Azusa Street Movement or Azusa Street Revival for the street where the church meetings were held.

A revival is a series of consecutive nightly church services for which, in most cases, a well known minister is brought in to preach and to provide religious counseling for church members or those seeking conversion from sin. Special choirs or singing groups are sometimes imported, or the resident church choir provides music for each service. Since the services are designed to revive the current membership and attract new members, one of the important features of the revival is the "altar call." During this part of the service, those who have decided to join the church or seek membership through counseling or instruction come to the altar or, in sanctuaries where there is no altar, to the railing that would normally enclose the altar and kneel or stand to be welcomed by the visiting minister and the resident preacher. In earlier days specific benches or chairs ("mourners' benches") were provided where those seeking membership would sit. (Such seats were always located in the front of the church very near the pulpit or lectern, close to the preacher.) Most revivals are held for only one week, although some congregations hold two-week revivals. A nightly collection is taken in order to pay the preacher for his service.

The Azusa Street Revival, however, differed from previous revivals in four very important ways: the movement was initiated by and for African Americans; the principal element of becoming "saved, sanctified, and filled with the Holy Ghost" depended on the experience of "speaking in tongues"; African Americans invited white people into the service and insisted on complete interracial participation; and the principal music produced by the revival reflected African American religious concerns and musical sensibilities.

Although the 1906 Azusa Street Revival was initially a series of services by and for African Americans, the seeds of the revival were planted as early as 1867 when a small group of white Methodists, seeking a perfect relationship with Christ, organized the National Camp Meeting Association for the Promotion of Holiness with the goal of discovering "spiritual perfection." The zeal of this Holiness faction soon embarrassed and antagonized the larger body of Methodists. By 1903 Charles Parham (1873–1929), a leading minister in the faction, opened a Bible school in Houston to teach the tenets of this new theology. Despite the complete segregation of Parham's classes and religious services (African Americans had to sit outside the classroom and at the back of the room or outdoors at services), the new theology began to attract a few African Americans. One of the first was William Joseph Seymour (1870–1922), who learned of Parham's work from the Reverend Mrs. Lucy F. Farrow, an African American minister of the Holiness church.

In 1906 Neely Terry, who met Seymour while he was studying with Parham, contacted Seymour and asked him to come to Los Angeles to serve as pastor of her twenty-member congregation of Holiness members. The invitation came at a time when there was a very small network of African Americans who believed in the Holiness movement. The Baptist and Methodist churches had served the needs of African Americans as far back as slavery, and by the turn of the century when these congregations were constructing their own church buildings and calling ministers from throughout the United States to serve as their pastors, it was not unusual for a Holiness preacher to relocate to a city thousands of miles away if he or she could minister to a faithful flock. The social situation in the South also contributed to physical movement. The Ku Klux Klan was conducting its night rides throughout the South, Jim Crow laws or practices were already in place in several towns, and the North, Midwest, and West were being touted as places where African Americans could find equality. These factors must have impressed Seymour for he accepted Neely's invitation.

When he arrived in Los Angeles (either in late February or early March of 1906), he preached Holiness and divine healing. Seymour was accepted with enthusiasm and gratitude by his small flock. His popularity began to spread in Los Angeles, which inspired him to introduce a doctrine in which he had long believed: baptism with the Holy Ghost, manifested by speaking in tongues. His belief was based on the description of Pentecost in Acts 2:4, which describes the activities of Christ's disciples fifty days after the Crucifixion when the Holy Ghost descended upon a gathering in the form of tongues of fire accompanied by the sound of the wind "rushing." Everyone present received the power to speak in a language understood by each member of the multilingual crowd. In the modern version of speaking in tongues, or glossolalia, the language is unknown, except to one or more of the group anointed to translate the message.

Seymour began a series of sermons that addressed this tenet. On April 9, 1906, he found a true believer with the manifested sanctification of Jennie Evans (1893–1936). Jennie Evans, whom Seymour married in 1908, had "come through"—she had been saved, sanctified, and filled with the Holy Ghost. She was saved when she made a conscious decision to lay aside "every weight that so easily beset" humans and to serve the Lord, treat her fellow human beings as children of God, pray constantly, and walk in a path that would lead to heaven after death. She became sanctified when she chose to consecrate herself and live free from sin (or at least to make a great effort to do so). And she was filled with the Holy Ghost when her relationship to God and Jesus reached such a point of ecstasy that she was able to allow the Lord to speak through her in a tongue that has never been translatable. This incident was not the first time that speaking in tongues had been practiced (J. T. Nichols, in the book *Black Pentecostalism* (1982), reported that this phenomenon was quite common among those who "received the fire.") However, this was the first entire church doctrine that was based on speaking in tongues as proof that one had received the Holy Ghost.

Word of Jennie Evans' "coming through" spread quickly throughout Los Angeles and then to other parts of the United States. Crowds flocked to Seymour's church, the Apostolic Faith Gospel Mission, located at 312 Azusa Street, with people "falling under the spell of the Holy Ghost" in great numbers. *The Apostolic Faith*, a newspaper published by Seymour and his congregation, carried such headlines as "Los Angeles Being Visited by a Revival of Bible Salvation and Pentecost as Recorded in the Book of Acts" and "The Promised Latter Rain Now Being Poured Out on God's People."

1906 edition of The Apostolic Faith

While Seymour used the word "apostolic" in the name of his church, he considered himself and his congregation Pentecostal, distinct from Holiness congregations that did not believe that tongue speaking was necessary for entry into heaven. Pentecostalists also shouted (a holy dance, mentioned in Psalm 149:3), indulged in the act of humility (washed one another's feet, based on John 13:5), and experienced visions and trances. Such was the character of the services of the Azusa Street Revival.

It is ironic that while the African Americans of the Azusa Street Revival invited white people into the revival and treated them as religious equals, social racism eventually split the group into black and white congregations. Parham, a white man, had been Seymour's teacher and mentor. However, although Parham believed in sanctification, he did not like the emotionalism associated with speaking in tongues and would not advocate it in his preaching. Parham and many of the white attendees withdrew in 1908, and Parham participated in the formation of the white Pentecostal congregation, the Assemblies of God, founded in Hot Springs, Arkansas, in 1914.

While the theology and practices of the Azusa Street Revival were new, they were in no way comparable with the unique music that accompanied these services. As members of the congregation "came through," they would celebrate their victory with a song. The congregation witnessed singing in tongues, much of which was never translated into English. *The Apostolic Faith* of September 1906 carried an article entitled "Holy Ghost Singing." The article stated that a song in an unknown tongue was interpreted as follows:

> *With one accord, all heaven rings*
> *With praises to our God and King*
> *Let earth join in our song of praise*
> *And ring it out through all the days.*

Beginning in the last quarter of the nineteenth century, white composers began publishing gospel hymns that were strictly organized with eight bars to the verse and eight bars to the chorus. The melodies were simple but attractive, and the rhythms were marked by an abundance of dotted eighth notes. Perhaps the most interesting aspect of these hymns was the pairing of soprano and alto against tenor and bass, with the female voices singing alternately with the male voices. But these hymns—always sung with the same notes, chords, and rhythms—contained no provisions for the improvisation so much a part of the African American musical style. Also, they did not contain the all important altered scale degrees and intricate rhythms that separate gospel hymns from the gospel songs sung in the African American congregations. One gospel hymn that was extremely popular during the revival was "In the Sweet By and By" by J. P. Webster (1819–75). The song is concerned with an overwhelming desire to go to heaven and be with the Lord, because once a person received the gift of the Holy Spirit, there was nothing more to seek on this earth. Among other popular Protestant hymns sung at the revival were those of Ira David Sankey (1840–1909), composer of "A Shelter in the Time of a Storm," and William Howard Doane (1832–1915), composer of "What a Friend We Have in Jesus" and "Pass Me Not O Gentle Savior."

Negro spirituals were often sung during the more emotional parts of the services. Songs that carried the message of a reward in heaven were especially favored for the shout:

> Get on board, little children
> Get on board, little children
> Get on board, little children
> There's room for many-a more.

"On board," a variation of "aboard," refers here to accepting Christ and the new religion by stepping onto the gospel train. During the slave era "get on board" would have meant to run away or would have been a call for help in the resistance effort. The last line of this song refers to "good room in my Father's kingdom"—the reward.

None of these songs, however, evoked the passion and frenzy produced by songs composed "under the spirit." Such songs usually consisted of one or two lines of poetry, a melody of only three or four tones, and harmonies as simple as those of a basic blues; they were delivered with a rhythm of both intricacy and complexity. These songs were led by soloists who had never considered studying voice and who, in most cases, neither read music nor gave much care to diction and articulation. But like the singers of the Negro spirituals of a century earlier, they sang with such power and conviction that their singing became as much of an attraction to the services and the religion as were the doctrine and practice. Often possessing voices that could be described as gravelly, whiny, or pinched, these singers nonetheless introduced a style of singing marked by a sincerity that was uncommon for the times.

Most of the songs composed spontaneously had no verse or contrasting section, but had a refrain in which the lead line would change with each call, while the congregation remained constant in its response:

> Leader: Latter rain is falling
>   **Congregation: Falling from on high,**
> Leader: Latter rain is falling
>   **Congregation: Falling from on high.**
>
> Leader: It's falling with power
>   **Congregation: Falling from on high,**

> *Leader: Mighty, mighty power*
> **Congregation: Falling from on high.**
>
> *Leader: Holy Ghost is falling*
> **Congregation: Falling from on high,**
> *Leader: Holy Ghost is falling*
> **Congregation: Falling from on high.**

Some of the songs requested the gift of the Holy Spirit:

> *Leader: Power*
> **Congregation: Power, Lord**
> *Leader: Power*
> **Congregation: Power, Lord.**
>
> *Leader: We need your power*
> **Congregation: Power, Lord**
> *Leader: We need your power*
> **Congregation: Power, Lord.**
>
> *Leader: Holy Ghost power*
> **Congregation: Power, Lord**
> *Leader: Holy Ghost power*
> **Congregation: Power, Lord.**

When the spirit was especially high, the congregation would respond to these songs by shaking their heads, swaying their bodies, clapping their hands, tapping or stomping their feet, and interjecting individual tonal and rhythmic improvisations onto an already rich palette of sound. The song leaders were the ministers, preachers, or singers whose authoritative voices were developed out of the necessity to cut through the responsive singing, clapping, stamping, and shouting of large congregations.

PENTECOSTAL MINISTERS AND SINGERS

By the 1930s Pentecostalism had become entrenched in the African American community not only by those who felt the Baptist and Methodist denominations to be inadequate but also by those who found traditional religion insufficient for their spiritual desires and needs. Despite protest and ridicule from the Baptists and Methodists—or perhaps because of it—Pentecostal denominations separated themselves from the Baptists and Methodists and created a service style, music, language, behavior, dress, and an attitude about their place among Christians. "Heaven or Hell" became their principal preachment.

Gospel music was selected as the illuminating force behind this theology and developed over all other types of sacred music. When hymns were sung by these congregations they were "gospelized." Services were nothing less than ecstatic with forceful and jubilant singing, dramatic testimonies, hand clapping, foot stamping, and beating of drums, tambourines, and triangles (and pots, pans, and washboards when professional instruments were not available). When a piano could be begged, borrowed, or bought, a barrelhouse accompaniment served to bring the spirit to earth. It was not uncommon for a shouting session to last for thirty or forty-five minutes, with women fainting and falling to the floor (where they would sometimes lie for twenty or thirty minutes) and men leaping as if they were executing a physical exercise or running around the church several times.

Members of these congregations addressed each other as "sister" (woman) and "brother" (man) and were collectively known as "saints." They greeted each other with a "holy" kiss and flavored their conversation with such phrases as "praise the Lord," "hallelujah," and "thank God." They found scriptures that supported a subdued style of dressing for women so that their arms, legs, and heads would be covered at all times. Congregation members were easily recognizable because the sisters wore long skirts long after they had passed from fashion; a dark suit, white shirt, and dark tie identified the brothers. They were never seen in places where many other Christians were seen: bars, theaters, movie houses, dances, parties, community picnics, or locations for "hanging out." Because they felt that they had found the one true way of connecting with the Supreme Being, they reduced their association with other Christians, often refusing to attend services at other churches or join other churches in ecumenical services. This behavior was perceived by some other Christians as a show of superiority or exclusivity. Strangely, this did not deter the other Christians from attending Pentecostal services (mainly to hear the singing and the preaching), although in many cases these services were viewed as a show and Monday mornings were filled with comments about who "shouted the longest at the sanctified church last night." Despite the levity at the expense of the "saints," people returned to hear the new gospel music. It was not long before some of the same people who first found the services comical found themselves shouting and singing gospel.

Any discussion of the first group of minister-singers influenced by the Azusa Street Revival would necessarily begin with Charles Price Jones and Charles Harrison Mason. Jones (1865–1949) was born in Texas Valley (near Rome), Georgia, and reared in Kingston, located between Rome and Atlanta. His mother died when he was seventeen, and thereafter he wandered throughout Mississippi, Arkansas, Tennessee, and Oklahoma. He was self-taught and began preaching in 1885. In 1887 he settled for a short time in Cat Island, Arkansas. There he was licensed to preach in the Baptist church. Soon afterward he entered the Arkansas Baptist College at Little Rock, and after his graduation in 1891, taught for a short period. He later accepted the pastorate of several small churches. While serving as the minister of the Tabernacle Baptist Church (the college church) in Selma, Alabama, Jones found himself in need of a deeper experience of grace. After fasting and praying for three days and nights, Jones accepted sanctification—that is, he decided to live free from sin. On a trip to Jackson, Mississippi, in 1894, he came under the influence of the Holiness movement and consciously decided to serve the Lord.

Joining with other ministers of the Baptist denomination who were attracted to Holiness, Jones called a Holiness convention on June 6, 1897, in Jackson. Among those present were W. S. Pleasant, J. A. Jeter, and Charles Harrison Mason. During the next convention in 1898, this Holiness faction decided to change the name of the principal church within their faction from the Mt. Helm Baptist Church to the Church of Christ. They were sued by the Baptist Association and dismissed from the communion. They held their first independent convention in Lexington, Mississippi, in 1899.

When word of the Azusa Street Revival came to the members of the Holiness convention in 1906, the group decided to attend. Jones did not attend the Azusa Street Revival himself but supported the visit of the church representatives Mason, Jeter, and D. J. Young. After these three returned to Mississippi, Jones and Mason could not agree on the interpretation of some of the scriptures that served as the basis of the revival, and the two separated. Half the group sided with Jones, who immediately organized the Church of Christ (Holiness); the other half sided with Mason, who organized the Church of God in Christ.

Jones was a self-taught but prolific composer of songs for his congregation, composing more than a thousand songs. He began publishing in 1899 with his hymnal, *Jesus Only*. This was followed with *Jesus Only, Nos. 1 and 2* (1901), *His Fullness* (1906), and *Sweet Selections* and *His Fullness Enlarged* (also 1906). The first official hymnal for the congregation, *Jesus Only Songs and His Fullness Songs*, was published in 1940. Among his most popular compositions are "I'm Happy with Jesus Alone," "Where Shall I Be when the First Trumpet Sounds," and "Jesus Only."

Jones's compositions are unique in early gospel because they cut through much of the rhetoric of late nineteenth- and early twentieth-century hymn writing. His songs move directly to the feelings and expressions of a group of people who, even after having been freed from slavery *by law*, still find no possible solution to problems on this earth, but who dismiss this earth and turn to the one still believable source of recompense: God in Christ. His attitude toward religion and the earthly life is eloquently expressed in his most famous composition, "I'm Happy with Jesus Alone":

VERSE
There's nothing so precious as Jesus to me,
Let earth with its treasures be gone;
I'm rich as can be when my Savior I see,
I'm happy with Jesus alone.

CHORUS
I'm happy with Jesus alone,
I'm happy with Jesus alone;
Tho' poor and deserted, thank God, I can say
I'm happy with Jesus alone.

Jones earned a respected position in gospel music. He was clearly the leader of one of the most respected Holiness groups in the South, and he was the first composer of gospel music to write for members of the Seymour movement. However, Jones based his entire doctrine on the New Testament in which no instruments are mentioned in the worship of Jesus. For this reason Jones felt that instruments were unnecessary in his services, even though as gospel has developed, the piano has become the principal accompanying instrument. Although the congregations of the Church of Christ (Holiness) sang with enthusiasm, they used no instrumental accompaniment and discouraged excessive emotion. These congregations have not produced any professional gospel singers. Yet considering the number of Jones' compositions in traditional piano-accompanied gospel singers' repertoires, he is secure in his position as one of the pioneering composers of this music.

"I'm Happy with Jesus Alone" by Charles Price Jones

Charles Harrison Mason (1866–1961) was born in Prior Farm (near Memphis), Tennessee. He was educated in the public schools of Memphis, although his attendance at school was infrequent. In 1878, when Mason was twelve years old, the family moved to Plumbersville, Arkansas. A prolonged and intense fever overtook him in 1880, and after a miraculous recovery he was converted and baptized in the Mt. Olive Baptist Church near Plumbersville, where his brother was the pastor. He preached his first sermon in 1893 and immediately entered the Arkansas Baptist College. He remained there for only three months, then left to become a traveling evangelist.

Mason met Jones in 1895 and joined his small body of Baptist ministers who were seeking a greater spiritual involvement than the Baptists offered. At the insistence of this small body of Holiness believers, Mason attended the Azusa Street Revival and remained there for approximately five weeks. He spoke in tongues and thereby received the Holy Ghost in March 1907. Later that year he settled in Memphis, where he began a series of services that attracted a large following. After the dispute with Jones over doctrinal issues, which resulted in each minister founding his own congregation, the two founders worked together only intermittently. Mason was elected overseer (later bishop) of his denomination, the Church of God in Christ. By 1934 the denomination had a membership of 25,000; in 1971 the membership was listed as 425,000, and reached a total of five million members by the early

1990s. COGIC, as it is called, is now the largest predominately black Pentecostal church in the world.

Mason was not a musician but a preacher who felt the need to stir his congregations with thematic songs at crucial moments in the service or sermon. He never personally published his songs, even though during his long life he composed many and led his congregations in song fests. His songs were not written down until the first denominational hymnal, *Yes, Lord!*, was published in 1982.

Mason contributed two significant compositions to Pentecostalism and eventually to the African American church. The most popular is the shout song, "I'm a Soldier in the Army of the Lord." The other is "Yes, Lord," also known as COGIC chant because of its limited number of tones, unpulsed tempo, and simple harmonies. The chant became so popular in the 1970s that most gospel singers ended an extremely fast shout song with:

> *Yes, Lord, Yes, Lord*
> *Yes, Lord, Yes, Lord*
> *Yes, Lord, Yes, Lord.*
>
> *We need your help, we need your help*
> *We need your help, we need your help*
> *We need your help, we need your help.*

"I'm a Soldier" likewise became so popular that it moved into the folk music repertoire, and by the time of its publication in 1982, was sung by both African American Christian congregations and gospel singers:

> *Leader: I'm a soldier*
> **Congregation: In the army of the Lord,**
> *Leader: I'm a soldier*
> **Congregation: In the army.**
>
> *Leader: I'm a sanctified soldier*
> **Congregation: In the army of the Lord,**
> *Leader: I'm a sanctified soldier*
> **Congregation: In the army.**

Leader: The Holy Spirit is my rifle
Congregation: In the army of the Lord
Leader: The Holy Spirit is my rifle
Congregation: In the army.

Mason exerted a strong influence on the development of gospel music by encouraging its performance at his services and among his congregations. He learned church music and structure in the Baptist church, where two deacons would lead the Baptist lining hymns and the congregation would sing them, alternating songs with prayers. While in the COGIC, Mason fashioned a service in which each member of the congregation was encouraged to lead the other members of the congregation in a song. Even new communicants who had not sung in public were expected to lead songs as soon as they were "saved." This song was followed by a testimony, which was an elaborate statement of thanks for life, health, strength, a job, spouse, child, and family—interspersed with stories of having overcome serious trials—that ended with a plea for all who "know the worth of prayer" to pray for him or her.

At the conclusion of the testimony another singer would lead a song followed by another testimony. The responsibility of each member to lead songs resulted in the development of strong singers throughout the congregation. Familiar Pentecostal shout songs ("I'm a Soldier in the Army of the Lord," "Power, Lord," and so on), along with gospelized standard Protestant hymns, became the repertoire of the congregation. While there was no overt competition among the singers, early on those singers who were able to ignite the congregation into a shout became congregational celebrities. They were singled out and called on to sing a solo or sing with each other during special parts of the service (before the sermon, during the offering, and so on). It was in this manner that a style of singing, first conceived in Los Angeles, developed in such southern cities as Memphis, Jackson, and Little Rock. Performers of gospel music from COGIC would eventually include such luminaries as Sister Rosetta Tharpe, Andrae Crouch, Walter and Edwin Hawkins, the O'Neal Twins, the Banks Brothers, the Boyer Brothers, and Vanessa Bell Armstrong.

Of the thousands who traveled to California, hoards were from the East Coast and brought the message and the music back with them. Among the Pentecostal denominations founded as a result of the Azusa Street Revival were the Church of the Living God; the Pillar and Ground of the Truth, founded by Mary L. Ester Tate (1871–1930); the Triumph Church and King of God in Christ, founded by Elias Dempsey Smith (c.1872–1908); the Church of the Living God, founded by William Christian (1856–1928); and the Church of God and Saints in Christ, founded by William Saunders Crowdy (1847–1908). The shout music of the Azusa Street Revival became the principal music of these congregations. Elder D. C. Rice (1880–c.1950) was a well-known Pentecostal minister from Alabama who recorded several of the songs sung during Pentecostal worship. Two of his most famous recordings are "Testify," in which he is accompanied by his congregation and a trombone and "I'm in the Battlefield for My Lord," in which he is accompanied by trumpet. All instruments were employed during his services.

In addition to Jones and Mason, two other Pentecostal ministers figured prominently in the development of gospel, although neither was a composer. They were Samuel Kelsey (1906–93) and Smallwood Edmond Williams (1907–92). Kelsey, born in Sandville, Georgia, received the Holy Ghost in 1915 and began preaching at the age of seventeen. After an association with the Pentecostal denomination called the First Born Church of the Living God, he joined COGIC in 1923. He moved to Washington, D.C., and founded the Temple Church of God in Christ where he not only encouraged gospel music within his congregation but also used his church as a performance venue for traveling gospel singers. Kelsey became a celebrity in 1947 when his recording of the gospelized spiritual "Little Boy," an elaboration of the story of Jesus preaching in the temple, became a gospel music hit.

Williams was even more dedicated to receiving traveling gospel singers than Kelsey. A native of Lynchburg, Virginia, he came to the Pentecostal church through a denomination known as the Church of Our Lord Jesus Christ of the Apostolic Faith, an organization in the direct apostolic line of Seymour and Robert Clarence Lawson (1883–1961). Lawson, from New Iberia, Louisiana, settled in Indianapolis in 1913 and came under the influence of Garfield Thomas Haywood (1880–1931), who championed Seymour's denomination. Lawson eventually moved to New York City where in 1919 he established the Refuge Church of Our Lord Jesus Christ of the Apostolic Faith. The Refuge Church became one of the principal performance venues for gospel music in New York City. Williams moved to Washington, D.C., in the early

1920s and founded the Bible Way Church of Our Lord Jesus Christ of the Apostolic Faith. Williams' daughter, Pearl Williams Jones, became a leading gospel singer, pianist, and scholar of the 1960s.

PENTECOSTAL MUSIC
OUTSIDE THE PENTECOSTAL CHURCH

While most of the new music was being created and performed in Pentecostal churches of the Deep South, African Americans were leaving the South daily to find better jobs, cleaner houses, safer neighborhoods, and greater opportunities for their children. Wherever they went they took the music with them and introduced it into their new community. Beginning with the Great Migration immediately following the Emancipation Proclamation in 1863, African Americans began settling just north of the Deep South, or moving into the Midwest. Some traveled only as far north as Virginia, while others settled in Pennsylvania, New Jersey, and New York. Other routes that were followed were from Mississippi to Chicago and Arkansas and Texas to California.

This influx of African Americans from the Deep South inspired several composers to attempt to capture the fervor, energy, and anxiety of southern Christians' "old time religion" in song. Perhaps the first of these was William Henry Sherwood, who flourished during the 1890s. Little is known of Sherwood other than that he appears to have lived his entire life in Petersburg, Virginia, where he owned an orphanage for African American children, and that he was a composer who conducted both a choir and a band. He is significant in gospel music because he appears to have been the first composer to take advantage of the return to the roots movement of the small body of freed slaves that eventually flocked to Azusa Street.

In 1893 Sherwood published a collection of gospel hymns and other songs under the title *Harp of Zion*. Like most collections published during that time, Sherwood's included hymns by several other composers, as well as a substantial number of his own songs. Of further significance is the fact that Sherwood was the first African American to publish songs that were decidedly cast in the Negro spiritual, pre-gospel mode. The melodies, harmonies, and, to an extent, the rhythm, all forecast music that in less than thirty years would be called gospel. His most famous composition, "The Church Is Moving On," enjoyed popularity as late as 1927 as evidenced by its inclusion in *Spirituals Triumphant, Old and New*, published that year by the National Baptist Convention Publishing Board. The publishing board was first drawn to Sherwood when news reached them in 1893 that he was about to publish his *Harp of Zion*. They contacted him and secured the plates, and with a few revisions, published his *Harp of Zion* as their *Baptist Young People's Union National Harp of Zion* in the same year.

Sherwood's songs are limited to few words, and call and response are written into the song. In his works the melody is simple but catchy, the harmony includes only three or four chords, and the rhythm leaves spaces for expansion. While the verses of the song attempt to tell a story, the refrain foreshadows that of a gospel song, with all of its concomitant parts, as in the refrain of "The Church Is Moving On":

> *Moving on,   moving on*
> *(moving on)   (moving on)*
> *Oh, the church   is moving on*
> *(Oh, the church)   (moving on)*
>
> *Moving on,   moving on*
> *(moving on)   (moving on)*
> *Oh, the Church*
> *(oh, the church)   is moving on.*

Less than a decade after Sherwood published his collection of gospel hymns, Charles Albert Tindley (1851–1933) of Philadelphia joined the ranks of preachers who would make significant contributions to the new music. Tindley, born in Berlin, Maryland, taught himself to read and write. At about the age of seventeen, he married Daisy Henry, and in 1875 they moved to Philadelphia to find a better life. While working first as a hod carrier and a sexton at the John Wesley Methodist Episcopal Church (the Methodist Episcopal Church, as it was then called, would become the United Methodist Church in the early 1970s), Tindley enrolled in correspondence school to complete his education and prepare for the examination to become a minister. He passed the examination, and beginning in 1885, he pastored congregations in Cape May and Spring Hill, New Jersey; Odessa, Delaware; and Pocomoke and Fairmont, New Jersey. He then received the call to Ezion Methodist Episcopal

Church in Wilmington, Delaware, where he was eventually appointed as presiding elder of the Wilmington District. Yet a greater honor awaited him: in 1902 he was called back to Philadelphia to the pastorate of the Bainbridge Street Methodist Church, the new name for the church where Tindley had served as sexton. Starting with a congregation of fewer than two hundred members, this eloquent, self-taught intellectual and, at the same time, spiritual-singing preacher built his membership to more than ten thousand members and amassed a budget of thousands of dollars.

"Leave It There" by
Charles Albert Tindley

His fame as a preacher, orator, civil rights worker, and caretaker for the downtrodden of Philadelphia has been overshadowed by the more than forty-five gospel hymns—interpreted as gospel songs even during his life time—that he left as his legacy. Tindley was the first recognized composer of gospel music, whether they are called gospel hymns or gospel songs. In the 1940s and 1950s, when gospel was first recognized as an acceptable African American musical art form, Tindley's songs were the first to be presented. Among his most popular songs are "What Are They Doing in Heaven?," "Nothing Between," "Some Day" (more commonly called "Beams of Heaven"), "Stand by Me," and "Let Jesus Fix It for You." Two of his compositions are so important to gospel music that they are considered standard repertoire, meaning that if one is called a gospel singer, one must to be able to sing these songs from memory. The first of these is "Leave It There," of which the second and last lines of the refrain now serve as a popular religious response or catch phrase in African American speech:

> *Leave it there, leave it there,*
> *Take your burden to the Lord and leave it there;*
> *If you trust and never doubt,*
> *He will surely bring you out,*
> **Take your burden to the Lord and leave it there.**

The second and by far the most popular composition by Tindley is his 1905 masterpiece, "We'll Understand It Better By and By":

VERSE 1

We're tossed and driven on this reckless sea of time,
Somber skies and howling tempest oft succeed the bright sunshine;
In that land of perfect day when the mists are rolled away,
We will understand it better by and by.

CHORUS

By and by when the morning comes,
When the saints of God are gathered home;
We'll tell the story how we've overcome,
For we'll understand it better by and by.

Like many of the songs created during slavery, this twentieth-century song spoke both to social and religious themes. Written during the rise of the Ku Klux Klan and before the Great Depression (which would further disenfranchise a group of people barely getting by), its refrain of "We'll Understand It Better By and By" struck a core chord in the hearts of African Americans and helped shape the music that would be called gospel. This was accomplished in no small way by the interpretation provided by the people who lived under the shadow and spirit of the Azusa Street Revival.

THE EMERGENCE OF THE JUBILEE QUARTET: THE JEFFERSON COUNTY SCHOOL

Almost simultaneous with the development of music and its performance style in the Pentecostal/Holiness churches was the development of another African American sacred music that was not born in the church, but in the workplace: the jubilee quartet. The impetus for creating this music was the 1905 decision of Fisk University to feature a male quartet singing Negro spirituals instead of the small mixed choir of male and female voices that had presented this music to the world since 1871. Fisk was not the only school to feature jubilee singers or a jubilee quartet, for such groups enjoyed great popularity. Hampton, Tuskegee, Utica, Mississippi, and Wilberforce universities were among the early schools that had jubilee singers.

As the men who sang in quartets while they were in school graduated or left, they went on to teach at less accredited schools or returned to their home communities. There they organized male quartets and modeled them after the Fisk Jubilee Quartet. James Weldon Johnson stated in 1925 that one could "pick up four colored boys or young men anywhere and the chances are ninety out of a hundred that you [would] have a quartet." Although they may not have been aware of it—though it is unlikely that they could remain ignorant of the Pentecostal/Holiness congregations springing up around them and the music sung there—they, like the singers from the Pentecostal/Holiness churches, were participating in the development of the African American gospel song and style. Even at this early stage of gospel, the Pentecostal/Holiness singers sang with more passion, seeming abandon, and consequently more improvisation than was sanctioned in the Baptist and Methodist churches, thus creating a unique style of singing. The early quartets avoided the most exaggerated vocal techniques for two reasons: of greatest importance was the fact that they could not, or would not, expose themselves to the ridicule that was heaped on and associated with Pentecostal/Holiness singers, who were often described as wild and savage. The quartet singers, were, in the main, Baptist, and following the admonitions of their denominational leaders, sought to "elevate the musical standards of the denomination." The Baptists had by the late 1910s developed their own style of singing, which, as exemplified in the Negro spiritual and the new white Protestant gospel hymn, was less frenzied and considered more refined than the Pentecostal/Holiness style. The Baptist singers remained close to the melody, only occasionally interpolating a stock phrase such as "yes, Lord," "thank you, Jesus," or "you know what I mean." A trained vocal sound was preferable to the rough "field" sound, and slow songs were favored over shout songs. A concert demeanor—standing straight and tall in one location with little use of the arms in gesturing—was considered proper, and standard Protestant hymns were more popular than the short and repetitive songs of the Pentecostal church.

Congregational response to the singing of the new church-directed quartets, who soon called themselves jubilee quartets after the Fisk Jubilee Quartet, was in the traditional church mode, with the congregation responding with "amen," "hallelujah," and "praise the Lord." It was impossible to maintain the Fisk Jubilee Quartet repertoire, style of singing, or stage behavior under this kind of religious enthusiasm. It was not long before these quartets began borrowing from the singing style of the Pentecostal/Holiness singers.

The quartet singers operated in the structure of a very disciplined club—that is, they elected officers, paid dues, had regularly scheduled rehearsals, wore uniforms, and arranged formal engagements for singing. The Pentecostal/Holiness singers were less formal, singing spontaneously during any church service and more as a participant in the service than as a special singer or guest. The quartet's organizational concept served the jubilee quartets well, for as Kerrill Rubman observed in *From Jubilee to Gospel in Black Male Quartet Singing*:

1. *Quartet singing (of both sacred and secular music) has been a widespread and respected pastime for Black men—a way for the musically talented to use and improve their skills without special training or instruments and*

2. *[Quartet singing provided] a way for Black men to travel and earn income, recognition, and status when few other avenues were open to them.*

To these observations could be added: .

3. *Quartet singers found another opportunity to express their belief in God and their Christianity in* public. *This was inspired by a desire—not to become famous but—to be another "witness" for the Lord.*

One of the university singers who went on to teach at a high school in Lowndes County, Alabama, was Vernon W. Barnett, a graduate of Tuskegee Institute (now Tuskegee University). One of his students in quartet singing was R. C. Foster (b. 1899), who came to Bessemer, Alabama, in 1915 to work in the mines. Foster formed a group of men into a quartet that sang as entertainment during their lunch period and in the evenings after work. Within a few months the group was singing in their local churches. The early quartets of Bessemer and Birmingham (Jefferson County), Alabama, found their audience from the beginning in the church and therefore created their music for the church rather than the concert hall.

Foster named his group the Foster Singers, after himself, and they featured a repertoire of Negro spirituals, standard Protestant hymns rendered in the jubilee quartet style, and the relatively new gospel hymns of both white and black composers. The Foster Singers were the first black male quartet formed in Bessemer, Alabama—and consequently the first quartet to begin the transition from the university-based and European-informed quartet to what would become the gospel quartet. Foster became the founder of the black gospel quartet movement

The group's original members were R. C. Foster, tenor; Norman McQueen, lead; Fletcher Fisher, baritone; and Golius Grant, bass. Selected and trained by Foster, these singers, all employees of Woodwards Old Mine, were literally the first cousins of the university jubilee singers. They sang much of the same repertoire and dressed in the black trousers and dinner jackets of their forerunners, comported themselves on stage with formal behavior, and considered themselves practitioners of university-style quartet singing "brought home."

The jubilee style of the Foster Singers, and those who followed them, featured four male singers in vocal ranges from tenor to bass, with the second tenor often serving as the soloist on call-and-response songs; close barbershop-like harmony emphasizing sharp and clear attacks and releases; a relatively close blend, but not so close that certain individual vocal qualities could not be heard above the other singers; a variety of vocal devices such as scooping, sliding, and ending words with just a hum; and a dynamic level extending from the softest whisper to the loudest explosion. The original difference between the jubilee quartets and those of the universities was one of vocal color. The color preferred by university quartets was one associated with singing the European art songs of Shubert and Schumann or one that could be employed in singing opera. Without proper training in the technique of placing the tone "in the head," the jubilee quartets placed their tones as they would if singing in a regular church service and therefore brought a certain "homeness" to their sound. Free to be rhythmic, not in the university sense but in the church sense, the singers placed greater emphasis on rhythmic accentuation, and this accentuation was accompanied by a slight movement of the body (never allowed among the university-trained singers), eventually leading to marking time by moving gently from left to right and a quiet slap on the thigh. Negro spirituals were sung with more rhythmic accentuation than was applied by the university singers, and gospel hymns were soon featured in the repertoire of the jubilee quartets.

What these first jubilee quartets did not realize, however, was that they were influenced by the audience's loud vocal response to their singing, even during their singing. In fact, the quartets had gradually adjusted their style to fit the response of the audience for which they were singing, the African American church congregation.

Therefore, while they thought of themselves as a local Fisk Jubilee Quartet, they were in fact the first participants in a gospel music tradition. In retrospect, then, the Foster Singers, and those who followed, were the creators of the "folk" gospel style.

The significance and influence of the Foster Singers cannot be overestimated for they began and inspired the quartet movement in Alabama where they were soon joined by the Famous Blue Jay Singers and the Birmingham Jubilee Singers, both of which were organized in 1926, and in 1929 by the Ensley Jubilee Singers and the Ravizee Singers.

By 1926 Charles Bridges was recognized as the leading quartet trainer of Jefferson County. Bridges was born in Pratt City, a suburb of Birmingham, in 1901. After graduating from Parker High School in Birmingham, where he studied voice with high school music teacher Julia Wilkerson, Bridges sang with the Dolomite Jubilee Singers before he organized the Birmingham Jubilee Singers. Members of the original group were Bridges, lead; Leo "Lot" Key, tenor; Dave Ausbrooks, baritone; and the legendary Ed Sherrill, who, according to Doug Seroff, the historian of the Jefferson County Quartet Movement, was the "heaviest" (deepest-voiced) bass of all the Jefferson County singers. The Birmingham Jubilee Singers, known for their close harmony and the energetic leading style of Bridges, became Alabama's first professional quartet, beginning their recording career in 1926. One of their most famous recordings was "I Heard the Preaching of the Elders." As one of Columbia Records' most-recorded black vocal groups, they toured the vaudeville houses of New York City, Chicago, and elsewhere with stars like Ethel Waters in the 1920s. Until this group was disbanded in the 1930s (upon the death of Dave Ausbrooks), they were rivaled in gospel quartet singing only by the Silver Leaf Quartette.

The Ensley Jubilee Singers maintained Birmingham's reputation as a quartet town until early 1980 when they ended the live radio broadcasts they had presented since 1942. The group, always closely associated with the Williams family of Ensley, was formed while they were teenagers singing on the street corners of Ensley, in the local churches, and for "uptown" parties. By the 1930s they were regarded as one of the leading quartets of Jefferson County. Original members were brothers James, Rufus, and Leroy Williams and their cousin, Charlie Jamison. Over the years the group boasted such prominent lead singers as Willie Love, who later joined the Fairfield Four, and Lon "Big Fat" Hamler.

The Ravizee Singers was one of the first groups to include women, which was unusual but permitted here because the Ravizee was a family group. Original members of the group were Mary Ravizee, first tenor; Hattye Ravizee, second tenor; Reverend Issac C. Ravizee, lead and first bass; and William Ravizee, second bass. In later years sister Leola Ravizee sang second tenor. The group relocated to Bessemer in 1935 to be near brother Reverend S. H. Ravizee, whose location in Bessemer even before the group moved there entitled them to be a part of the Jefferson County singers. The Ravizees were known for their slow and moderate gospelized Baptist hymns.

Jefferson County was the home of many jubilee groups and enjoyed a reputation as the leading quartet center in the South for many years. The influence of the movement begun by R. C. Foster and his singers was soon felt throughout the South.

THE JUBILEE QUARTET MOVEMENT SPREADS

Jefferson County was not the only place where quartets began to flourish, for as early 1919 in Norfolk, Virginia, the seat of the Tidewater area, a community quartet from the Berkley section of town began singing in churches in Norfolk and Portsmouth. Named the Silver Leaf Quartet, it included in its membership Melvin Smith, first tenor and lead; William Thatch, falsetto voice; William Boush, baritone; and Ellis McPherson, bass. Like two other groups that helped to identify Tidewater gospel, the Harmonizing Four and the Golden Gate Quartet, the Silver Leaf Quartet sang in a smoother vocal style than the groups of Jefferson County and was more heavily influenced by popular music than were Jefferson County groups. Interested from the beginning in the harmonies of popular music—that is, harmonies other than the simple chords found in hymns and Negro spirituals—the Silver Leaf Quartet was one of the first to investigate the complex chords that later would be associated with vocal jazz groups. More interesting, however, was the inclusion of a falsetto voice in the quartet. The falsetto is an African Americanism inherited from African tribal singing (Richard Jobson discussed African falsetto singing in a 1623 book). Whereas most quartets employed a first tenor—some of whom were described as light as an "Irish" tenor—as the top voice, in the Silver Leaf Quartet the falsetto of William Thatch would often soar over the other voices of the group.

Their interest in popular music was instrumental in their decision to accept an extensive booking as the Cavalier Singers, the name under which they sang secular

The Harmonizing Four, the most popular gospel quartet of the Tidewater, Virginia, region

music, at the exclusive Virginia Beach Cavalier Hotel in 1947. From that time on the group sang both sacred and secular music, but they maintained their reputation as a jubilee quartet. The group retired in 1979, but reveled in the fact that they had influenced the Golden Gate Quartet, the most famous jubilee group of the 1930s and the 1940s.

A number of other quartets were formed in the 1920s. In 1921 in Nashville, Tennessee, a group of young boys organized a quartet and named themselves the Fairfield Four, in honor of their church, the Fairfield Missionary Baptist Church. In 1927 the Harmonizing Four was organized in Richmond, Virginia, while the Dixie Hummingbirds of Greenville, South Carolina, organized in 1928. The late 1920s witnessed the first of two halcyon times that the black gospel quartets would experience.

CHURCH SINGING ACCOMPANIED
BY PIANO, GUITAR, AND OTHER INSTRUMENTS

The quartet movement of the 1920s coexisted with the Pentecostal movement, although there was one major difference: quartets celebrated the *a cappella* tradition while the Pentecostal/Holiness groups, generally, accompanied their singing with percussion instruments, banjos, harmoniums, melodiums, and eventually piano. The early 1920s witnessed the emergence of a group of gospel singers from the Pentecostal/Holiness movement, most of whom accompanied themselves, or were accompanied, on various instruments. Several of these singers served as song leaders for Pentecostal preachers and the emerging Pentecostal/Holiness church.

Blind Arizona Dranes

Arizona Dranes (c.1905–c.1960) was the most prominent of the early sanctified singers and the first-known gospel pianist. Dranes was known as the "Blind Gospel Singer" in the early 1920s. Her blindness is generally conceded to have resulted from an attack of influenza, an epidemic of which swept Texas in the early 1900s. She served as song leader and pianist for Emmett Morey Page (1871–1944), Riley Felman Williams (c.1880–1952), and Samuel M. Crouch, Jr. (1896–1976), all of whom became bishops in COGIC.

Page, a native of Mississippi, received sanctification in 1902. In 1907 when he met Charles Harrison Mason, Page received the Holy Ghost. In 1914 Mason assigned him to the Texas where he held his first state convention that same year. Within a few years Page was also assigned as "overseer" (superintendent) of Texas, Arkansas, Oklahoma, New Mexico, Louisiana, Missouri, California, and parts of Tennessee, Mississippi, and Wisconsin. On a visit to Texas he met Arizona Dranes, a singer in the new sanctified style who was developing a style of piano playing that did not detract from the fervor of the singing, but complemented it in an ecstatic way. Whenever Page was in Texas Dranes served as his song leader and pianist.

Williams, born in Memphis, Tennessee, was one of the second generation of ministers who joined Mason in "planting" or "working out" new churches for his denomination. "Planting" or "working out" a Pentecostal church involved finding a community that was even slightly ready to support a sanctified church, relocating to that community, becoming visible among the religious community, and after establishing a reputation as a devout Christian, introducing the new religion through services in homes (as Seymour did) or in converted storefronts. Church "planters" often held "street meetings" in front of popular businesses or borrowed the sanctuary or basement of an established church when the church was not occupied (this happened rarely but was significant in the development of Pentecostal churches). The planter remained until the new congregation had a strong identity and would then move to a new community and begin the process again. Planters were highly revered, to the extent that some churches took on the name of the planter, as did Flowers Temple Church of God in Christ in Winter Park, Florida, named after its planter, J. J. Flowers.

Williams traveled throughout the South conducting revivals and setting up churches, many of which were pastored by ministers whom he ordained. During his travels in Texas in the early 1920s he, too, encountered Arizona Dranes, who became his song leader.

After traveling with Williams, Dranes returned to her hometown of Dallas, Texas, and became the pianist and song leader for Crouch, who eventually became the First Assistant Bishop of COGIC. Crouch earned this honor through his travels throughout the United States preaching Pentecostalism and setting up COGICs, the activity which brought him to Dallas in the middle 1920s. In Texas he began an association with Dranes that lasted throughout her career as a recording singer. In the early 1930s Crouch moved to California where he continued planting churches. He eventually settled in Los Angeles, where he founded the Emmanual Church of God in Christ. In the early 1960s the pianist for his church was his nephew, Andrae Crouch (b. 1942).

While Dranes was serving as song leader for Crouch in Dallas, Richard M. Jones (1892–1945), pianist and a talent scout for Okeh Records, attended one of Crouch's services and heard her. Recognizing her talent and the sensation she would generate among black Christians, he negotiated a contract for Dranes with his record label after she made a test recording in Chicago. Dranes had secured a traveling companion and gone to Chicago where she recorded a Negro spiritual/gospel version of "My Soul Is a Witness for My Lord." The producers were highly impressed, not only with her singing, but with her piano playing as well.

Her piano playing was a combination of ragtime, with its two beats to the bar feel, octave passages in the left hand, exaggerated syncopation in the right hand, and heavy full and ragged (syncopated) chords of barrelhouse piano, and the more traditional chords of the standard Protestant hymn. What Dranes brought to the style was what became known as the "gospel beat," emphasizing a heavy accent on the first beat in musical units of two beats and beats two and four in musical units of four. In addition to the accents on the primary pulses, Dranes filled in the space between the accented beats with octave and single note runs. The right hand's playing was characterized by repeated notes and chords and few—but well-chosen—single-note motives (runs), while the left hand played octaves. Most of her playing was in the center of the keyboard, with excursions into the very bottom and top of the keyboard during passages normally reserved for breaks in the music.

Her singing style, which influenced many later gospel singers, was remarkable for its piercing quality that cut through the clapping and stamping of church services. Located in range between a soprano and an alto, her voice was marked by nasality, but with clarity of pitch, and was treated like a drum when, with emotion and fervor, she shouted out the lyrics of songs. This is nowhere more clearly demonstrated than on her 1928 recording of "I Shall Wear a Crown." In addition to introducing a gospel piano style, Dranes sang with a true backup group, rather than a congregation, and rendered several songs in 3/4 time, which would become the 12/8 rhythm of gospel in the 1950s. Between 1926 and 1928 she recorded over thirty songs for Okeh Records and was one of their most commercial religious music artists.

Other Blind Gospel Singers

Dranes was only one of a cadre of blind singers who turned to gospel in the early 1920s, many of whom became recording artists. This is perhaps no coincidence: the Pentecostal/Holiness church placed heavy emphasis on healing and many of these singers were awaiting healing; the music was new and catchy; and donations were given with less pity and guilt when the blind person exhibited a talent.

Washington Phillips (1891–1938) was the second most popular blind gospel singer after Arizona Dranes. A Texas native who also died there after several years in an insane asylum, Phillips possessed a clear, but scratchy voice that could nonetheless melt the heart of the meanest man. His simple delivery, accentuation of key lyrical phrases, and crystal clear sincerity even on recordings made him a popular recording preacher and singer in the late 1920s. Accompanying himself on the dolceola, one of several variances of the dulcimer (played like a piano), Washington is known today by the following lyrics:

VERSE
I want to tell you the natural fact,
Every man don't understand the Bible alike.

CHORUS
But that's all now, I tell you that's all;
But you better have Jesus now, I tell you that's all.

The opening of his 1927 recording of "Denomination Blues" was a sacred song based on the secular song "Hesitation Blues."

Blind Mamie Forehand, accompanied by her guitar-playing husband, A. C. Forehand, was one of the sanctified street singers from Memphis who did not fit the mold of the traditional Pentecostal shouter. Not only was her voice thin with a decided quaver not always used for vocal effect, her delivery was deliberate and measured. Yet she was one of the highly regarded sanctified singers of the 1920s, in spite of her advanced age at that time. She accompanied her singing by playing antique small cymbals (which are completely unrelated to the full-sized symphonic cymbals used in most gospel music accompaniment), while her husband accompanied her on guitar. When he sang, he accompanied himself on the harmonium, one of the earliest gospel keyboard instruments. The Forehands' legacy depends almost entirely on their recordings of "Wouldn't Mind Dying if Dying Was All" and the more famous "Honey in the Rock."

Among other blind gospel singers active during the 1920s was Blind Joel "Joe" Taggart, who recorded thirty gospel songs. Taggart possessed a strong voice, delivered lyrics with authority, and played guitar with noticeable skill. His recordings of "Handwriting on the Wall" and "I Wish My Mother Was on That Train" testify to his reputation as one of the strong singers of the 1920s. Blind Roosevelt Graves and Blind Willie Johnson, who often performed with his wife Angeline, made significant contributions to guitar-accompanied religious singing. Graves and Johnson both sang secular music as well. Charles Tindley's "Take Your Burden to the Lord" was recorded by both artists, first by Graves, then by Johnson one year later.

Sighted Gospel Singers

The gospel style of singing—though it was not yet called gospel but jubilee singing in public and sanctified singing in private—provided the perfect avenue for blind people to make a living and was preferred over selling pencils or standing on street corners with cups. The blind singers were joined by sighted soloists, duos, and quartets, some of whom, although inspired by the Pentecostal/Holiness singers, performed in a style not unlike that of the early jubilee quartets. The less frenzied, more controlled singing of the Baptists and Methodists coexisted with the energetic, florid, and "spirit-induced" singing of the sanctified saints. While Sister Sallie Sanders offered a rousing, spirit-informed version of gospel/spirituals in a 1923 recording session, the Nugrape Twins (Matthew and Mark), at the same session, recorded songs with a classically trained pianist who played a classically informed introduction, paused for the singers to commence, and carefully followed them through their songs. The difference between the two performances is so distinct that clearly, even without a name, *gospel* had become a distinct style of singing.

This style is more obvious in the singing of the legendary Sister Bessie Johnson, a Mississippi evangelist or a woman preacher (in COGIC or in similar denominations, women are not allowed to be called Elder or Reverend). Sister Johnson's voice, while that of the average alto, could summon up a deep and dark quality and assume the growling timbre associated with the African American folk preacher. Her singing partner, Sister Melinda Taylor, on the other hand, possessed a voice that was deep and resonant. Both Johnson and Taylor, along with Sally Sumler, were members of the Sanctified Singers. "He's Got Better Things for You" (1929) was one of their popular recordings. Sister Johnson's recording of "Telephone to Glory" illustrated the depth of her range and her ability to "growl," a technique that would not become popular among most gospel singers until the 1950s.

Sister Cally Fancy, a Chicago gospel singer and direct contemporary of Bessie Johnson, featured a repertoire of songs that commented on social issues of the day. Her recordings of "Everybody Get Your Business Right," about the rash of tornados that plagued the United States between 1928 and 1930, and "Death Is Riding through the Land," a realist's reaction to the perceived folly of the League of Nations in 1920, illustrate her style and repertoire.

Race Records

The preponderance of recordings of African American preaching and gospel singing as early as the mid-1920s testifies not only to the popularity among black people of this kind of African American religion and its music, but also to white people's fascination with it. The phenomenal sale of so-called "race records" (recordings produced using African American performers for the African American audience) between 1924 and 1949—when the term "rhythm and blues" was added to the Billboard list of records sold—is documented by Paul Oliver in *Songsters and Saints* (1984). This scholarly book on the popularity, sales, and importance of race recordings has a chapter on gospel singing and preaching but still does not tell the complete story. Gospel music and African American preaching were discovered by the record com-

panies in the early 1920s, and as early as 1924, record companies began recording and marketing these songs. They often went to small towns and recorded in churches, homes, and bars. Companies small and large had two or three preachers or singers on their rosters. The major recording companies that recorded gospel in the 1920s and 1930s were Okeh, RCA Victor, Vocallion, Paramount, and Columbia.

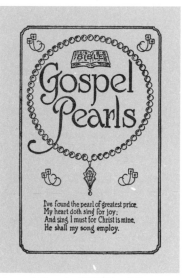

Gospel Pearls *(1921) with songs by Charles Albert Tindley,* Lucie Campbell, *and Thomas Andrew Dorsey*

Gospel Pearls

Early gospel brought a new excitement to religion in the African American community. Like any sensation, it attracted new followers daily. The most genuine and inspiring music, however, was performed within Pentecostal and storefront Baptist churches. The music was infectious and mesmerizing, and the Pentecostal/Holiness movement presented a problem to the Baptists and Methodists. At first, because Holiness congrega-

tions waved their arms in exaggerated fashion at moments of ecstacy, shouted (executed a holy dance), and on occasion fainted or went into trances, few people sought membership in their congregations. However, in the late 1920s and early 1930s when the Holiness church began to make inroads into the membership of the major Baptist and Methodist established churches, the ministers of these churches saw the Holiness church as a threat, both to their membership and to their power.

At the same time, members of the budding African American middle class saw the Holiness church and its service as an attack on the accomplishments, positions, and progress they had worked so hard to attain.

Despite this feeling of shame and anger in the African American community, as early as 1921 the National Baptist Convention, the largest organization of African American Christians in the United States, formally recognized the power and beauty of this new music. In that year they published *Gospel Pearls*, the first collection of songs published by a black congregation using the term "gospel" to refer not only to the "good news" but to the new kind of song and singing that was stirring the nation. *GP*, as it is commonly called, was edited by Willa A. Townsend (1880–1947), a professor of church worship, music, and pageantry at Nashville's Roger Williams University. Townsend was ably assisted on the church editorial committee by such luminaries as Lucie E. Campbell, E. W. D. Issac, Sr., and L. K. Williams, all of whom played major roles in the development of music in African American Baptist churches after 1900. As musical associates, Townsend was flanked by a coterie of emerging Baptist gospel singers, as noted in the preface to this collection:

> *"Gospel Pearls" is a boon to Gospel Singers, for it contains the songs that have been sung most effectively by Prof. Britt, Mrs. J. D. Bushnell, Prof. Smiley, Prof. Nix, Mrs. Williams, and other prominent singers, telling of His Wondrous Love through song.*

While the music committee, the signatory of the preface, identified this group as "gospel singers," they did not mean singers in the tradition of Arizona Dranes and Sallie Sanders, but a new and different style of singing that sought to capture the ecstasy of the Holiness church singers but without the excesses. Excesses were interpreted as singing at the extremes of the register with a volume usually reserved for outdoor song, interpolating additional words into the text, hand clapping, and occasional spurts of shouting. This *GP* style of gospel singing leaned heavily on the nineteenth-century Baptist lining hymn tradition of singing songs in a slow tempo and elaborating each syllable with three to five embellishment tones.

Of the 163 songs in *GP*, 143 are standard Protestant hymns, gospel hymns by white composers, or patriotic songs such as "Battle Hymn of the Republic." In a section entitled "Spirituals," Townsend included "Stand by Me" by Charles Albert

Tindley and "Shine for Jesus" by E. C. Deas. In the first untitled section, Townsend included four other songs by Tindley, including "We'll Understand It Better By and By" and "Leave It There," several songs by E. C. Deas and Carrie Booker Person, "I'm Happy with Jesus Alone" by Charles Price Jones, and "If I Don't Get There," the first gospel song published by Thomas Andrew Dorsey. The late 1921 edition of *GP* (the first edition was published in early 1921) became so popular that the National Baptist Convention Publishing Board decided to use the original plates for all subsequent issues. The 1921 version of *GP* was still a saleable item in the early 1990s without any changes or additions. With the publication of the collection and the large membership of the National Baptist Convention, gospel music, as it was now called, began to spread among black Christians, endorsed by the respectability of the National Baptist Convention. *Gospel Pearls* crossed denominational music boundaries and by the 1930s was found in the pews of Baptist, Methodist, and Pentecostal churches.

Gospel Pearls and Gospel Singing

The publication of *Gospel Pearls* profoundly affected the singing of gospel music in the African American community because Baptists no longer had to attend Pentecostal, Holiness, or sanctified churches to hear the music. They could now hear this music in their own churches on Sunday mornings; for the shouting kind of gospel they still had to go to the source. There were now two styles of singing gospel: one that emphasized singing in which the spirit dictated the amount of embellishment, volume, and improvisation that was applied, and a second that, while attempting to incorporate the dictates of the spirit, tempered the rendition to the musical taste of the Baptist congregation. The Baptist style of singing gospel inspired the development of gospel groups and soloists who heretofore had been attracted to the music but found no way to participate, given their sense of moderate vocal and physical indulgence. One of the first groups to emerge was the Tindley Gospel Singers, also known as the Tindley Seven, organized in the Tindley Temple Methodist Episcopal Church in Philadelphia and named in honor of the pastor, Charles Albert Tindley. This group, organized in 1927, was unique in two respects: they were the first male gospel group to be accompanied by piano, although the piano accompaniment was much more like hymn playing than gospel singing, and while their basic repertoire was the gospel hymns of Tindley, they sang other songs, principally those found in *Gospel Pearls.*

Golden Gate Quartet

Another group to emerge following the publication of *GP* was the Golden Gate Quartet, the most famous gospel quartet before the Golden Age of gospel. The Golden Gate Quartet, a name that had been used for African American high school quartets since the 1890s, was again used for a group that attended Booker T. Washington High School in Norfolk, Virginia, in the late 1920s. Its original members were Henry Owens, lead; Clyde Reddick, tenor; Willie "Bill" Johnson, baritone; and Orlando Wilson, bass. Reddick was later replaced by Willie Langford but returned to the group in the 1950s. Their style was, at first, similar to that of barbershop quartets and jubilee singers, emphasizing close harmony with precise attacks and releases (they were influenced by the Mills Brothers as well as by jubilee singers and gospel quartets). Most of their repertoire consisted of Negro spirituals, to which they applied a rhythmic beat, not unlike that associated with blues and jazz. In the late 1930s, they began to include songs of Thomas A. Dorsey, Lucie Campbell, and Charles A. Tindley and applied a few of the techniques of the sanctified singers.

Beginning in 1935 the Gates appeared in live radio broadcasts, first from the 50,000–watt station WBT in Charlotte, North Carolina. Their harmony, rich vibrato-laced tones, and rhythmic accentuation made them an early radio favorite among black and white listeners. In addition to other elements exploited by jubilee singers and gospel quartets, the Gates could imitate trains, boats, cars, whistles, and motors with their voices (probably inspired by the Mills Brothers). Often used as background for solos, these nonmusical sounds became a trademark that set the Gates apart from other groups. Their WBT broadcasts reached much of the eastern United States and brought them to the attention of Victor Records, for which they began recording in 1937. During their first session, they recorded a spirited version of the Negro spiritual "Jonah," and it became an immediate hit among race records.

The popularity of their recordings and radio broadcasts prompted John Hammond (1910–87) to feature them in the famous 1938 Carnegie Hall "From Spirituals to Swing" concert. By the end of the concert the Gates had become the toast of New York. They moved to a national CBS live broadcast, and in 1941 they performed at Franklin Delano Roosevelt's inauguration (later they recorded "Why I Like-a Roosevelt," which became a big hit).

Because the Gates produced a sound that appeared to devote more attention to the techniques of polished barbershop/jubilee/popular music than to praising God, they were often mistaken for popular music singers (snapping their fingers for rhythmic accentuation and swaying their bodies in syncopated movement helped create the confusion). They soon attracted a large audience that had no particular interest in religion, only in music. After appearing at Cafe Society in New York in 1940 they began to perform more secular music—and gospel music presented in a secular manner—and eventually presented themselves as both jubilee and popular singers.

After World War II black gospel quartets began to proliferate, and the Gates were then only one of several popular quartets attempting to grab the same audience. Too involved in a style that had been more than twenty years in development, the Gates chose not to switch to pure gospel and around 1950 found themselves with a very small black audience. By 1955 the group had undergone several personnel changes and was not able to recreate their sound from the 1930s and 1940s. They thereby lost their entire black audience as well as much of their white audience. They made their first trip to Europe in 1953 where they became an instant hit (gospel quartets had not yet toured Europe). They immediately moved their headquarters to Paris where, through many personnel changes, they have remained, confining their touring to Europe. Some of their early hits include "Shadrack, Meshack, and Abendigo" and Tindley's "What Are They Doing in Heaven Today?"

The Southernaires

Another extremely popular quartet, one that often appeared with the Golden Gate Quartet in their early New York days, was the Southernaires. Organized in New York City in 1929, this group was formed to sing in local churches. During its early period the group rehearsed at Williams Institutional Colored Methodist Episcopal Church (CME) in Harlem and the following year began broadcasting over radio stations WMCA and WRNY. In 1933 the group began a series of broadcasts from the NBC Blue Broadcast under the title "The Little Weather-Beaten Whitewashed Church" that lasted more than ten years. Their broadcast "featured traditional spirituals and secular southern folksongs, as well as sermonettes, recitations, and guest speakers

The Dixie Hummingbirds

who emphasized the accomplishments of African Americans." Although they mixed secular and barbershop, jubilee, and gospel quartet styles into one musical melange, the Southernaires were most highly regarded as a gospel and jubilee quartet. From 1939 to 1941 they recorded jubilee and gospel songs on the Decca label.

Gospel Music on the Eve of the Golden Age

By the early 1940s gospel music was thoroughly entrenched in both the African American community and its churches. It did not go unnoticed, however, outside the African American community, and on December 23, 1938, when John Hammond staged the famous "From Spirituals to Swing" concert in Carnegie Hall, he included the Mitchell Christian Singers and the Golden Gate Quartet, along with Sister Rosetta Tharpe, a gospel singer who accompanied herself on guitar. The next year Sister Tharpe recorded jazz versions of gospel songs with Lucky Millender (1900–66) and his band, and the Georgia Peach appeared with a quartet singing gospel songs at Radio City Music Hall. In the early 1940s, the Dixie Hummingbirds appeared at Cafe Society, and Ernestine B. Washington, the wife of a Holiness minister, recorded gospel with jazz trumpeter Bunk Johnson (1879–1949).

From the services held on Azusa Street in Los Angeles around the turn of the century evolved a music that began to challenge the Negro spiritual as the favored sacred music in the African American community. This new gospel music spoke in more immediate tones, both musically and textually, to the difficult life of being both black and Christian in the United States during the first two decades of the twentieth century. While the music began in the Pentecostal churches and moved into the community through jubilee quartets, it was spread throughout the nation by radio, recordings, and concerts by traveling gospel singers. The Sunday afternoon gospel concert was becoming a fixture in Baptist churches along with the pre-service gospel concert in Pentecostal churches. Occasionally even Methodist congregations received gospel singers into their sanctuaries.

By 1940 the *a cappella* male gospel quartet had been perfecting its style for more than twenty-five years, and this refinement was reflected in public preference at concerts. The newer piano-accompanied gospel singers coming into prominence at the middle of the century were less developed and still searching for a precise style of executing this music. On the one hand, the piano freed the singers from supplying the complete rhythmic foundation; on the other hand, it restricted absolute freedom of harmony because harmony was supplied by the piano. Between 1940 and 1945, the piano-accompanied group solved its accompaniment problems and was ready to challenge jubilee quartets for prominence within the emerging gospel audience.

Live broadcast of Mahalia Jackson at New York's WOV

Move On Up A Little Higher: 1945–55

*B*eginning as early as the mid-1930s, piano-accompanied gospel joined with the *a cappella* jubilee quartet to provide greater variety in this new music. The gospel choir, organized as early as 1932, could now be found in many Baptist and Pentecostal sanctuaries, with occasional performances in Methodist churches. By 1945 there were very few people in the African American community who had not heard gospel music. Jubilee quartets, who heretofore had only flirted with the virtuosic techniques of the Pentecostal gospel singers, now embraced those techniques and sought to create a music that would wreak emotional havoc. What exactly was this new music called gospel?

Gospel music was, by 1945, a sacred folk music that had its origin in the slave songs, field hollers, Baptist lining hymns, and Negro spirituals of the slave era and standard Protestant hymns and especially composed songs. These songs were adapted and reworked into jubilant expressions of supplication, praise, and thanks by the urban African American. The harmonies were as simple as those of a hymn or the blues, but gospel's rhythm, always personalized by singers into the accents and cross-pulses of their speech, walk, and laughter, was intricate and complex—yet precise and clear enough to inspire synchronized movement. As important as the music were the practices employed in its performance. So great were these practices that by the mid-1940s they defined gospel style.

The gospel style features exaggerated improvisation as its driving force. Of special interest in gospel singing is the variety of timbres that make up the gospel sound, representing the diverse musical personalities of those singers who created the style: Arizona Dranes sang in a tense, almost shrill mezzo-soprano; Mamie Forehand had a contralto voice that she used in a low, almost lazy manner of singing; Washington Phillips and Joe Taggart possessed "dirty" baritone voices and were very much influenced by the blues in their singing; Willie Johnson sang in a hoarse, strained voice, not unlike that of a sanctified preacher. Yet each sang with the passion of a convinced Christian.

A gospel piano style had been developed based on the "rhythm section" concept, in which the middle of the piano is used to support the singers by doubling the vocal line in harmony; the left bottom portion of the keyboard serves as the bass fiddle, and the right upper portion acts as a solo trumpet or flute, playing countermelodies and "fill" material at rhythmic breaks.

The text of gospel songs speaks of the Trinity, blessings, thanks, and lamentations, and the manner in which the text is delivered is more important than the melodies and harmonies to which they are sung. Despite the fact that gospel songs were sung for others to hear, it was paramount that the singers *use* singing to communicate their feelings about Christianity. It was, therefore, not unusual to witness a singer *singing* through her problems. It was common for the congregation to become so moved that they forgot their own problems for days, while others transcended the weights of this world through the music.

During the first ten years of the Golden Age of Gospel (1945–55), the style of music reached a level of near perfection and amassed a devoted audience. Gospel moved from shabby storefront churches with a few untrained singers dressed in threadbare black or maroon choir robes to the gospel-group extravaganzas of New York's Joe Bostic or New Jersey's Ronnie Williams. The singers of the new generation exhibited extraordinary control and nuance, dressed in blazing pastel gowns and bright suits, and were accompanied by nine-foot Steinway grand pianos and

Hammond organs with Leslie speakers. A "singing," as gospel concerts were called, generated as much excitement as an appearance by Duke Ellington or Louis Jordan and provided an opportunity for the church folk in the African American community to view the finest in clothing, hair styles, and automobiles. But this new emphasis on opulence and grandeur did not interfere with the audience experiencing, through the music, a religious ecstacy heretofore unmatched in the twentieth century.

THE LEGACY OF WORLD WAR II: RADIO AND RECORDINGS

The years of World War II had stimulated unprecedented economic growth in the United States. Southern African Americans, mainly through benefits such as the G.I. Bill and its economic stimulus, were able to move to large northern and midwestern cities, secure high-paying jobs, buy homes, and send their children to better schools. However, many of these transplanted southerners were uncomfortable with the more formal worship services of the North and Midwest and felt the need to recreate the spirited and informal religious church services and music they had enjoyed back home. As enterprising record producers from labels such as Apollo, Gotham, Excello, Atlantic, Imperial, black-owned Vee-Jay, Savoy, Specialty, Peacock, Chess, Aladdin, and King scouted for the new secular music—soon to be called rhythm and blues—they also looked to the churches for music that would satisfy hard-shell Christians as well as lovers of rhythm and blues. Almost every major city boasted at least one gospel soloist, group, or quartet that was recording or waiting for the call to record.

Like the recordings of rhythm and blues, gospel recordings were, according to Portia Maultsby, a leading authority on rhythm and blues, first produced by "small, independent record companies founded by entrepreneurs. Some of the companies were established by white jukebox vendors who catered to black communities." In cities where there was no record store owned by African Americans, white record store owners stocked black gospel and would make special orders. James C. Petrillo (1892–1984), president of the American Federation of Musicians, led a strike in 1942 banning the union's members from making recordings until the record manufacturers agreed to pay the union a fee for every disc produced. According to Nelson George in *The Death of Rhythm and Blues*, "Records cut prior to the ban, plus some primarily vocal recordings and scattered bootleg sessions (falsely said to have been recorded before the ban), made up the bulk of record releases during the next two years." The strike lasted until 1944, by which time many of the major record labels were no longer interested in gospel. New recording companies like Apollo and Gotham, eager to fill this void, stepped in and made African American gospel music a major business.

While gospel provided spiritual uplifting through the two or three songs rendered during a church service and the two hours of a concert, radio and recordings became the principal source for listening to gospel every day and all day. Gospel quartets had begun to perform live as early as 1933 when the Southernaires began a series of broadcasts on stations WMCA and WRNY in New York City. This musical diversion soon became so popular that it was picked up by stations in other cities. Such groups as the Golden Gate Quartet, the Swan Silvertones, the CIO Singers (from the Congress of Industrial Organizations union), the Soul Stirrers, and the Wings Over Jordan Choir joined the Southernaires for Sunday morning or weekday broadcasts. These early black gospel quartet broadcasts were not only an innovation in African American musical culture, but also in the history of American radio, for while African American swing bands had had live radio broadcasts in cities like New York and Chicago, African American sacred music had been confined to the church. Few black-owned radio stations were in existence in 1930, and the few that were active found greater sponsorship in playing jazz and blues recordings.

Radio in the 1940s was not yet the black-owned and black-programmed radio that became popular in the last quarter of the twentieth century. There were African American disc jockeys (DJs) on only a few stations, working three or four hours daily, while white DJs on other stations and at other times affected the timbre, rhetoric, and booming voice of African Americans. Regardless of who was broadcasting, radio had become the means through which small-town America could hear gospel on any Sunday and, in most cases, either before seven o'clock in the morning or after ten o'clock at night on weekdays. Gospel radio became a much desired reality in the mid-1940s, and stations from New York to Tennessee featured the gospel hour with Deacon Jones (a black DJ) or Brother Paul (a white DJ). Among the most prominent stations on which gospel could be heard were WDIA (Memphis), WXLW (St. Louis), WLOF (Orlando), WDBJ (Roanoke, Virginia), WNOX (Knoxville), WLIB (New York City), WIS (Columbia, South Carolina), WLAC (Nashville), WOKJ (Jackson, Mississippi), and WMMB (Miami). None of these stations were black owned.

While most of the stations covered a listening audience within a radius of twenty-five miles or less, WLAC of Nashville covered such a large area that it became the black radio station for the United States. With 1,510 kilocycles (the station was advertised as having 50,000 watts) in early 1940s, the station could be heard for thousands of miles during the day. After nine o'clock at night, when many stations left the airwaves, WLAC literally covered the nation. Playing easy listening music during the day, WLAC featured rhythm and blues and gospel at night. The station had three DJs who programmed music especially designed for black audiences. Each featured forty-five-minute segments of rhythm and blues alternating with fifteen-minute segments of gospel. The station was important not only because it featured race music at night but also because it was one of the first radio stations to sell items over the radio, expanding the mail-order industry. Through the mail from WLAC, African Americans bought baby chicks, hair pomade, recordings, garden seeds, choir robes, and skin-lightening cream advertised between the sounds of James Brown, LaVern Baker, and the Dixie Hummingbirds.

The three DJs (none of whom were black) that became "brothers" were Bill "Hoss" Allen, known as the "Hossman," Gene Noble, and John "John R" Richbourg. Depending on the hour of broadcast, the DJs were sponsored by Randy's Record Shop of Gallatin, Tennessee, or Ernie's Record Mart of Nashville. The principal gospel music DJ, however, was John R (b. 1910), who offered record packages of five records for $3.98, and for those who ordered within the next seven days, an additional free record.

At the height of WLAC's popularity in the early 1950s, the station covered thirty-eight states and had eight million to twelve million listeners. Kip Lornell, who studied gospel quartets in Memphis, reported that the Spirit of Memphis Quartet told him that it "was possible to drive from Atlanta to Los Angeles and never miss one of John R's broadcasts." John R and WLAC became part of the fabric of the gospel network early on.

The gospel radio programs needed an abundance of gospel recordings, of which there was no shortage. Not since the 1920s had record producers in such large numbers scoured the black community for religious music.

Few gospel recording artists ever received a fair accounting or money for the records sold. As was the case in other forms of black recorded entertainment, gospel was a gold mine for ripping off the artists. The rip-off was manifested in several ways: record producers paid artists for fewer records than were sold (artists did not see the books), records were distributed in areas where the artists did not perform and therefore had no knowledge of the market, the artists were not advised that they themselves were paying for the recording session and they would receive no money until the cost of the session had been paid, and the reprehensible act of signing a group as a tax write-off and investing no money to promote their recordings. In order to offset their losses—singers had little leverage to negotiate more advantageous contracts—singers would purchase hundreds of recordings at a reduced price from the producer and sell them during their concert tours. The singers themselves left the stage or pulpit and moved through the audience selling records. This was often the only way they were able to make money from the recordings. While gospel artists knew they were not receiving the money they deserved from the recording industry, they were nonetheless grateful for recording contracts.

GOSPEL ON THE HIGHWAYS AND BYWAYS

A contract and the resulting recording could ensure singers a large crowd when they performed. Every singer sought to ensure a recording contract by courting gospel DJs (serious payola was not a major factor in the gospel recording industry), calling them from distant places on their tours, sending postal and Christmas cards, and making great ceremony when they attended concerts.

Despite many discomforts and problems, professional gospel singers—those who had given up their weekday jobs to sing—traveled throughout the United States during the rain, snow, sleet, or 120 degree temperatures to sing gospel before whomever would listen in any church or school auditorium. Having to perform in the African American church uniform of some combination of black and white (for economic reasons) or threadbare black or maroon choir robes and being accompanied on an old upright piano, often out of tune, these singers forged ahead to bring their message of "good news" in a new melodic, harmonic, rhythmic, and spiritual form. Often leaving home under the most dreadful circumstances, reaching their destination and converting new souls became more important to these singers than comfort during their travels. Soloists, quartets, and groups with their accompanists traveled in dilapidated cars, on trains, and in buses, and sometimes in a combination of all these modes of travel. If cars broke down, singers would call sponsors or promoters and request financial assistance to make their engagements, or if they were relatively close to the place of performance, ask that they be picked up. Sometimes performers were up to two hours late.

Nonetheless, most singers preferred automobile travel. Riding buses or trains meant having to travel in the "colored" section. On trains only one porter (or none at all) was assigned to two or three cars. Seats in these cars were seldom in good repair, and luggage sat on passenger seats for lack of storage room above. Few food services were offered, and bathrooms were seldom cleaned. Many of the bus stops had no provisions for African Americans, requiring them to stand outside a side window of a restaurant for food service.

Many buses and trains arrived at a specific designated point at one or two o'clock in the morning. Upon arrival, singers had to find transportation to the "colored" hotels or rooming houses in town if no sponsor or friends could meet them. (During the 1940s and 1950s white taxi entrepreneurs began to dispatch taxis for the "colored" section of town, which alleviated this problem to a degree.) Except on visits to cities such as New York or Chicago, most singers had to stay in the one hotel or rooming house that would accommodate African Americans. If no rooms were available, friends or even strangers met on the street could direct singers to homes that took in "overnight" boarders. Rather than endure this travail, singers would use their church network or family and friends to arrange accommodation. In many towns where singers were performing for two or more days, dinner invitations from church members or concert attendees were eagerly accepted. Sometimes the sponsor of multiple concerts would arrange to have the singers dine at a different home each night.

When singers discovered that they would have to depend on restaurants and cafes for food, they would go to the local grocery store and stock their suitcases with crackers, potato chips, pork rinds, peanuts, potted meat, sardines, and pickled pig feet. Such action was necessary because many of the African American restaurants and cafes during the 1940s were run by people who worked at other jobs during the day and only opened their establishments after they completed their other jobs. Many restaurants did not open until six o'clock in the evening.

Whether singers lived in homes, hotels, or rooming houses, there was the perennial problem of preparing their uniforms for the stage. Early on both men and women began to travel with one or two irons to press uniforms before a performance. While ironing in the home of a friend or family would be easy—often the host would volunteer to do the work—hotels and rooming houses usually made the singers pay extra for the electricity used. To make up for this extra charge, sometimes three and four people would sleep in one room, some in the one bed, some in chairs, and some on the floor.

Singers would bring extra posters or placards with them and, on the day before the concert, place them in stores and on signposts in the African American community to ensure proper advertising for the concert. This was especially crucial when the singers felt that the promoter was not sufficiently sophisticated in concert promotion. Many promoters—at first, all black—were gospel DJs who had no experience in concert promotion; some were ministers who assigned work to parishioners who were inept, and others were singers who thought that their names should be enough to guarantee a crowd.

By the early 1950s transportation problems had earned gospel singers such a reputation for late arrival at concerts that it became necessary to assure the public beforehand that the singers were indeed in town. In cities like Chicago, New York, and Detroit, a Sunday afternoon or evening concert appearance required that the singers be featured in one or two selections at one of the more popular churches so that the news of their arrival would spread before performance time.

Singers often performed with a guarantee of sixty percent of all collections or offerings. When paid admission to concerts began in the early 1950s, it was the custom for one or two of the singers to sit or stand at the door of the performance room or in the box office and collect (sometimes sell) tickets to ensure accountability for the number of persons attending a concert and the correct percentage they were due. Most singers required an advance two weeks before the concert. This advance, called a "guarantee," was necessary for two reasons: in many cases singers did not have the money to travel to the performance, and promoters were notorious for reporting a smaller amount of money than was collected, thereby cheating the singers of their full percentage of the money. Singers felt that if they were going to be cheated it would be better to get at least some money for the performance. If a group agreed to present a concert for a fee of $500, $200 would be the requested guarantee; the remaining $300 was due at the intermission of the concert. While this plan appeared fail-safe, it seldom worked. Singers were left to collect whatever money they could. It was usually necessary to present the concert once they were in town so they would have enough money to return home.

While many professional singers appeared to be "on the road" in the 1950s, many more could have been had they not had to work so hard to bring their music and message to the people. The dedicated pioneers who persevered became part of American and world history. One of the first was Thomas Andrew Dorsey.

GOSPEL IN CHICAGO

The seeds for a gospel community had been planted in Chicago by COGIC minister William Roberts (1876–1954), a Mississippi native who was "saved" under Charles Harrison Mason. After serving as Mason's deacon for a few years, Roberts was called to preach and went to the Windy City in 1917 to plant a church, where he introduced sanctified singing to his small congregation.

Charles Henry Pace (1886–1963) had moved to Chicago from Atlanta at age thirteen, and although he studied the European masters in his piano lessons, he came under the influence of the new gospel music and composed and conducted a style of this music at the Beth Eden and Liberty Baptist churches. In 1925 he formed the Pace Jubilee Singers, a conservative gospel group that, with Hattie Parker as soloist, reached a new peak in gospel in 1930 with their recording of Charles Albert Tindley's "Stand by Me."

Chicago was thus primed for a genuine gospel movement, and Thomas Andrew Dorsey seized the day. With a group of gospel musicians from Chicago and the surrounding area (sometimes extending more than two hundred miles), Dorsey created a vigorous gospel community. The leaders of this community were Dorsey, Sallie Martin, and Theodore R. Frye.

Thomas Andrew Dorsey

By 1945, it was difficult to avoid gospel music in the African American community. Although gospel had been created in the Pentecostal/Holiness churches of the South, the National Baptist Convention formally adopted it in 1921. And because Chicago was the center of music making for the National Baptist Convention, this city became the center for the development of gospel. For many years the leader of the "Chicago school of gospel" was Thomas Andrew Dorsey (1899–1993). Born in Villa Rica, Georgia, thirty-eight miles from Atlanta, Dorsey was the oldest of three children born to the Reverend Thomas Madison Dorsey, a graduate of what is now Morehouse College, and Etta Plant Dorsey, an organist. The Dorsey family moved to Atlanta in 1910, by which time young Thomas was able to play the pump organ for services at which his father preached, having first studied piano with his mother and then with a Mrs. Graves. Dorsey was encouraged in his musicianship by band members who accompanied acts at the 81 Theater, a vaudeville house on Atlanta's Decatur Street, where, since age eleven, he had worked selling nickel soda pop.

Thomas Dorsey and his female quartet, consisting of Bertha Armstrong, Dettie Gay, Mattie Wilson, and Sallie Martin, 1934

Atlanta's 81 Theater, the principal performance house for black artists of the Theater Owners Booking Association (TOBA), presented the most popular black entertainers on the traveling circuit. Among the entertainers who performed there were Gertrude "Ma" Rainey (1886–1939), the first great female blues singer and leading blues singer of the 1920s; pianist Eddie Heywood; and the comedy team of Butter Beans and Susie. Dorsey absorbed their influence, paying particular attention to the blues and to barrelhouse piano, and was soon able to duplicate their chords, riffs, and runs. He featured his new playing style at house and rent parties and teas sponsored by women's organizations.

Desiring a better musical education than he thought he could secure in Atlanta, Dorsey moved to Gary, Indiana, in 1916. His principal job there was working in a steel mill, but when he was not at the mill, he played piano in various local jazz bands. Settling permanently in Chicago in 1918, he enrolled for a short time in the Chicago College of Composition and Arranging. After only a few months in Chicago, he began playing with such well-known local jazz groups as Les Hite's Whispering Serenaders, a band that once included Lionel Hampton (b. 1909), and his own group, the Wildcats Jazz Band, the traveling band for Ma Rainey.

In 1925 he joined with Hudson Whittaker (1900–81), known as "Tampa Red," in a duo. The two produced "Tight Like That" in 1928, and the tremendous success of this double entendre song was the catalyst for several other duets, most of which were successful records. In late 1928, while working with Tampa Red, Dorsey suffered his second nervous breakdown in two years and decided to retire from music. During a two-year recuperation, a minister told him that he was "not as sick in the body as in mind" and that if he would use his music for God he would be healed. Dorsey accepted this as a warning that he should return to the music of his Christian roots.

This return would mean a radical change for Dorsey (Baptists, like Pentecostalists, did not believe that you could play blues, the devil's music, and still be a Christian), because for so long he had denied his "calling" to both the spoken and musical ministry. He had been converted as a small boy in Villa Rica and continued playing for church services even as he became involved with the blues. He kept his blues playing from his parents and most church members did not go to the places where he played, although if any had, they would not have mentioned his playing for they would not want it known that they had been to such places.

When Dorsey attended the National Baptist Convention in Chicago in 1921, he had no plan to return to the church, as he was having what he considered a successful career as a blues pianist. His intentions were changed when he experienced a second conversion during one of the services. The Reverend W. M. Nix, a Birmingham, Alabama, native, delivered a stirring gospel rendition of the 1907 hymn "I Do, Don't You?" by Edwin O. Excell (1851–1951) that was characterized by improvisation like that found in the singing of the sanctified singers. Dorsey, according to his biographer Michael W. Harris, declared:

> My inner being was thrilled ... my emotions were aroused; my heart was inspired to become a great singer and worker in the Kingdom of the Lord—and impress people just as this great singer did that Sunday morning.

Despite this second conversion, Dorsey's return to the church lasted only a few months. During that brief time, however, he composed a gospel song, "If I Don't Get There," for the second edition of *Gospel Pearls*, published in late 1921. The song remains number 117 in the hymnal. Dorsey's first published gospel song, it is a fairly sophisticated indication of what his songs of the 1930s and 1940s would be, capturing as it did the sonorous language of the common folk set to a melody of only six (scale) tones, four chords (one more than in the blues of the 1920s), and a refrain of repeated lines:

VERSE

Dear friends and kindred have gone from this world,
To dwell in that city so fair,
Hard trials and troubles no longer they share,
They'll be disappointed if I don't get there.

CHORUS

If I don't get there, if I don't get there,
They'll be disappointed with hearts in despair,
Dear father and mother, sweet sister and brother,
Kind kindred and others, if I don't get there.

When this gospel song did not propel Dorsey into the forefront of gospel singers, he felt there was nothing to do but return to the world of secular music. Then the minister's words "not as sick in the body as in mind" finally struck a chord with Dorsey in 1928, and in 1930 he renounced secular music and became a full-time gospel musician. It was a tumultuous two years between 1928 and 1930 for Dorsey because he had no church community to replace the community he had established in blues. At the same time his blues-playing friends were regularly offering him jobs. He had no occupation other than music and without his blues and jazz engagements he could not make a living. But after playing only a few blues jobs, Dorsey set about meeting church musicians and attending sacred music concerts. To earn a living, he began composing gospel music and peddling song sheets throughout Chicago, although he was often the butt of jokes and humiliation.

Determined to serve the Master through his gospel music, he organized one of the first gospel choirs at Chicago's Pilgrim Baptist Church in 1932 and secured as his pianist the young adult Roberta Martin, who would become a leading force in gospel within ten years. In the same year he opened the first publishing house for the exclusive sale of gospel music by African American composers, and the following year, along with Sallie Martin, Magnolia Lewis Butts, Theodore R. Frye, and

Beatrice Brown, organized the National Convention of Gospel Choirs and Choruses, Incorporated (NCGCC). The members of Dorsey's NCGCC were directors and choirs in Baptist churches throughout the United States. Each annual convention, held in a different city, brought forth a new batch of songs that choir directors could teach to their local church choirs.

Dorsey was particularly skilled at writing songs that not only captured the hopes, fears, and aspirations of the poor and disenfranchised African American but also spoke to all people. Marked by catchy titles, many of which became part of the religious rhetoric of African American Christians, these songs had simple but beautiful melodies, harmonies that did not overshadow the text, and open rhythmic spaces for the obligatory improvisation that identified gospel. Indeed, during the 1940s there were periods when all gospel songs were referred to as "Dorsey."

There has been no more imposing figure in gospel than Thomas Andrew Dorsey, and for his contribution to the music, he was named early on "Father of African American Gospel Music" and was celebrated as such in the 1983 documentary *Say Amen, Somebody*. His most popular composition, "Take My Hand, Precious Lord," second only to "Amazing Grace" in popularity in the African American community, has been translated into more than forty languages and has even been used as a prayer.

It is ironic that one of the most beloved of all Christian hymns, "Take My Hand, Precious Lord," was born of tragedy. In 1932 Dorsey and Theodore R. Frye left Chicago en route to St. Louis, Missouri, to organize a gospel choir. After traveling only a few miles Frye remembered an important engagement and requested that Dorsey return him to his home. Dorsey took the trip to St. Louis alone. Upon his arrival at the church in St. Louis, he found a telegram waiting for him. The telegram said that his wife had suddenly become extremely ill and that he should return to Chicago at once. Dorsey's wife was in the last stages of pregnancy, and when he finally returned home he found that his wife had died. The baby had been born without difficulty but unfortunately died within two days. He retired to his "music" room and remained there for three days. Dorsey said that when he came to himself after three days he went to the piano and, using as inspiration a white Protestant hymn, "Must Jesus Bear the Cross Alone" by George N. Allen (1812–77), composed this song:

Precious Lord, take my hand,
Lead me on, let me stand,
I am tired, I am weak, I am worn;
Through the storm, through the night,
Lead me on to the light,
Take my hand, precious Lord, lead me on.

It was one of several Dorsey compositions sung at his funeral in Chicago on January 28, 1993.

Sallie Martin

The first genuine gospel singer to attract Dorsey's attention was Sallie Martin (1896–1988) of Pittfield, Georgia. Martin arrived in Chicago in 1927, by way of Cleveland, Ohio, with her husband and son after a hard life in her small Georgia town. From baby-sitting, cleaning houses, cooking, and washing clothes, Martin became a church singer, singing hymns and spirituals for Sunday morning services, Wednesday evening prayer meetings, and revivals. When she moved to Chicago she became affiliated with the Pentecostal church, but retained an association with the National Baptist Convention, the denomination into which she was born. When Dorsey began his gospel movement in 1930, Martin attempted to become his associate. Dorsey considered her singing style unrefined, filled with whoops, slides, groans, and most abominably, physical steps while singing, a practice associated with shouting in the Pentecostal church.

Another bone of contention that Dorsey had to reconcile was Martin's inability to read music and her complete disinterest in learning to do so. While Martin had been brought up in the Baptist church and had sung there as a young girl, her mature singing had developed in the Pentecostal church. At that time the Pentecostal church did not use hymn books, preferring to sing relatively simple refrains such as those of the Azusa Street Revival. Since such music could be learned so quickly and improvisation was so important to the style, reading music was unnecessary. Dorsey was aware that most choir members did not read music, but many soloists did, especially those who were good enough and sang enough to develop favorable reputations. Even though he did not care for Martin's singing he recognized her celebrity as a local singer. Dorsey would soon discover that the ability to read music was extremely rare in gospel choirs, and that teaching music without reading it would become his method of working with gospel choirs.

Martin devised a plan to win Dorsey's attention. Whenever she knew that Dorsey was to appear at a local church, she arranged to appear on the program or lead a song during the service. Singing a repertoire of sanctified songs, she was able to stir the church into a frenzy. She auditioned for Dorsey three times but was rejected each time. Through the intervention of Theodore R. Frye, Dorsey agreed to accept her as a member of a trio he formed in 1932 to demonstrate his songs. It was a year before Dorsey assigned her a solo, and although he objected to the dark color of her voice, her tendency to purposely insert a break in the voice at the beginning and ending of phrases, and her curt manner of addressing him, he could not deny the fact that she possessed a special relationship with church audiences: they responded enthusiastically to her singing of his songs.

Sallie Martin had a keen sense of finances: at the height of her career in the 1960s she was reportedly the wealthiest woman in gospel, having accumulated more money than either Roberta Martin or Mahalia Jackson. She knew how to market sheet music, save on printing, charge for voice lessons, and save money. Dorsey was little concerned with such matters, delegating such responsibilities to Martin once their partnership was solidified. She organized his music store, hired assistants to work at the counter, and kept records of the inventory. After a few short months of working with Dorsey, she was able to show a profit for his business—a feat that had eluded Dorsey. This success was not achieved without many stormy sessions between Dorsey and Martin. Martin was argumentative and adversarial by nature and was constantly on the attack. Their heated discussions were often caused by Martin's statement to Dorsey that "you have something here [his compositions] but you just don't know what to do with it [he was not an aggressive salesman]." The same kind of tenuous relationship was to mark her association with Willie Mae Ford Smith, her partner in Dorsey's convention, as documented in 1983 in *Say Amen, Somebody*.

In 1932 Martin joined Dorsey in organizing the NCGCC, and served as first vice president from its organization until her death. In 1940, with gospel song composer Kenneth Morris and with financial backing from the Reverend Clarence H. Cobb, she opened the Martin and Morris Music, Inc. in Chicago, a publishing company she codirected until 1975. In 1940 she also formed the Sallie Martin Singers with whom she traveled throughout the United States and Europe (the singers disbanded in 1975). She was an active supporter of Martin Luther King, Jr., and represented him at the 1960 ceremony marking independence in Nigeria. Her visit to Africa inspired her to make financial contributions to the Nigerian Health Program. As a result, a state office building in Isslu-UKA, Nigeria, was named in her honor.

Martin was unlike other Chicago singers in that she never attempted to smooth out her rough-hewn voice. She adopted the sanctified style of shout singing and was known for her Holy Ghost jerks and steps. When taken over by the spirit, her dark alto would soar above a shouting crowd on such songs as "I Claim Jesus First and Last" and Dorsey's "It Don't Cost Very Much" and "I'll Tell It Wherever I Go." Of all her recordings, she is best known for her duet with Alex Bradford of "He'll Wash You Whiter Than Snow" in which she matches Bradford note for note and nuance for nuance as he, with a voice much like that of a young Louis Armstrong, wailed and squalled through one of the most joyous jubilee songs of the 1950s.

Despite her adversarial relationship with Dorsey that endured until the 1980s, when Dorsey retired from composing, Martin was Dorsey's right hand in his gospel ministry. In recognition of her contributions to gospel music and her work with Dorsey, she was accorded the title of "Mother of Gospel" by the NCGCC.

Theodore R. Frye

The third person in the triumvirate established by Dorsey was Theodore R. Frye (1899–1963). Born in Fayette, Mississippi, Frye moved to Chicago in 1927. Having studied piano and voice as a child and having served as soloist and choir director in his hometown, Frye eagerly sought a musical camaraderie in Chicago with musicians who not only read music but who were not afraid to sing with the "spirit." He found this in Dorsey. With Dorsey as his pianist, he quickly developed a reputation as a singer who could "move a house," meaning that he was generally successful in arousing the emotions of a congregation. His light baritone was perfectly suited to the new gospel songs: enough volume in the low register to give a solid reading of the theme and enough notes in the upper register to display varied techniques while improvising. He and Dorsey became close friends and served as codirectors of the junior choir at Chicago's Ebenezer Baptist Church; Frye became sole director in 1932 when Dorsey assumed the directorship of the gospel choir at Pilgrim. In 1933, a year after cofounding the NCGCC, he and Roberta Martin formed the Martin-Frye Quartet of young boys from Pilgrim's Junior Choir. Although Frye composed the popular "Sending up My Timber up to Heaven" (1939) and "God's Power Changes Things" (1949), he is more popularly known as the revisionist of "I'm Going to Walk That Milky White Way" (1948), first recorded by the CBS Trumpeteers in 1948 and a popular hit again in the late 1980s through a recording by the gospel/jazz *a cappella* group, Take Six. His compositions, like Dorsey's, are characterized by a poetic use of black rhetoric, singable melodies, and syncopated rhythms.

In the 1940s Frye became an associate of Mahalia Jackson and figured prominently in her second recording session for Apollo Records in 1947 that produced her greatest hit, "Move on up a Little Higher." He was a cofounder of the National Baptist Music Convention (1948), an auxiliary of the National Baptist Convention that was organized to train musicians for the denomination. Frye worked with Lillian Bowles and Dorsey in their publishing firms and finally opened his own publishing house in 1948.

Magnolia Lewis Butts

A close associate of both Dorsey and Frye was Magnolia Lewis Butts (c.1880–1949). Butts had served as the director of the Youth Choir of the Metropolitan Community Church since 1928, and when Dorsey organized the gospel choir at Pilgrim, she followed his lead and adopted gospel music for her group. She changed the name of her choir to the Metropolitan Community Church Gospel Chorus in 1932 when she became a cofounder of the NCGCC. While Butts was known then as a great gospel soloist whose small but prominent alto voice could fill a large hall with spirited singing, she is remembered today principally as the composer of "Let It Breathe on Me" (1942), a composition that even in the early 1990s was still being sung during the call to prayer and meditation in many African American services:

> *Let it breathe on me, let it breathe on me,*
> *Let the breath of the Lord now breathe on me;*
> *Let it breathe on me, let it breathe on me,*
> *Let the breath of the Lord now breathe on me.*

Unlike most of Dorsey's associates, Butts never opened a publishing firm, but published her songs through the Bowles Music House, whose catalogue was purchased by Sallie Martin in 1959 for the Martin and Morris Music Company.

Roberta Martin

Dorsey's Chicago school of gospel inspired many younger musicians to adopt his style and join his followers. Roberta Martin (1907–69) had been with Dorsey since he organized the gospel choir at Pilgrim in 1932. She had heard gospel before she met Dorsey, however, and in a 1964 interview Martin described her introduction to gospel:

> I've been playing in churches nearly all my life, ever since I was so high. I started down at Pilgrim where I was the pianist for the Sunday School. At that time I was just interested in church hymns, anthems, choir music and secular songs. The first time I heard gospel singing as such, was this lady and the men—Bertha Wise and her Singers [from Augusta, Georgia]. Miss Wise played the piano for them. They came to our church, and oh, did we enjoy them. Actually, they were famous—they would go around to the National Baptist Convention and sing. They were not exactly singing gospel songs, but spirituals like gospel songs and the one that interested me the most was "I Can Tell The World About This." This was in 1933 [1932?].

Martin's experience with the Wise Singers was evidently before her assignment as the pianist for Dorsey's choir. In either case, in 1933 she and Frye organized the Martin-Frye Quartet, and by 1935 when she changed the name of the group to the Roberta Martin Singers, she had become a convert to gospel.

Roberta Evelyn Martin was one of six children born to William and Anna Winston in Helena, Arkansas. She moved with her family to Cairo, Illinois, when she was ten, by which time she had studied the piano with her oldest brother's wife and had already been a pianist for the Sunday School. While attending the Wendell Phillips High School in Chicago, she was inspired by her teacher, Mildred Bryant Jones, to study to become a concert artist. However, when she was invited to become the pianist for the Young People's Choir at Ebenezer Baptist Church, she began to devote her talents to church music.

Eugene Smith, Archie Dennis, Delois Barrett, Roberta Martin, and Gloria Griffin as the Roberta Martin Singers

After working with both Dorsey and Frye, she decided to enter the field of gospel and selected several young boys from Ebenezer and Pilgrim to become the Roberta Martin Singers. The original members were Eugene Smith (b. 1921), Norsalus McKissick (b. 1925), Robert Anderson (b. 1919), James Lawrence (1925–1990), Willie Webb (b. 1919), and Romance Watson (b. 1925). Inspired by Bertha Wise and her singers, and undoubtedly because even as a youngster Martin possessed a dark, rich contralto that could easily mix with the male timbre, she set about developing a gospel sound with no bass, but rather a dark treble sound with the vocal elasticity that the new music required. Eugene Smith, who was only twelve years old when Martin first assembled the group, sang first tenor, Watson sang second tenor, Webb was the high baritone, and Anderson the low baritone. Martin filled in when one of the boys took the lead. In the early 1940s when Martin decided to add female voices to her group, she selected Bessie Folk (b. 1928) and Delois Barrett (b. 1926) and refined the "Roberta Martin gospel sound and style."

The Martin style was one of refinement in songs, singing style, and piano and organ accompaniment. Although her inspiration came from the Pentecostal shouters, she felt that she could not duplicate this fiery kind of singing and instead attempted, with great success, to capture their zest with well-modulated voices. She began the tradition of each member serving as both soloist and background singer. Rather than encouraging a lead voice with increasingly aggressive background singing, she took the opposite approach, assigning a hum as response instead of an energized repetition of the lyrics. This practice encouraged the audience to pay more attention to the delivery of the text and melody by the lead singer. This technique worked well with slow, lyrical gospel ballads; for jubilee or fast-paced songs Martin returned to the original Pentecostal/Negro spiritual practice of call and response with the background voices spurring the leader on to a vocal frenzy.

Martin was equally well known for her piano style, which was marked by nuance and refinement rather than virtuosity. She played mainly in the middle of the piano, introducing chords—magnificently voiced—that she borrowed from the Western European classical music she had studied and that were new to gospel. She emphasized the first beat of each musical unit in the middle of the piano and provided her own response by answering this beat with secondary beats at the upper ranges of the keyboard. One of her trademarks was bringing a song to a "ritard" (slowing down) at the end, followed by cascading chords all the way to the upper extremes of the keyboard.

She opened the Roberta Martin Studio of Music in 1939, and one of her first publications was the gospel standard "He Knows How Much We Can Bear." Her first composition to become a gospel standard, "Try Jesus, He Satisfies," was written and published in 1943. Among her other famous compositions are "I'm Just Waiting on the Lord" (1953) and "God Is Still on the Throne" (1959). Unlike Dorsey, who published only his own compositions, Martin published songs by other composers, as long as they were songs her group sang. In this way she advertised her inventory. She published and her group sang compositions by James Cleveland, Lucy Matthews, Sammy Lewis, Kenneth Woods, Alex Bradford, and Dorothy Norwood. Her most famous publication was her theme song, "Only a Look" by Anna Shepherd.

Martin began recording in the late 1930s, and during the thirty-six-year career of the Roberta Martin Singers, she earned six gold records for selling a million copies of a song or an album. She was one of the first singers to refuse to permit her group to perform in secular venues. She did, however, accept an invitation to perform at Gian-Carlo Menotti's Spoleto Festival of Two Worlds in Spoleto, Italy, in 1963. She was honored for her groundbreaking work in gospel by a colloquium and concert at the Smithsonian Institution in 1982.

Eugene Smith and Gospel Blues

In 1941 Eugene Smith, a member of the Roberta Martin Singers, composed "I Know the Lord Will Make a Way, Oh Yes, He Will." His composition became extremely important because it gave another formal structure to composers of gospel and would continue to intrigue composers even into the 1980s.

Smith, the most flamboyant of the Martin Singers and the manager of the group from 1947 until it disbanded in 1969, could have easily led his own group. With his penchant for caressing the lyrics and tones of a gospel ballad (a slow gospel song that often tells a serious or melancholy story) and his ability to deliver a shout song not unlike his Pentecostal preaching friends, Smith was approached on several occasions to leave the Martin Singers and form his own group. He chose not to but made a contribution to gospel that was possibly greater than the formation of a group. "I Know the Lord Will Make a Way, Oh Yes, He Will" is now recognized as *gospel blues*. While, at first hearing, gospel blues bears none of the formal characteristics of the blues made famous by Bessie Smith (1884–1937) or B. B. King (b. 1925), their structural relationship becomes clearer on closer examination.

The most obvious characteristic of the blues is its constant harmonic progression. That is to say, whether the blues is "Fine and Mellow" by Billie Holiday (1915–69) or "Everyday I Have the Blues" by Memphis Slim (Peter Chatman, b. 1915), each with a different melodic line, the harmony that supports the melody for each is the same. The harmony, explained in musical textbooks as I-IV-V and embellished with as many additional chords as there are performers, is the harmonic foundation over which each composer lays a new or different melody.

"I Know the Lord Will Make a Way, Oh Yes, He Will" is as true to the gospel blues structure as "Everyday I Have the Blues" is to the secular blues. Both use a constant harmonic scheme: secular blues is composed of a three-line poem with an AAB rhyme scheme, while gospel blues is composed of a four-line poem with an AABA rhyme scheme. Secular blues requires three units (three four-bar phrases) of musical time to express its poetry, while gospel blues requires four units of musical time. Also, a different middle and closing section are incorporated into gospel blues. Secular blues text treats a dire situation that worsens in the last line, while gospel blues speaks of a hope that is guaranteed and celebrated in the third line with the first line repeated as the last, giving symmetry to the poem. For example:

SECULAR BLUES—"STORMY MONDAY"
They call it stormy Monday, but Tuesday's just as bad
[rhyme—A; musical time—four bars]
They call it stormy Monday, but Tuesday's just as bad
[rhyme—A; musical time—four bars]
Wednesday's worse, and Thursday's oh, so sad
[rhyme—B; musical time—four bars]

GOSPEL BLUES—"I KNOW THE LORD WILL MAKE A WAY, OH YES, HE WILL"
I know the Lord will make a way, oh yes, He will
[rhyme—A; musical time—four bars]
I know the Lord will make a way, oh yes, He will
[rhyme—A; musical time—four bars]
He will make a way for you, He will lead you safely through
[rhyme—B; musical time—four bars]
I know the Lord will make a way, oh yes, He will
[rhyme—A; musical time—four bars]

"I Know the Lord Will Make a Way, Oh Yes, He Will" revived interest in the first gospel blues composition, "When the Storms of Life Are Raging, Stand by Me" by Charles Albert Tindley, and inspired such later compositions as "I'm Going to Die with the Staff in My Hand" and "Lord, I've Tried."

Robert Anderson

While Eugene Smith remained with the Martin Singers, three other members left to organize their own groups. The first was Robert Anderson, followed by Willie Webb and Delois Barrett. Having come to Chicago from his native Mississippi as a small child, Anderson followed other young, musically inclined children to Metropolitan

Community Church where Magnolia Lewis Butts directed the children's choir. He never studied piano formally but, like many other pianists and organists in the African American church of the period, learned to play by ear and often assisted Roberta Martin with the Sunday School choir. Anderson cared little for traveling so when the Martin Singers began to do so full time in the early 1940s, he decided to establish a solo career. This was a momentous step for Anderson, because he had one of the most unusual voices in gospel, a true baritone singing in a style similar to such then-popular singers as Billy Eckstine and Bing Crosby. Although he came from Mississippi, the adopted home of Charles Harrison Mason, Anderson never adopted a shouting style of singing gospel. His style was marked by fullness of tone, few embellishments, and little physical activity while singing. Yet his attention to phrasing, purity of tone, and dynamic style brought the same kind of response from audiences as Eugene Smith did using the theatrics of the Pentecostal church.

Anderson organized several groups to sing with him even as he continued his solo career, hoping to find other singers who would bear some of the responsibility of leading songs. Most successful was the Gospel Caravan, which he organized in 1947. Unlike those he organized before and after, this group was composed of all women and included seventeen-year-old Albertina Walker, who within a few years would leave Anderson to organize her own group. Serving as his own accompanist, Anderson developed a reputation as a stirring singer, conductor, and composer. While he performed the compositions of Dorsey, Frye, and Martin with enthusiasm, none of these performances equaled the renditions of his own compositions. The 1950 recording of his 1947 composition "Prayer Changes Things" has yet to be equaled in its reading of the lyrics and forceful delivery of the melody, especially in its sing-a-long style chorus:

> Oh yes, I know prayer changes things, oh yes, I know
> Prayer changes things,
> When I was out on the stormy, raging sea;
> I was hungry, I was sick, I was filled with misery,
> Along came Jesus and He rescued me,
> That's why I know that prayer changes things.

Like Dorsey, Roberta Martin, and Sallie Martin, Anderson opened a publishing house, Robert Anderson's Good Shepherd Music House, in Gary, Indiana, in 1942, through which he published his compositions. Anderson was the only member of the Chicago school of gospel to publish outside Chicago. Among his other popular compositions were "Why Should I Worry?" (1945) and "Oh Lord, Is It I?" (1953).

Norsalus McKissick

Norsalus McKissick was not a composer, but as the second youngest of the original Roberta Martin Singers, he was so instrumental in presenting the gospel ballads sold by Martin that he deserves special mention. Like Eugene Smith, McKissick came to Ebenezer Baptist Church from Metropolitan to join the Youth Choir organized by Roberta Martin and Theodore R. Frye in 1933. Slight of stature and the quietest member of the Roberta Martin Singers, McKissick did not possess a golden baritone like that of Robert Anderson, but rather a slightly brassy baritone, extraordinary breath control, and a sense of phrasing unmatched in gospel even into the 1990s. Called a "deliberate" singer, that is, one who is always slightly behind the beat, allowing time for each syllable to become an independent unit within itself, McKissick could work through a ballad in such a way that the listener was transported into the situation about which he sang. Throughout his long career with the Martin Singers (1933–69), there was always a rush of audience emotion when he sang, "I was lost in sin and sorrow," the opening line of Dorsey's recasting of the Negro spiritual "Old Ship of Zion." He was no less at home with Roberta Martin's gospel arrangement of the white Protestant hymn "The Old Account Was Settled." He reached new heights of interpretation with Alex Bradford's "Saved Till the Day of Redemption" in the mid-1950s.

Kenneth Morris

Although he never worked directly with Dorsey, Kenneth Morris (1917–88) came under his influence early on and patterned much of his career after Dorsey's. Morris was born in New York City and took piano lessons from grammar school through high school. Like most child pianists of the church, he occasionally served as pianist for the Sunday School, but by his teen years, his interest was focused on impromptu jam sessions with other teenage boys from his neighborhood. After graduating from high school, Morris entered the Manhattan Conservatory of Music where he studied traditional Western music theory—but with the hope of becoming a jazz musician. While he was at the conservatory, the Kenneth Morris Jazz Band, which grew out of the jam sessions, received an invitation to perform in Chicago at the 1934 World's Fair. His group was a success, but Morris contracted tuberculosis and had to leave the band.

Rather than return to New York to recuperate, Morris decided to remain in Chicago. For entertainment during this period he occasionally "sat in" with a group of Chicago jazz musicians, all of whom could read and write music. The news of the group reached Lillian Bowles, owner of Bowles Music House, who approached Morris in hopes that he could recommend a scribe to write down in musical notation the songs composed by those who were technically illiterate and could not do so themselves.

Mrs. Bowles (c.1884–1949), originally from Memphis, Tennessee, but a long-time resident of Chicago, had opened a publishing house in the late 1920s. Gospel was one of several types of music she published, along with blues, jazz, and ragtime. Although Bowles' publications were mainly skeletons of what an improvising performer was expected to play, the scribe who wrote out the music needed to know the several styles. In most cases scribes did not alter in any way what composers sang or played for them—people who did that were called "arrangers." However, Morris did not know this when Mrs. Bowles approached him and he took the job, which he considered a good find since it was not strenuous and was indoors. Although he was initially disappointed, Morris worked at the Bowles Music House from late 1934 until 1940. He filled a position that had been previously held by Charles Henry Pace, who left Chicago in 1936 for Pittsburgh, Pennsylvania, where he established the Pace Music House shortly afterwards.

During Morris' tenure with Bowles he transcribed such popular gospel songs as "God Shall Wipe All Tears Away" (1935) by Antonio Haskell, "I'm Sending My Timber up to Heaven" (1939) by Theodore R. Frye, and in the same year, a 1937 composition attributed to Mrs. Bowles—and in 1937 the first song recorded by Mahalia Jackson—"God's Goin' to Separate the Wheat from the Tare." Although he transcribed other kinds of music during his years at Bowles, Morris reported in an interview for a 1986 symposium of his music held at the Smithsonian Institution that he was transcribing so much gospel music that he began to lose interest in the other types.

The Reverend Clarence H. Cobb (1907–79), known as "Preacher," often visited the Bowles store to select new music for his church choir. As founder and pastor of Chicago's First Church of Deliverance, Cobb was one of a few preachers in the town who welcomed gospel music. Mrs. Bowles felt that Preacher should meet her new scribe, who could not only play gospel music, but transcribe it as well. Preacher was so impressed with the musicality of Morris that he persuaded him to become choir director at his church. Morris not only accepted the position, arranging for and directing the choir, but in 1939 he revolutionized gospel singing by introducing the Hammond organ as a gospel instrument. When the piano and Hammond organ were paired, they created the ideal accompaniment for gospel: one instrument would sustain tones while the other was rhythmically active; one instrument could affect the vibrato of the voice while the other instrument could be struck like the patting of feet; and one instrument could imitate a bass fiddle while the other instrument tinkled the highest keys like a harp being plucked. These two instruments became the standard accompaniment for traditional gospel until 1970, when a newer style of gospel, called "contemporary," introduced the synthesizer.

Morris became almost as significant a publisher as he was a composer. When he and Sallie Martin realized that Dorsey was publishing only his own compositions and Roberta Martin was publishing only what her singers sang, they saw a tremendous opportunity. By publishing the music of those who had no connection to either the Dorsey or Roberta Martin publishing houses, they could serve a large number of new composers. Their company, Martin and Morris Music, Inc., became the leading publishing house in Chicago. Among their composers were Alex Bradford, James Cleveland, (composers sometimes published with as many as five houses), Sam Cooke, W. Herbert Brewster, Lucie Campbell, and Dorothy Love Coates. Morris transcribed all their compositions, although some composers, such as Lucie Campbell, could notate their own music.

Morris would pay fifteen dollars for each song that he accepted from new or relatively known composers. Well-known composers such as Cleveland and Bradford would haggle over song fees and, depending on their fame at the time of their song submission, could receive as much as fifty dollars for a song. This was an important victory for the composers, for that payment was all that they received from Martin and Morris. On the other hand, Morris would copyright the song in the composer's name and would sell song sheets or books that included the song to the composer at a reduced rate.

Morris, responsible for demonstrating and selling music at the store in addition to transcribing music, still found some time to compose, and from 1940 until the mid-1960s produced some of the most important songs in African American gospel. His first hit came in 1940 with "I'll Be a Servant for the Lord," made famous by the popular Ohio-based choir Wings Over Jordan. On a train trip from Kansas City to Chicago, Morris exited the train on one of its stops to get some fresh air and heard one of the station porters singing a song. He paid little attention at first, but after he reboarded the train the song remained with him and became so prominent in his mind that at the next stop, he left the train, took another train back to the earlier station, and asked the porter to sing the song again. Morris wrote down the words and music and published the song "Just a Closer Walk with Thee" that year, 1940, adding a few lyrics of his own to provide more breadth. Within two years the song became a standard in gospel music, eventually becoming a standard in jazz, and then moving into the realm of American folk music, known and sung by many.

In 1944 Morris published his most popular song, "Yes, God Is Real." The song opens with a strong declaration of the inability of mortals to understand the universe and to survey all its wonders:

> *There are some things I may not know,*
> *There are some places I can't go.*

The song then immediately shifts to an equally strong statement of confidence, proclaiming what people can understand and their joy in such knowledge:

> *But I am sure of this one thing,*
> *That God is real for I can feel Him deep within.*

In 1946 Morris published the second most popular song in his catalogue, "Christ Is All." Following the Morris formula for lyric writing—that is, stating the problem in the verse of the song, it begins:

> *I don't possess houses or land, fine clothes or jewelry,*
> *Sorrows and cares in this old world my lot seem to be;*

Continuing the formula he brings the verse to a close in the last two lines of the inevitable solution:

> But I have a Christ who paid the price way back on Calv'ry,
> And Christ is all, all and all this world to me.

Morris songs are distinguished from Dorsey and Roberta Martin in this problem-solution aspect of verse writing. His melodies and harmonies were those of 1940s gospel whereby three or four chords supported the melody of five or six tones, limiting the tones of the melody so that the words would not be overshadowed by any musical elements. His "Eyes Hath Not Seen," composed in 1945, goes beyond his usual harmonic language to introduce new and modern chords into gospel that were not completely adopted by gospel composers until the 1960s. Among his more than five hundred songs are several gospel standards, including "Jesus Steps Right in When I Need Him Most" (1945), "Dig a Little Deeper in God's Love" (1947), and "King Jesus Will Roll All Burdens Away" (1947).

Emma L. Jackson

Emma L. Jackson, who flourished from 1940 to 1960, was a staunch supporter of the music of the National Baptist Convention. Deciding to follow the "sound of gospel," she relocated from New Orleans to Chicago in the early 1940s. She first made an impression on the city as a soloist capable of "rocking a church" with both the old Baptist moan and the newer gospel songs. She is credited with introducing Dorsey's "Take My Hand, Precious Lord" at the National Baptist Convention, a song she kept in her repertoire throughout her performance career. Encouraged by Dorsey to write her own songs, in 1942 she composed "I'm Going to Die with the Staff in My Hand":

> I'm going to die with the staff in my hand,
> I'm going to die with the staff in my hand;
> Sometimes I reel and I rock from side to side,
> I'm going to die with the staff in my hand.

Jackson wrote her song for a choir rather than a small group, and when it was performed in the mid-1940s by nearly a thousand voices at the National Baptist Convention, the organists, pianists, and choir directors were participants. They brought the song back to their local choirs, and it soon became extremely popular.

"I'm Going to Die with the Staff in My Hand" served to introduce Jackson to the gospel public. However, by far her most popular song was "Don't Forget the Family Prayer," composed in 1945 and published in her newly formed publishing house, Jackson Studio of Music:

VERSE
Prayer will keep your home together,
Bring your wand'ring child back home;
Prayer will make you love your neighbor,
Don't forget the family prayer.

CHORUS
Don't forget the family prayer,
Jesus goin' to meet you there;
When you gather round the altar,
Don't forget the family prayer.

Jackson's lyrics were set to a melody that could be remembered and sung after only one rendition. The song captured the essence of Chicago gospel: a simple solution to a difficult problem, but a solution that requires total trust in God; singers who delivered songs with a conviction that would normally be confined to the privacy of one's home; a beat that would not permit a listener to remain uninvolved in the singing; and vocal virtuosity that had not been imagined before the Azusa Street Revival. Jackson's song evoked a passion that had not been experienced by African Americans since slave meetings. The African American nuclear family had been given no respect during the slave era, and families were often broken up, with mother going to one plantation, husband to another, and the children to yet another. In post-slavery times husbands often had to work away from home (sometimes as far as a hundred miles), coming home only on weekends. Often families were, for one reason or another, fatherless. Jackson's song presents, if only for the length of the song, a family obviously composed of both mother and father eagerly awaiting the return of their child from some wayward journey. "Don't Forget the Family Prayer" was and still is popular because of strong African American belief in family and prayer.

Willie Webb

The second singer from the original Roberta Martin Singers to form a group was Willie Webb. Webb (b.1919), like Frye and Anderson, came to Chicago from Mississippi as a small boy. Hearing of the opportunities afforded young musical talent, he joined Anderson, Smith, and McKissick at Metropolitan and sang under Magnolia Lewis Butts. Like Anderson, he did not wish to travel; but unlike Anderson, Webb developed into a virtuoso pianist and organist and was soon recruited to play for and direct local church choirs in the Chicago area. Before "Little" Lucy became the substitute pianist for the Roberta Martin Singers, Webb often replaced Martin at the piano.

He never felt secure enough about his solo voice to lead songs, but he was skilled at arranging songs to fit any voice, teaching all the parts of the chord to singers, and accompanying them on piano or organ. He organized an all-male group in the late 1940s that sang in the Chicago area. In 1949 he founded a mixed group not unlike that of his mentor Roberta Martin, that could express his compositions with an attention-getting flair. The group was composed of, among others, such well-known singers as new Chicago resident Alex Bradford, Ozella Weber, Oralee Thurston, and Webb himself. While Webb has been accorded a certain celebrity for having introduced Alex Bradford to the gospel world—Bradford was the lead singer on Webb's 1951 recording of "Every Day and Every Hour"—many gospel music lovers remember him as the composer of his "I'm Bound for Higher Ground" (1945), a popular gospel standard for twenty years, as was his 1947 composition entitled "He's All I Need."

"Little" Lucy Smith

The Reverend Lucy Smith (1874–1952), founder and pastor (1920–52) of Chicago's All Nations Pentecostal Church, arrived in Chicago in 1910 from her native Athens, Georgia, with ten children. While working as a dressmaker to support her family, she became active in the Olivet Baptist Church. In 1914, however, reacting to the news of the Azusa Street Revival, Smith received the baptism of the Holy Ghost. She founded a healing ministry in 1916 and four years later built one of the first churches in Chicago to receive sanctified singing. Her granddaughter (b. 1928) was known as "Little" Lucy.

Little Lucy showed spectacular musical aptitude from age four when she got on the piano stool and began picking out tunes that she had heard in church. At age ten her grandmother sent her to Roberta Martin for piano lessons. Little Lucy mastered the gospel style in two years and transferred her piano skill to the organ. At age twelve, she became the organist at her grandmother's church and was as much a drawing card as her grandmother.

When she was sixteen, Little Lucy suggested to Roberta Martin that Martin meet her father, who by that time was divorced from her mother. The meeting took place, and through a strange set of circumstances, Martin married Little Lucy's father. Martin then began to teach Little Lucy music theory and voice. In the mid-1950s Little Lucy organized the Lucy Smith Singers, whose members were Catherine Campbell, Sarah McKissick (wife of Norsalus McKissick), Gladys Beamon, and Smith. Her most famous composition was "I'll Never Let Go His Hand," while the most famous recording for the Lucy Smith Singers was "Somebody Bigger Than You and I." In the early 1960s she became the official pianist for the Roberta Martin Singers.

Other Composers Associated with Chicago Gospel

Dorsey and his associates (which did not include the Pentecostal gospel singers because they seldom associated—even musically—with non-Pentecostal singers) inspired others to turn to gospel. One of the most important of these second generation associates of Dorsey was Sylvia Boddie.

SYLVIA BODDIE

Sylvia Boddie, wife of the Reverend Louis Boddie, pastor of the Greater Harvest Baptist Church of Chicago (one of the principal venues for gospel performance during the 1940s and 1950s), composed more than one hundred songs, many of which became gospel standards. Because the choir of her husband's church was the principal vehicle for the performances of her songs, she composed most of them for large groups. Chief among her compositions is the gospel standard "Now Lord" (1948), in which she delivers a prayer to the Master as if talking to a neighbor across the back yard fence:

Now Lord, now Lord, now Lord, now Lord,
You've been my burden bearer, you've been my all and all;
I need you when troubles grieve me, I need you when friends deceive me,
Now Lord, please hear me when I call.

VIRGINIA DAVIS

Virginia Davis' "I Call Him Jesus, My Rock" (1950) bears a close relationship to Sylvia Boddie's "Now Lord" and was dedicated to Sylvia Boddie's husband. Davis (b. 1904) occasionally served as a choir director and soloist in Chicago but earned her living as a musical scribe for most of the major publishing houses in Chicago. (She perfected this skill while serving in the same capacity for Lillian Bowles.) She opened a publishing house for a short time but found that all her potential customers had lucrative contracts with other houses at an advance of fifteen or twenty-five dollars per song, so she returned to working with Frye, Jackson, and others as a freelance scribe. She was at her best in arranging songs for gospel singers. She also wrote several songs that enjoyed huge popularity for a short time. Her most famous song, recorded by Clara Ward and the Ward Singers among others, has a sing-a-long chorus built of few words but attached to a memorable melody supported by the sparse harmony that the gospel of the 1940s and 1950s required:

Chorus
Calling Jesus
   My rock
I need you Jesus
   My rock
Hear me Jesus
   My rock
I'm calling Jesus
   My rock
I know He won't deny me
   Jesus—Jesus
For He's walking right beside me
   Jesus—Jesus

> *Church, I call Him Jesus—*
> > **My rock**
> *I call Him Jesus*
> > **My rock.**

The lyrics literally sing the call and response and elicit the kind of audience participation that invariably results in a shout.

VIOLA BATES DICKINSON

A choir director and organist in Chicago churches since the early 1940s and still working in such a capacity in the early 1990s, Viola Bates Dickinson opted for texts that were more progressive than the resurrected Negro spiritual/Pentecostal texts commonly associated with early gospel. Despite what was considered a large number of words, the chorus of her 1942 composition "It's My Desire to Do Thy Will" was a popular hit:

> CHORUS
> *It's my desire to do Thy Will, bear my cross up ev'ry hill,*
> *Tho' the way is sometimes drear, still I know that Thou art near.*
> *You can righten ev'ry wrong, you can change a heart of stone,*
> *Lord, you know it's my desire to do Thy Will.*

BEATRICE BEALE

Beatrice Beale, an associate of Dorsey's since the early 1930s, made no pretense of a progressive slant in her most famous composition "Great Day" (1951). A choir director and pianist who successfully made the transition from standard Protestant hymns to gospel, Beale enjoyed reaching a wide audience through songs that would immediately invite participation:

> VERSE
> *The saviour's face we'll see, with the Lord we shall be,*
> *In that land beyond the sea when we all gather home;*
> *No more sorrow will we know, peace and joy shall overflow,*
> *We shall rest for evermore when we all gather home.*

CHORUS
It will be a great day when we all gather home,
It will be a great day when we all cease to roam;
We will shout hallelujah, over in the land of Beulah,
It will be a great day when we all gather home.

To be sure, Chicago resonated with gospel in the 1940s and early 1950s. While Dorsey had been ridiculed and even turned out of a few churches, not ministers, the burgeoning middle class, nor music conservatories could halt the speed at which gospel was growing. When main-line or old-line churches, as they were called at that time by the educated and the black intelligentsia, refused in the 1920s and 1930s to allow gospel music in their sanctuaries, many young men and women withdrew from established congregations such as Quinn Chapel African Methodist Episcopal (AME), Bethel AME, Olivet Baptist, and others, some of which were members of the National Baptist Convention. These young people organized independent congregations where the principal music was gospel. Of extreme significance is the fact that these new gospel churches were being organized by the generation that had rejected gospel in the first decade of the twentieth century when they heard it in its rawest form in the Pentecostal church. These were also the same people who nonetheless did not protest when a more refined and sedate style of gospel singing was touted by the National Baptist Convention after the publication of *Gospel Pearls*. By the mid-1930s, they had adopted gospel and were willing to fight for its presence in their churches.

Such concerns, however, were far from the minds of Dorsey and his associates in the late 1930s and early 1940s, and without a backward glance they forged a path into American music and culture that allowed gospel to enter the mainstream. But first they needed to find one person or group who could break through the stalwart resistance presented by, of all people, the African American church.

Almost unnoticed by Dorsey and his associates were a cadre of soloists and groups who were more than capable, ready, and willing to stake their reputations on the presentation of this music. Chief among them was Mahalia Jackson.

MAHALIA JACKSON

Mahalia Jackson (1911–72) was the only child born to Charity Clark and Johnny Jackson, Jr. Mahala, as she was christened at birth, grew up in a tightly knit family of devout Baptists who could be found every Sunday morning at the Plymouth Rock Baptist Church in New Orleans. The family enjoyed the music of the church, and although none showed the interest or talent to join the choir, like the other worshippers they participated in the singing of the Baptist lining hymns, standard Protestant hymns, and Negro spirituals, accompanied by a keyboard instrument, usually a harmonium, melodeon, pipe organ, or piano. The singing inspired church members to get "happy" on occasion, but that music did not prepare them for the style of music that they heard on the Sunday morning when little Mahala made herself known to the congregation. According to Jackson's biographer Laurraine Goreau in *Just Mahalia, Baby* (1975):

> At four, with a voice twice as big as she was, Halie ranged before the Plymouth Rock pulpit in its children's choir, singing loud and clear … Jesus Loves Me.

By twelve she was a member of the junior choir at the Mount Moriah Baptist Church, where members regularly requested her to sing "Hand Me Down My Silver Trumpet, Gabriel."

It would be many years before Mahala realized the most important influence on her singing style—the singing she heard in a sanctified church a few doors from her house. Unlike the Baptist churches with their single weeknight service, the Wednesday night prayer meeting, the early sanctified saints would meet two or three evenings each week for services that lasted almost until midnight. In her 1966 autobiography *Movin' on Up*, Jackson described her relationship to those sanctified churches:

> I know now that a great influence in my life was the Sanctified or Holiness Churches we had in the South. I was always a Baptist, but there was a Sanctified Church right next to our house in New Orleans.
>
> Those people had no choir and no organ. They used the drum, the cymbal, the tambourine, and the steel triangle. Everybody in there sang and stomped their feet and sang with their whole bodies. They had a beat, a powerful beat, a

Mahalia Jackson sings "Move on up a Little Higher"

rhythm we held on to from slavery days, and their music was so strong and ex-
pressive it used to bring tears to my eyes.

I believe the blues and jazz and even rock 'n' roll stuff got their beat from the
Sanctified Church.

Although Mahala had been unaware of its influence, her ability to sing with the seeming abandon of the sanctified shouters was apparent to the congregation at Plymouth Rock and would become more apparent through the years.

As Mahala's voice changed from soprano to alto, she listened for hours to the recordings of popular blues singers Mamie Smith, Bessie Smith, and Ma Rainey and attempted to capture their nuances and volume. She then blended this sound with that of the sanctified singers, and by the age fifteen her vocal style was formed: from Bessie Smith and Ma Rainey she borrowed a deep and dark resonance that complemented her own timbre; from the Baptist church she inherited the moaning and bending of final notes in phrases (what W. C. Handy called "worrying over a note"); and from the sanctified church she adopted a full-throated tone, delivered with a holy beat and the body rhythm to accent that beat. While it may appear strange that none of her influences came from gospel singers, it should be remembered

Three gospel divas: Sister Rosetta Tharpe, Madame Ernestine B. Washington, and Mahalia Jackson

that gospel was only arriving in New Orleans as Mahala was leaving, and other than the sanctified church, the only singing she heard outside of the Baptist church was that of the emerging gospel quartet. That sound would also have a lasting influence on her style.

Mahala's Aunt Hannah, who lived in Chicago, invited her to that northern city, and shortly after Thanksgiving of 1927, Mahala made the journey. She accompanied her aunt to church on her first Sunday in Chicago, and as reported by Goreau in *Just Mahalia, Baby*, "as the spirit rose up in her, Halie stood up to witness, her way: 'Hand me down my silver trumpet, Gabriel.'" The big Chicago church, with its formal service not unlike the solemn dignity of the white Baptist church, was shocked

Gospel promoter Johnny Myers and Mahalia Jackson

by the unsolicited solo from the congregation, but they could not deny the beauty of the voice nor the sincerity of the singer.

In 1929, dissatisfied with the reception of her singing in the old-line churches of Chicago, Mahala accepted the invitation of the three Johnson Brothers—Robert, Prince, and Wilbur—to join their singing group, which had one other female singer, Louise Lemon (Jackson had joined the Greater Salem Baptist Church because of this group). The Johnson Singers became not only the stars of Greater Salem Baptist Church, pastored by the father of the Johnson Brothers, but also the first organized gospel group in Chicago.

After only a few years with the Johnson Singers, Mahalia, as she now chose to call herself, became exclusively a soloist. Her style of singing, full throated, bending a note here, chopping off a note there, singing through rest spots and ornamenting the melodic line at will, confused trained pianists but fascinated those who played by ear. Teenager Evelyn Gay from COGIC, who with her sister, Mildred, would become one of the major gospel duos of the 1950s, played for Mahalia for the sheer pleasure of it. Mahalia soon became a fixture on local gospel concerts. She also served as a soloist for politicians, often traveling to surrounding towns to accompany them or to sing at rallies in their stead.

She met Thomas A. Dorsey in 1928, and he attempted to secure her as his song demonstrator, although he was a little concerned about the melodic liberties she took with his music. In retrospect, it is crystal clear that Mahalia Jackson was never a Baptist singer, except when she sang songs in the Baptist lining hymn tradition. Such songs as "Even Me," "Amazing Grace," and "In My Home over There" show the kind of treatment of the melody line, restrained improvisation, and most of all the legacy of the older styles of African American religious music that the Baptists treasured. If Jackson sang a song that had a solid beat serving as the rhythmic foundation, she exhibited the aggressive style and rhythmic ascension that was found only among the Pentecostal singers. And for all his credit as the "Father of Gospel," Dorsey was a Baptist at heart and fostered a Baptist style of singing.

Jackson was not always inclined to follow the Baptist style of singing, especially when she was caught up in the spirit. Dorsey was legitimately concerned with what she would do to his songs. On the other hand, Jackson was taking Chicago by storm, and Dorsey wanted to be a part of that storm. The decision, however, was not for Dorsey to make, and it was not until 1930 that she accepted his invitation. In 1937 the two became a team for fourteen years, during which time Mahalia would accompany him to his concerts and sing his songs whenever she was not giving concerts of her own. Their relationship was a warm one, although in later years Jackson came to resent Dorsey's insistence that she learned everything she knew about gospel from him.

Realizing that certain doors were not open to her because she had no voice training and could not read music, she was persuaded by one of her friends to audition for a voice teacher, Professor Kendricks, for voice lessons at four dollars an hour. In 1932 their first and only meeting resulted in an admonition from Professor Kendricks:

Young woman, you've got to stop that hollering. That's no way to develop a voice, and it's no credit to the Negro race. White people could never understand you. If you want a career, you'll have to prepare to work a long time to build that voice.

Mahalia left his studio, and that was as close as the lady who sang gospel at one of the inaugural parties of President John F. Kennedy ever came to a voice lesson.

Despite Professor Kendricks' opinion, by 1937 her reputation as a gospel singer had become so great that J. Mayo "Ink" Williams (1894–1980), artist and repertoire director for Decca Records, Race Division, and producer of many of Ma Rainey's recordings, approached her to record four songs with piano for the Decca label. She and her pianist for the past two years, Estelle Allen, had their first recording session on May 21, 1937, in Chicago. Mahalia wanted to use organ on gospel, which she thought would enhance the slow songs, although it had not been tried before. She recorded "God's Goin' to Separate the Wheat from the Tare" by Lillian Bowles and "Oh, My Lord" with piano. Then Allen moved to the organ and pumped away on "God Shall Wipe All Tears Away" by Antonio Haskell (from her hometown of New Orleans) and the standard Protestant hymn "Keep Me Every Day." These recordings received little attention and despite the pleas of Ink Williams, Decca would not record Mahalia again. In fact it was seventeen months before Decca recorded another gospel artist (on October 31, 1938, they held their first session with Sister Rosetta Tharpe).

Despite the commercial failure of her first recorded songs, Mahalia set about to cultivate a national career. She traveled throughout the Northeast and to several states in the South, in addition to appearing annually at the National Baptist Convention. When she felt that the revenue from these concerts did not provide sufficient income, she enrolled in the Chicago branch of Madame C. J. Walker's famous beauty school. After completing her course, she opened a beauty salon in Chicago and confined her traveling to weekends. Ever the entrepreneur, she opened a two-chair shop and rented out the second chair so that she could afford to pay the rent even when she traveled.

While she was a beautician, Johnny Meyers, the most prominent African American concert promoter in New York City, booked Mahalia into New York's Golden

Gate Auditorium. One of the attendees at this concert was Bess Berman, owner of Apollo Records. Berman had under contract at the time such African American secular music performers as Billy Daniels, Arnett Cobb, and Dinah Washington and gospel singers including Clara Hudman Gholston (the Georgia Peach) and the Dixie Hummingbirds. Despite a few problems between the two strong-willed women, they agreed to one recording session of four sides. On October 3, 1946, Mahalia, with her pianist Rosalie McKenny, recorded "I Want to Rest," "He Knows My Heart," "I'm Going to Tell God All about It," and "I'm Going to Wait until My Change Comes." Although these recordings did not garner much public attention, Mahalia's interview on the Studs Turkel radio program from Chicago created a wave of interest and, because of this publicity, Berman was persuaded to record her again.

Gospel DJ Joe Bostic and friend presenting flowers to Mahalia Jackson after her performance at a Baptist Church in the Bronx

Producer Art Freeman was dispatched to contact Mahalia, and the two agreed that she would record a song that she had used as a warm-up before her first recording session. The song had been surreptitiously secured for Mahalia by Theodore R. Frye from a concert that the Brewster Ensemble of Memphis had given the year before in Chicago. (In the 1930s and 1940s copyrights were not secured until a number of years after a song had been introduced—for example, Dorsey composed "Precious Lord" in 1932, but it was not copyrighted until 1938.) Using an early tape recorder, Frye recorded the leader of the group, Queen Candice Anderson, singing "Move on up a Little Higher." Freeman hit upon the idea of recording the song in two parts since the 78 rpm recordings of the time could accommodate only three to three and one-half minutes per side. With James "Blind" Francis (b. 1914) on organ and James Lee (b. 1915) on piano, Mahalia recorded "Move on up a Little Higher" on September 12, 1947. The recording made gospel history, and the career of Mahalia Jackson was established.

The piano part was left off the recording, leaving the tremolo-based Hammond organ as the only accompaniment. This sound had not been heard in gospel before. Francis set up a moderately slow tempo, unifying the accompaniment with a triplet figure that would emerge each time Mahalia would take a rest. The result was an extraordinary display of call and response—but not between soloist and choir, but between soloist and instrument. Mahalia, in the time-honored southern black tradition, "stands flat footed and sings this song." She employs a scooping technique so that there is no clear movement from one note to the other; instead, she connects each note to the other by sliding through all the notes of the melody.

Side One set up the story of the journey from earth to heaven, while Side Two related Mahalia's meeting with all of the heroes of the Bible, as well as family members and friends. The journey is characterized by an ascending melody line from a low to a high tone, bringing the phrases to a close with the voice dropping down the tones of a blues-like scale as easily as water falling over a rock. In her usual style, she brings Side One to a close with obligatory ritard. Side Two of the record opens with the voice completely open and soaring above the accompaniment:

> *Move on up a little higher, meet with Old Man Daniel.*
> *Move on up a little higher, meet with Paul and Silas.*

Since each one of the statements melodically travels a short distance and turns on itself to be repeated, the melodic action is held in place for several phrases, while the element of repetition serves its function to get the message across. Each full chorus is ended with Mahalia shouting, "It'll be always 'howdy, howdy,' and never goodbye." The rhythm is so freely intricate that only after hearing the song is one capable of appreciating the number of rhythmic strains that were simultaneously combined, while the embellishments rival those of a coloratura soprano (think of birds chirping). The big, dark, liquid, burnished contralto of Mahalia signaled this recording as a masterpiece. And this is exactly how it was received by the public when it was released in January 1948.

The success of the recording secured for Mahalia a weekly network radio show. She became the first gospel singer to broadcast the pure sanctified gospel as host and star of her own CBS radio program, which premiered on Sunday, September 26, 1954. With Mildred Falls on piano, Ralph Jones on organ, and a white quartet conducted by the show's music director, Jack Halloran, Mahalia began a series of broadcasts that would ensure her career into eternity.

A successful number of recordings at Apollo followed. Among the most popular were "Just over the Hill," "These Are They," and "In the Upper Room." Mahalia was by this time so popular that Columbia Records felt that she could become a crossover artist, and on November 22, 1954, she had her first recording session with that powerful company. Columbia Records made Mahalia Jackson an international star and the "World's Greatest Gospel Singer," but many gospel singers and people from the African American church felt that the singing was not the same as it had been on Apollo Records. Much of this criticism was due to the repertoire assigned to Mahalia on Columbia. The popular music market wanted "Rusty Old Halo" and "You'll Never Walk Alone," while the African American church audience wanted "When I Wake Up in Glory" and "If We Never Needed the Lord Before." Mahalia solved the problem by creating two performance styles: one for the recording studio and the other for live performance.

With Mildred Falls she went on to star on the "Ed Sullivan Show" in 1956, at the Newport Jazz Festival in 1958, and at one of the inaugural parties for President John F. Kennedy in 1960. She sang just before Martin Luther King, Jr., delivered his famous "I Have a Dream" speech at the March on Washington in 1963 and sang Thomas A. Dorsey's "Take My Hand, Precious Lord" at King's funeral in 1968. She sang all over the world before church people, kings, and queens and at her beloved National Baptist Convention. She was on a concert tour in Germany in 1971 when her heart began to beat so slowly that she knew it was her last performance. Through beauty of voice, extraordinary technique, and through her Christian conviction, Mahalia Jackson, more than two decades after her death, is still considered the world's greatest gospel singer.

JAMES LEE

While Mahalia Jackson earned success as a soloist—and she was most often presented as such—she enjoyed singing with choirs, groups, and in duets. One of her favorite singers was her hometown compatriot, James Lee. Lee came to Chicago as a teenager in the early 1930s and quickly aligned himself with emerging gospel singers Robert Anderson, Eugene Smith, and Theodore R. Frye. He always held a unique position among these men and in the gospel movement because of his unusual voice. Lee could sing tenor but only with great effort, and shortly after arriving in Chicago he turned to his true voice, that of a counter-tenor, with the range of a soprano. He became one of the principal soloists in the Greater Harvest Baptist Church gospel choir and in 1949 persuaded Robert Anderson to direct the choir. His greatest popularity, however, rested on his singing soprano to Mahalia Jackson's alto on such compositions as Lucie Campbell's "He Understands, He'll Say 'Well Done'" and the hymn "I Can Put My Trust in Jesus."

SALLIE MARTIN SINGERS

With the opening of their music publishing company in 1940, Sallie Martin and Kenneth Morris had to devise a method of advertising their inventory. Dorsey advertised his music during his convention and Roberta Martin featured her music with her singers. Some consideration was given to organizing the Kenneth Morris Singers, for which Sallie would be the lead singer and Kenneth would serve as pianist, composer, and arranger. But because Kenneth could both transcribe and play music, while Sallie was only able to sing, they decided that Sallie would organize a group of singers and feature the inventory from the Martin and Morris Music, Inc.

In late 1940, Martin selected four young women and formed the Sallie Martin Singers. Among the early members were Dorothy Simmons (b. 1910), who with Doris Akers would later form the Simmons-Akers Duo. The others were Sarah Daniels, Julia Mae Smith, and Melva Williams. The pianist for the first group was Ruth Jones (1924–63), who in 1943 left the group to build a career as a secular music singer under the name Dinah Washington.

Cora Juanita Brewer (b. 1927) joined the group in 1942, and even though her parents were alive and living in Chicago, Martin adopted her and she became famous as Cora Martin. Although Brewer's parents loved her and could well afford to bring her up, they saw her dreams for a gospel singing career coming true only with someone like Sallie Martin. They gave up their daughter willingly to Martin; however, Brewer continued to maintain a close relationship with them. Brewer and Martin enjoyed a loving relationship until Martin's death at age ninety-two.

In the fashion of the day, most of Sallie Martin's songs featured a lead soloist with the rest of the group providing the response. Simmons possessed a brilliant soprano; Ruth Jones, who sang and played the piano, had a brassy light alto; Cora's alto was strong and capable of rapid embellishments; and Sallie's "bass" could soar into her upper register when she delivered a shouting song.

The group's signature sounds, however, were the unrefined, uneven, and yet warm voice of Sallie and the brilliant alto of Cora. While Cora could deliver the sweet gospel ballad with sincerity and conviction, Sallie was known to "rock the house" with explosive attacks, releases, and soaring slides, occasionally accented by a quickly executed shouting step. Under the name of the Sallie Martin Colored Ladies Quartet, the group gained notoriety when, in 1944, they appeared as special guests in the crusades of the legendary evangelist Aimee Semple McPherson (1890–1944). One newspaper review stated that "The Sallie Martin Colored Ladies Quartet possess [sic] ... exceptionally fine voices blended together." And indeed this blending, along with tightly arranged harmonies (initially arranged by Kenneth Morris) and the solo voices of Sallie and Cora, became the trademark of the Sallie Martin Singers. Among their most outstanding recordings are "Eyes Hath Not Seen," a Kenneth Morris composition in which Cora shows the full range of her voice and technique, and Sallie's aggressive handling of "Thy Servant's Prayer, Amen."

THE GOSPEL QUARTETS IN CHICAGO

The male quartet movement, while created and developed in the South, had become so popular by the mid-1940s that it could no longer be contained at home. In the 1920s and early 1930s, such cities as Bessemer, Alabama, Richmond, and Nashville served as fertile ground for gospel quartets, in part because of their proximity to the African American colleges and universities where the quartet movement began. But by the early 1940s, quartets began springing up in the North and Southwest, where there was not only an audience desperate for "home grown" church music, but an economy that could import southern singers. Another drawing card was the the manner in which the male quartet had created the quartet world.

When southern quartets began leaving the South to take their music throughout the United States, they presented themselves not only as upstanding and talented members of the community, but as a group of African American men who could and did serve as role models for other African American men. When they arrived at the church or school auditorium for a concert, they were dressed exactly alike in sharply pressed business suits with white shirts and respectable ties (the tuxedos and white dinner jackets of earlier times had been discarded). Each member of the group sported a fresh haircut or a freshly marceled hairdo, and the breath of each singer was kept fresh by the constant use of Sen-sen, a breath freshener. To maintain this freshness, it became a rule that smoking was not to be permitted outside the car that brought the singers.

Inside the performance hall, quartet members sat together in the pews or on stage, and when they were announced for performance, while still seated they began singing their "theme song." In many cases theme songs dealt textually with the group and included such material as where and when they were organized, who the members of the group were, and the kinds of songs they sang. In other cases, theme songs were favorite compositions of such composers as Dorsey and Lucie Campbell, or a Negro spiritual. After one or two choruses, the quartet would sing its way to the stage and offer an A and B selection. As the B selection neared its end, the quartet would proceed back to its seats, continuing to sing while standing in place, and at the end of the song the group would turn to the audience and bow.

While quartets featured more four-part harmony singing than leader-group singing until the middle 1940s, they were still able to elicit a feverish response from the audience. On slow gospel ballads women showed their approval by "getting happy"—shaking the head in agreement, saying "amen" or "hallelujah," crying, screaming, or even fainting. On jubilee (moderately fast songs) or shout songs (very fast songs) women would clap their hands and execute a shout. Social restrictions (and even church restrictions) dictated that men only smile and "talk back" to the singers. Many singers insisted that while singing they were actually in a service rather than a concert and therefore encouraged the congregation to act as if they were in church. Usually, little encouragement was needed for the congregation to act in a churchly manner because they had come for that exact reason. During this period female gospel singers made their entrance on the national gospel scene and were beginning to elicit the same kind of audience response that the male groups drew. Within the next ten years, they would challenge the male groups for the most aggressive audience response.

In addition to their dress, behavior, and four-part singing, male quartets brought to audiences their experiments in the development of the soloist-oriented quartet.

Realizing that a soloist—out in front of the group—would require a rhythmic foundation over which he could spin his tune, quartets found the perfect background rhythm for slow gospel songs: seven even-punctuated sounds with one-beat rests. The problem was one of finding syllables to fit the seven pulses but not detract from the text of the soloist (most songs did not lend themselves to seven equal divisions). The problem was solved by the creation of a number of syllables that had no meaning, but possessed a *sound* over which the soloist would be free to spin a web of sorrow, joy, happiness, thanks, or any number of textual themes. The syllables selected were: "Oom-ma-lank-a-lank-a-lank." When these syllables were sung giving each syllable the same amount of time, a viable and much-beloved background chant was established:

> *Soloist: Just*   *a*   *closer*
> **Quartet: Oom-ma-lank-a-lank-a-lank**   **Oom-ma-lank-a-lank-a-lank**
> *Soloist: walk with thee*
> **Quartet: Oom-ma-lank-a-lank-a-lank**

For variety some quartets began using the phrase "Oh my Lord-y, Lord-y, Lord."

Armed with the newest sound in African American sacred music the black male jubilee quartets—soon-to-be gospel quartets—decided to present themselves in the gospel music center, Chicago. The first two such groups to venture into that piano-accompanied gospel territory were the Soul Stirrers from Texas and the Famous Blue Jay Singers of Alabama.

REBERT H. HARRIS AND THE SOUL STIRRERS

While the Soul Stirrers, perhaps the most famous and innovative of all gospel quartets, can hardly be discussed in gospel circles without some reference to Rebert H. Harris (b. 1916), the group was already ten years old in 1937 when Harris became a member. By 1926 gospel quartets had spread to Trinity, Texas, where baritone singer Silas Roy Crain organized a quartet at the Mount Pilgrim Baptist Church. This group of teenagers sang in a style close to that of the Fisk Jubilee Quartet and the other quartets that famous group inspired. Crain experienced frequent turnover in his quartet as young men graduated from high school and moved to larger cities for college and more profitable employment.

Around 1931 or 1932, Crain decided to move to Houston, one hundred miles away, to work in a rice mill. There he found several gospel quartets, but none impressed him as much as the New Pleasant Grove Singers that had been organized by Walter LeBeau in 1928 and named after the church they attended. Because their baritone had recently died, the New Pleasant Grove Singers asked Crain to join the group. Crain agreed, provided they change their name to the Soul Stirrers, the name of his former group, since "at one of the first performances of his teenage group, a member of the audience came forward to compliment them on how much they had stirred his soul, and from that day they adopted the name, Soul Stirrers." The New Pleasant Grove Singers accepted his request, and the group that was to set many trends in modern gospel became the Soul Stirrers.

The members of the original Soul Stirrers were Edward R. Rundless, lead; LeBeau, tenor; Crain, baritone; O. W. Thomas, bass; and Harris as first tenor. Quartet singing was not new to Harris. At ten he had formed a family group, the Friendly Five, to sing at the Harris Christian Methodist Church (named after his father, the pastor) in his hometown of Trinity, Texas. The group was composed of his brothers and cousins, and their repertory included a song Harris composed at age eight, "Everybody Ought to Love His Soul," and another he composed a year later that was to become a classic, "I Want Jesus to Walk around My Bedside."

While Harris attended Mary Allen Seminary in Crockett, Texas, for two years and was exposed to the Western European art music tradition of using the voice in a formal or subscribed manner, he resisted the operatic "head tone" of the quartet singing at his school and chose to place his voice between the head and chest so he could call on the power of his lower voice and the falsetto, in which he could essay his high range but without the opera-singer sound. His was a vocal sound never before heard in gospel—nor has it been heard since.

The addition of Harris to the Soul Stirrers signaled a change in gospel quartet music history. Harris precipitated or helped develop many new trends in quartet singing. His deep religious grounding, developed while attending his father's church, inspired him and the Soul Stirrers to approach their singing with an emotional intensity that until then had been considered too sanctified. He encouraged the singers to move around the stage as they sang, unlike the Fisk Jubilee Quartet and the quartets who had adopted their stage presence, and although he retained the tight harmonies that had been the trademark of gospel quartets, he encouraged a less rigid ensemble so that individual parts could develop integrity. Jesse J. Farley, who joined the group one year before Harris, was a bass with the ability to "thump" a bass line in the style of Jimmy Bryant of the Heavenly Gospel Singers, and while Harris moved the group's entire singing range higher than it had been, he still found the harmonic depth for Farley to provide a thumping bass. Finally, he persuaded the group to change their repertoire from Negro spirituals, biblical songs, and standard Protestant hymns to the songs of *Gospel Pearls* and such composers as Thomas A. Dorsey and Kenneth Morris.

The Soul Stirrers introduced the "swing lead," which amounted to two singers leading one song. In most cases one singer, usually a baritone, would sing the verses while the choruses would be assigned to a tenor. The swing lead style was most effective when one singer brought a song to a high level of intensity and the second lead (the swing leader) would work the audience into a frenzy. The swing leader, sometimes called a "utility" man—in such cases one singer would move from tenor to baritone to bass to lead—enlarged a quartet to a quintet; however, groups continued to use the designation quartet. In time additional members were added to quartets so that by the mid-1950s a quartet seldom involved only four singers but would often involve five to seven singers.

The Soul Stirrers made their first recordings under John Lomax at the Smithsonian Institution in 1936; their first recordings with Harris were made in 1939. One of the songs in that first session was the Harris composition "Walk Around." This recording, different from those being made at the same time by the Golden Gate Quartet, appeared less concerned with polished precision and popular music techniques and more concerned with touching some element in the soul that would bring a tear to the eye. The recording also was instrumental in distinguishing the gospel quartet from the jubilee quartet. The Soul Stirrers were able to arouse audiences to a feverish pitch, not only through their soulful singing, but also when Harris, overcome by the spirit, would jump from the stage and continue singing without missing a beat. Their popularity became so great that by 1944 they had concertized through forty-eight states. The Soul Stirrers were among the first religious group to have a sustaining weekly radio show of their own, broadcasting each Sunday morning for over ten years from Chicago's radio station WIND. To ensure the spread of the gospel quartet movement, Harris, along with several other quartet leaders, organized the National Quartet Association of America in 1947. Harris served as president of this group for many years, during which he patterned the organization on the Dorsey convention, setting up chapters in cities throughout the United States, conducting training sessions, and fostering the organization of teenage gospel quartets.

Harris' pure and clean tenor, along with his sincerity and coolness of storytelling in song, influenced the gospel quartet movement in a way that has yet to be paralleled. He not only inspired innovations in quartet singing but directly influenced the singing style of several gospel and soul singers, the most popular of whom was Sam Cooke, who took over the solo leadership of the group when Harris retired. Among others who credit Harris with directly influencing their style were Johnnie Taylor, Bobby Womack, and Paul Foster.

SILAS STEELE AND THE FAMOUS BLUE JAY SINGERS

While they did not rival the Soul Stirrers—their lead singers were not as commanding nor was the group as innovative—the quartet that came closest to capturing the public's fancy in the late 1940s and early 1950s was the Famous Blue Jay Singers. They earned their greatest popularity while based in Chicago, although they were formed and had honed their skills in Jefferson County, Alabama, which included such towns as Bessemer and Birmingham. Jefferson County was fertile territory for gospel (then still called jubilee) quartets. Among the groups organized in the area during the 1920s were the Sterling Jubilee Singers, the Shelby County Big Four, the Birmingham Jubilee Singers, the Ensley Jubilee Singers, and the Blue Jay Singers.

Sometime between 1925 and 1926, Charles Bridges of Pratt City, Alabama, who had moved to Birmingham to work in the mines, organized the Birmingham Jubilee Singers. They soon gained a local reputation as leaders of the new group of quartets that sang with the spirit, and in April 1926 they went to Atlanta for a recording session for the Columbia Record Company. Several of the songs recorded in that first session, including "Southbound Train," "He Took My Sins Away," and their signature song, "Birmingham Boys," met with only modest success among race record sales. But that success was sufficient to inspire several other groups to form and develop local and regional careers. Gospel quartet members maintained their day jobs and concertized in local areas during the week, but on weekends they would travel as far as two hundred miles for performances. The success of the Birmingham Jubilee Singers recording lit a fire under the Blue Jay Singers who decided that they too would seek a regional, if not national, career.

Around the same time that the Birmingham Jubilee Singers was formed, Silas Steele (b. 1913) from Brighton, Alabama, joined forces with Clarence Parnell, a former bass singer with the Pilgrim Singers, another local quartet, to form the Blue Jay Singers. Parnell had already gained local celebrity as a quartet singer, and Steele, a young baritone and the younger brother of James "Jimmie" Steele, leader of the Woodwards Big Four Quartet, was beginning to gain a reputation as an outstanding soloist in his church choir. Parnell and Steele "stole" (a tradition in gospel quartets) James "Jimmie" Hollingsworth, tenor, and Charlie Beal, bass, from the Dunham Jubilee Singers to form their group. Within a very short time the Blue Jays, featuring young Silas as the lead (he was only thirteen when he joined the group), were the biggest rivals of the Birmingham Jubilee Singers. Because Steele possessed extraordinary charisma and began to adopt the preaching style of singing introduced by the sanctified singers, the Jays usually "took the program" when they appeared on the same bill with the Birmingham Jubilee Singers.

The Jays' style was one that would influence gospel quartets for the next fifty years: they celebrated the beauty and character of the natural male voice with its low sounds and brassy, but warm, timbre; they sang with the power of the African American Baptist and Pentecostal preachers; they celebrated the African American tendency of gathering resonance from the fatty tissues of the mouth rather than placing the tone close to the bridge of the nose; and they were not afraid to celebrate the body in their rhythmic accompaniment to their singing. These are the qualities that they brought to their 1931 recording of "If You See My Savior," the first Dorsey song ever recorded by a gospel quartet.

The gospel quartet movement had spread to Dallas, Texas, and the Blue Jays began to divide their time between Dallas and Birmingham. On one of their trips home they recruited Charles Bridges, former lead singer of the Birmingham Jubilee Singers. He agreed, because since the death of Dave Ausbrooks, the stalwart baritone of the Birmingham Jubilee Singers, that group had become inactive for long periods, and Bridges felt that they would find no suitable replacement to revive the group. With the addition of Bridges, the Jays became one of the most popular quar-

Prominent Chicago Gospel Women

Although men most often organized gospel events and ceremonies, women were always the facilitators of such activities. This trend started in Chicago, the first center of gospel, with a group of gospel women who composed, sang, conducted vocal groups, played piano and organ, and published music for themselves and others.

Sylvia Boddie	Emma L. Jackson
Lillian Bowles	Mahalia Jackson
Magnolia Lewis Butts	Roberta Martin
Virginia Davis	Sallie Martin
Viola Bates Dickinson	Albertina Walker
Mollie Mae Gates	

tets in the quartet network. Their 1947 recordings of "I'm Bound for Canaan Land" and "Standing on the Highway" are perfect examples of the Jays' style, illustrating the swing lead technique between Steele and Bridges.

While in Texas the Jays became close friends and frequent performers with the Soul Stirrers (whom they might have influenced in the early days, although the Soul Stirrers surpassed them in popularity within a few years) and followed the Stirrers to Chicago in the mid-1940s. After settling in Chicago and seeing the development of a battalion of gospel quartets, Steele adopted the sanctified preaching style of talking through a song, which later became known as the "sermonette" before or during a song performance. His preacher shouts became legendary and marked a clear break with their original style of sweet singing in the jubilee style and a pronounced entry into gospel. They were one of the first quartets outside the Tidewater gospel quartets (Golden Gates, Silver Leafs, Harmonizing Four, and so on) to employ the "clank-a-lank" response as a rhythmic and syllabic accompaniment to a solo lead.

Although the Blue Jays flourished until the 1960s, by the late 1940s other groups had surpassed them in innovation and popularity, causing Steele to seek more current and fertile ground for his talent. By 1948, James Darling, one of the leaders of the Spirit of Memphis quartet, was able to report:

Silas Steele talked with me long distance and told me that his fellows was getting old and not well. They couldn't go on the road anymore and he didn't know nothing but singing.... He asked me if I thought I could get him with the Spirit of Memphis.... So I talked with the boys and they said yes.

Silas Steele left the Famous Blue Jays, the name they used by this time, and joined the Spirit of Memphis Quartet. While it meant a new career for Steele, it sounded an impending death knell for the Famous Blue Jay Singers, one of the most important musical organizations in the history of African American sacred music.

More Chicago Musicians

Three other Chicago-based musicians played prominent roles in the development of gospel though they never took to the road.

ALVIN A. CHILDS

Alvin A. Childs (1908–c.1972) was born to a Baptist preacher and his wife in Missouri. The family moved to Des Moines, Iowa, when Childs was an infant, and it was there that he received his education, which was tempered by the strictness of his Baptist household. Childs was fascinated by the joyous and rhythmic music of the Pentecostal church and without his parents knowledge began to attend services there. He was saved in 1922 and became a member of COGIC, in which he was ordained to preach in 1934. After several pastorates in Iowa and Illinois, Childs settled in Chicago in the early 1940s and became a member of the gospel community, often singing with Theodore R. Frye and Robert Anderson. He is known today chiefly as the composer of three gospel standards: "How Much I Owe," a song that became so popular in the late 1940s and early 1950s that it moved into the folk music realm and was adopted as a shouting chorus; "Sow Righteous Seeds," made famous by Robert Anderson; and "He's My Lord."

RALPH GOODPASTEUR

Ralph Goodpasteur (b. 1923), a native of Columbus, Indiana, came to Chicago in 1948 after having learned gospel music from the Los Angeles gospel community where he lived from 1942 until his move to Chicago. He, along with J. Earle Hines,

Chicago Music Publishing Dynasty

In the mid-1950s there were at least ten gospel music publishing houses in Chicago. Chicago held a virtual monopoly on gospel music publishing. Although Clara Ward had a firm in Philadelphia, Eugene Smallwood and Doris Akers had houses in Los Angeles, and Arthur H. Hughes had a small company in Miami, they all relied on Chicago to provide their major inventory. Gospel music publishing was so successful during the 1950s that according to Kenneth Morris, in an interview given to culture historian Bernice Johnson Reagon in 1986, during the 1950s he averaged $100,000 annually.

Robert Anderson's Good Shepherd Music House
(located in Gary, Indiana, but considered part of the Chicago school)

Bowles Music House
(Lillian Bowles)

Thomas A. Dorsey, Music Publisher

Theodore R. Frye Publishers

H & T Music House Publishers, Inc.
(Theodore R. Frye and Georgiana Rose)

Jackson Studio of Music
(Emma L. Jackson)

Martin and Morris Music, Inc.
(Sallie Martin and Kenneth Morris)

Roberta Martin Studio of Music

Sallie Martin House of Music
(1965–75—concurrent with Martin and Morris)

Pace Music
(1910–35—Charles Henry Pace)

carry the distinction of being the first two celebrated gospel choral conductors after Thomas A. Dorsey. Goodpasteur was brought to Chicago by C. H. Cobb to succeed Kenneth Morris as choir director at the First Church of Deliverance. (In the early 1950s Cobb began a series of midnight broadcasts of services from his church that could be heard in most parts of the United States because few radio stations broadcast after midnight.) Goodpasteur brought the same kind of harmony, precision, and intensity to his choir of seventy-five voices that Roberta Martin brought to the Martin Singers. The choir became a model for many gospel choirs around the nation (the group was selected to accompany Nat King Cole on a 1959 recording) and was responsible for introducing Kenneth Morris' "Jesus Is the Only One." Goodpasteur composed several songs for the choir, which received modest popularity. Among these songs were "Joy Bells Ringing in My Soul," "Precious is He," and "To Me He's So Wonderful."

CLAY EVANS

Clay Evans (b. 1925) began his public career as a singer, gained fame as a preacher, and since the 1970s has combined the two. As a child Evans often sang with his family group, led by his mother who was a gospel singer and pianist. As a teenager he was a member of the Lux Singers, a piano-accompanied gospel group, and the Soul Revivers, an *a cappella* male quartet that was often presented in concert with the Highway QCs when Sam Cooke was its lead singer. In 1950 Clay founded the Hickory Grove Baptist Church in Chicago with five members. The church soon changed its name to Mount Carmel and then to Fellowship Baptist Church, the name by which it has become famous. With a membership of five thousand (among whom were Sam Cooke, J. J. Farley, and Johnnie Taylor) and a recording choir of two hundred voices, Evans secured his sister LeDella Reid as his choir director and, since the mid-1950s, this choir has been one of the principal gospel choirs in the United States.

GOSPEL IN PHILADELPHIA

The Chicago school of gospel resonated throughout the nation. Male gospel quartets had been springing up around the country since the mid-1920s, and the 1940s saw the organization of a group of female singers that would bring gospel into the mainstream of American music. The rise of gospel throughout the United States owed no small debt to the Pentecostal church since they were "duty bound" to lift up their voices like a trumpet. Following the Azusa Street Revival virtually every small town in the United States found itself host to some branch of the Pentecostal church. Cities of 50,000 or more supported two or three Pentecostal congregations. Pentecostalism began its claim as the religion of the twentieth century as early as the 1920s. It was during this period that Ozro Thurston Jones (1891–1972) settled in Philadelphia. A native of Fort Smith, Arkansas, Jones was saved at age ten and began preaching in the COGIC shortly thereafter. He organized the youth department in that denomination in 1914 and in 1925 moved to Philadelphia and assumed the pastorate of the newly organized Holy Temple Church of God in Christ. Sanctified singing became a feature of church music in Philadelphia.

Elizabeth Dabney (c.1890–1967) came to Philadelphia from her native Virginia to attend college. After hearing a sermon preached by Jones she joined his church and became known in the city as one who could "get a prayer through." After marrying Thomas Dabney, a minister in her denomination, she helped him in his newly founded COGIC in the city. Upon Jones' death, Dabney became spiritual advisor for the congregation (COGIC laws prohibited her from assuming the pastorate). Her constant fasting and praying drew visitors from throughout the United States to her church, the Garden of Prayer Church of God in Christ. Both Jones and Dabney featured gospel music during their regular services and presented concerts of this music as a feature of their Sunday evening Young Peoples Willing Workers activities.

Gertrude Ward and the Ward Singers

Clara Ward and the Ward Singers

Gertrude Ward (1901–81), originally of Anderson, South Carolina, and her daughters, Clara (1924–73) and Willarene (b. 1922), were constant visitors to the services of Jones and Dabney and wanted to sing the kind of music featured in their services, but had no one to teach them. Staunch Baptists that they were, they considered it improper to request lessons from the pianist and soloist of churches to which they did not belong. However, Mrs. Ward knew that Thomas A. Dorsey and Sallie Martin were traveling throughout the nation organizing gospel choirs and groups and that the annual National Baptist Convention was held each year in a different city, so she hoped they might come to Philadelphia. Mrs. Ward was not able to get the convention into Philadelphia in 1935, but she was able to get Dorsey, Sallie Martin, and Ruth Jones (Dinah Washington) to be the guests for her special concert commemorating the number of years she had been singing in public, or her "anniversary" as it was called. (She had no special guest for her anniversary in 1934, opting to present for the first time the

Ward Trio, composed of Gertrude, Clara, and Willarene, who was called Willa). Mrs. Ward's singleness of purpose and tenacity—as exhibited in her quest for gospel music skills—would become her hallmark in later years.

Although in 1935 Mrs. Ward had been singing publicly for only four years, she delighted in recounting (and stating in her printed programs) the story of her beginning:

> *The year was 1931 when standing before a steaming tub at work, I heard the Master's voice say "Gertrude, leave this place and go sing the gospel." The rest is history.*

To her, gospel meant the word of the Lord and not the style of singing that she would adopt four years later during Dorsey's 1935 visit. The Ward Trio, with Clara playing the piano, adopted the music of Dorsey and began singing in Philadelphia churches with the gospel sound and style. They gained a local reputation as the leaders of the new music and by 1943 were ready to launch a national career. They chose the 1943 National Baptist Convention as the venue for their debut. With Clara playing the piano and leading one of the old Baptist lining hymns so dearly beloved by this congregation, the Ward Trio became the sensation of the convention. From that single appearance they were able to schedule a year of concert and revival dates throughout the National Baptist Convention network. Following that year of travel they entered the network of the entire African American church.

By 1947 Willa had married and begun to raise a family and was therefore not able to travel with the trio. Mrs. Ward added two singers to the group that helped create the Ward Singers' sound. Henrietta Waddy (1902–81), a South Carolinian like Mrs. Ward, possessed a rough and unsophisticated alto but was able to blend with the rather pure voices of Mrs. Ward and Clara. Drawing on her southern church behavior, Waddy would move throughout the audience as she sang, accenting the rhythm of songs with arm gestures. This activity brought a much needed physicality to the group, who had until then been considered great singers but too "stiff."

The second new member was Marion Williams (b. 1927) of Miami, Florida. Brought up in a Pentecostal church, Williams was well grounded in singing shout songs at very fast tempos, using fill-in words at points where the melody called for a rest, repeating words and melodic motives for intensity, and singing with a volume like few other singers. Her unique and most outstanding talent, however, was her

The Ward Singers, the first to replace choir robes with elaborate gowns

ability to soar effortlessly into the top of the soprano register with purity and volume. It was not unusual for Williams to sing eight or nine consecutive high Cs and then drop to the bottom of her register and deliver a growl in the manner of sanctified preachers. Her high notes were delivered most often on the syllable "ooh," although she occasionally used "ah." To give the sound more of a percussive accent, Williams would place a "wh" sound in front of "ooh," thereby producing the syllable "who." This device, now known as the "high who," became a standard practice in gospel and is used when going from the end of one chorus into the beginning of another, producing a seamless sheet of sound. The high who became a signature of the Ward Singers, as they were now called, and was sung by the entire group on their recording of Mary Lou Coleman's 1948 composition "Jesus."

The Ward Singers began recording in 1947, but it was not until 1949 that they found "Our God Is Able," the song that was to make them the most famous female group of the 1950s. The song's composer, W. Herbert Brewster, a Memphis-based minister in the National Baptist Convention, wrote elegant songs based on scriptural texts. Most of his music was performed by his own group, the Brewster Ensemble, led by Queen Candice Anderson. The Ward Singers appeared in a concert with the Original Gospel Harmonettes and heard them sing "Our God Is Able," which they had learned from the Brewster Ensemble.

Clara took the song and completely reworked it for the 1949 recording, dividing the lead between Williams and herself and adding a repetitive section at the end. The arrangement was unique and completely new to gospel. After five single notes played in the middle of the piano as an introduction, Clara sang the last four bars of the chorus to begin the song:

> *Clara: Surely*
> **Group: Surely**
> *Clara: Surely*
> **Group: Surely**
> *Clara: He's able*
> **Group: He's able**
> *Clara: To carry*
> **Group: To carry**
> *All: You through.*

The word "through" is sung to seven different tones on the two chords used in singing the "amen" at the end of a hymn. Each member of the group moved up and down in parallel fashion, creating simultaneous improvisation, another Ward Singer trademark that soon became a standard device in all gospel. After singing one verse, Clara begins a chorus during which she rehearses biblical situations in which the Lord worked miracles:

> *He was Daniel's stone a-rolling*
> *And Ezekiel's wheel turning,*
> *He was Moses' bush burning*
> *He was Solomon's "Rose of Sharon,"*
> *He was Joshua's mighty battle ax.*

As the chorus comes to an end, Williams begins a high who and holds a high A-flat until the second chorus begins, which she now leads. While Clara addressed previous miracles, Williams speaks to miracles the Lord will affect for those who follow Him:

> *He'll be your friend when you are friendless,*
> *He's a mother for the motherless, a father for the fatherless;*
> *He's your joy when you're in sorrow,*
> *He's your hope for tomorrow;*
> *When you come down to the Jordan*
> *He'll be there to bear your burdens,*
> *He's going to step in just before you*
> *At the judgment He's gonna know you.*

Where Clara ended her chorus singing the word "surely," pronouncing the word as it is spelled, Williams pronounced the word "showly." She repeats the word several times, each time with a response of the word from the group. "Surely, God Is Able" became one of the biggest hits in gospel and was sung by choirs and local groups throughout the nation.

Several new elements, while not being new to gospel, were made famous and became standard gospel music devices with this recording. Williams use of such

Clara Ward and the Ward Singers

phrases as "He's going to step in just before you, at the judgment He's gonna know you" is a practice held over from Negro spirituals in which a group of rhyming couplets are catalogued and when a variety of text or words for a contrasting section are needed, the singer selects an appropriate or favorite couplet and inserts it into the song. Among other famous couplets are:

> *I went in the valley, I didn't go to stay*
> *My soul got happy and I stayed all day.*
>
> *My hands got stuck to the gospel plow,*
> *I wouldn't take nothing for my journey now.*
>
> *If you get to heaven before I do,*
> *Look out for me 'cause I'm coming too.*

While less popular than couplets, quatrains are also a part of the folk poetry singers insert into songs:

You may not sing like Angels,
You may not preach like Paul;
But you can tell the love of Jesus
And say He died for all.

These "wandering" couplets and quatrains became standard practice after their use by Brewster in "Move on up a Little Higher," recorded by Mahalia Jackson, and the Ward Singers' version of "Surely, God Is Able." (Brewster originally published this song as "Our God Is Able." After Williams emphasized the word "surely" in the recorded version, he republished the song with the title "Surely, God Is Able.")

The third device employed by the Ward Singers in "Surely, God Is Able" was the repetition of the same musical elements to different words, bringing the progress of the music to a halt for a period resulting in a section of repetition called a "vamp." Clara knew that repetition is the most important element in African and African American music for getting its message across and employed it judiciously in this recording. The vamp became so important in gospel that for the next forty years there would be very few gospel songs that did not employ the device.

Another practice made famous by the Ward Singers was that of the immediate reprise. During the mid-1950s when the Ward Singers were at the height of their career, they would sing only six songs at each concert. Four songs were delivered before intermission, each of which was immediately followed by a reprise that was often longer that the initial performance. After the intermission came the two additional songs, each of them reprised, which brought the concert to a close. On those occasions when the spirit was exceptionally high, as many as two or three reprises would follow the initial performance.

The Ward Singers set the standard for all female gospel groups. They led the way in vocal arrangements, uniforms, dress (the Ward Singers eventually sang in sequined gowns), and mode of travel (Cadillacs with trailers). They were the first gospel group to wear exaggerated coiffured wigs at a time when women were ridiculed for wearing "false" hair. Mrs. Ward jealously protected her singers, demanded grand fees for performances, juggled programming so that the Ward Singers would appear in the most lucrative places on the program, and even resorted to taking up special collections when she felt they had been underpaid. These tactics would be employed by other groups in the future. She was also an entrepreneur, seizing on the idea of creating a second group of Ward Singers in 1951 that she called the Clara Ward Specials. This group traveled with the Ward Singers on double-billed concerts and also appeared in solo concerts, from which Mrs. Ward received a percentage. In 1954 Mrs. Ward and Clara opened the Clara Ward House of Music and published Clara's songs as well as those of Brewster that they featured in their concerts.

In 1958 Williams, Waddy, Kitty Parham (b. 1931), along with Frances Steadman (b. 1928), who had recently joined the group, withdrew from the Ward Singers and formed the Stars of Faith, a group that would enjoy tremendous celebrity for the next few years. With the loss of the original group, Clara never regained her status in gospel even though she organized several groups of singers after 1958. Her influence is still felt in gospel even more than twenty years after her death. She influenced many gospel and soul singers, among whom were Aretha Franklin and Della Reese.

Angelic Gospel Singers

Philadelphia's second gospel group, organized in 1942, began as a gospel choir called the Spiritual Echoes. They toured Philadelphia's churches on Sundays, gaining a citywide following. During the height of the choir's popularity, the leader of the group, Margaret Allison, had a dream in which her pastor asked her why she hadn't formed her own group. When she answered that she didn't know how to launch a group, her pastor replied, "The Lord will bless you in whatever you do, as long as you keep Him first."

Margaret Wells Allison was born in 1921 in McCormick, South Carolina, fifty miles north of Augusta, Georgia. When she was four, Allison's family moved to Philadelphia so that her father could find a better job. They prospered until the Great Depression, when the family went on welfare briefly until her father secured employment with the Works Progress Administration (WPA). Allison's parents attended the Little Temple Pentecostal Church in Philadelphia, and although she never sang in a choir, it was the training camp for most gospel singers (Pentecostal churches did not have choirs until the late 1940s). Allison was fascinated by the congregation's joyous gospel singing.

Allison studied piano for a short time when she was twelve and transferred her membership to the B. M. Oakley Memorial Church of God in Christ (the church that

Marion Williams would later join) where she had an opportunity to play for services. By 1942 the twenty-one-year-old Allison was ready to enter the gospel field. During her tenure with the Spiritual Echoes, she learned how to arrange for female voices, compose songs, play and sing at the same time, and introduce a song to an audience. Even though she had lived in Philadelphia since she was small, her musical contacts celebrated the old-fashioned southern style of church music, gospel, and hymns in which elements of slave singing were quite prominent: percussive attacks, sliding from one pitch to another, vocal interjections by each member of the group, and repetition of any portion of the song that struck a spiritual chord. By 1945 the tours of such groups as the Sallie Martin Singers (conducting singing revivals) had made this gospel style seem dated; however, many gospel music lovers still knew it and wished to hear it again. Allison built her new group on this old-time sound.

The name Angelic Gospel Singers came to her in the same dream in which her pastor had encouraged its organization. In 1944 Allison recruited two South Carolinians who had also relocated to Philadelphia—Lucille Shird, originally of Ashville, and Ella Mae Morris, a native of Greenville. The fourth member was her sister, Josephine McDowell.

The Angelics were to the Pentecostal congregations what the Ward Singers were to the National Baptist Convention. They sang in their denominational circuit throughout the United States, and by 1949, they were not only known throughout gospel circles but had scored the greatest success of their career with their rendition of Lucie Campbell's "Touch Me, Lord Jesus." (Although Allison states that the song was recorded in 1947, records indicate 1949 as the date of the session.) The Angelics were to have many hits during their long recording career, but no other record ever equaled the success of their first. Among their other hits were "When My Saviour Calls Me Home," which was the flip side of "Touch Me, Lord Jesus"; "Jesus, When Troubles Burden Me Down," the revival meeting song; "There's Not a Friend Like the Lonely Jesus"; and "Back to the Dust." Although not apparent from its early modest success, "Glory to the New Born King" (1950), became as popular in gospel music circles as "White Christmas" is in the popular music world:

> Jesus, Jesus, oh, what a wonderful child.
> Jesus, Jesus, so holy, meek and mild;
> New life, new hope to all He brings,

Listen to the Angels sing:
Glory, glory to the new born King.

Although the Angelic Gospel Singers introduced many gospel standards, their name is irrevocably associated with "Touch Me, Lord Jesus":

Touch me, touch me, Lord Jesus, with Thy hand of mercy,
Make each throbbing heartbeat feel Thy pow'r divine.
Take my will forever, I will doubt Thee never,
Cleanse, cleanse me, dear Saviour, make me wholly Thine.

Not only was the old time or early gospel music style presented in the Angelics' arrangement of this song, but Allison's piano gave the voices the kind of support that 1940s gospel required: basic accompaniment doubling the voice parts in the middle of the keyboard, rhythmic licks in the upper portion of the keyboard during the singers' rest periods, and percussive attacks with explosive releases at every open space in the rendition. "Touch Me, Lord Jesus" was picked up by radio stations across the country and reached Billboard's R & B Top 20 that year. It also became a silver disc selling well over 100,000 copies—a phenomenal success for the time. Ernie Young of Ernie's Record Mart, broadcast over WLAC, the principal national gospel radio program during the 1950s, used the song as its theme for over a decade.

Even though "Touch Me, Lord Jesus" was accompanied by piano, it possessed a male gospel quartet character. This may be because when she first organized the group, Allison knew no female groups other than the Ward Singers, so she patterned the Angelics after the Fairfield Four. The quartet element in the Angelics' sound prompted their management to couple them for several tours with the Dixie Hummingbirds, who had recently relocated to Philadelphia. The Angelics and the "Birds" toured as a package during 1950 and 1951 and recorded six singles together. Most outstanding among these recordings were "Dear Lord, Look Down upon Me" and "In the Morning."

The Angelics suffered a great loss in the late 1950s when both Shird and Morris retired from the group. For a while Allison traveled with her sister, Josephine McDowell, and a new singer, Bernice Cole; in later years, she added men to the group. The Angelics, however, remain one of the historic female groups of gospel.

The Davis Sisters

Another Philadelphia female group was the Famous Davis Sisters. Like the Angelics, this group from the Pentecostal church brought the spiritual and musical intensity of that congregation to their singing. Like the Ward Sisters, members of the Davis Sisters were born and reared in Philadelphia but inherited their parents' appreciation for southern religion and its music heritage. Additionally, they captured—and to a degree attempted to refine—the intensity of the sanctified church. However, when Ruth (Baby Sister) was given free reign in shout songs, the congregation ultimately responded as if they were in that "little wooden church out on a hill."

"Baby Sister" Ruth Davis, the leader of the Davis Sisters

The Davis Sisters were members of the Pentecostal sect called Fire Baptized. The Fire Baptized Holiness church, founded in 1908 by Bishop and Sister W. E. Fuller in Atlanta, Georgia, is a small, but prominent, congregation within the Pentecostal/Holiness apostolic denominations organized after the Azusa Street Revival. The Davis family was one of the first members of the Mount Zion Fire Baptized Holiness Church in Philadelphia after its founding in the late 1910s. And there the Davis children developed into great gospel singers. On special occasions the Mount Zion pastor would highlight the talent of his membership and called upon the young women to sing a selection. The Davis Sisters, organized in 1945, was initially led by the eldest sister, Ruth (1928–70), known as "Baby Sister." The other sisters in the group were Thelma (1930–63), Audrey (1932–82), and Alfreda (1935–89).

After establishing a reputation as "house rockers" in the Philadelphia area, the sisters made their official debut in 1946 at their parents' home in Port Deposit, Maryland, and then followed the Pentecostal circuit, performing in churches and schools in the Northeast. They began recording in 1947, by which time they had been joined by pianist cousin Curtis Dublin (1928–1965). Dublin provided an accompaniment style midway between the sanctified church and the nightclub, characterized by occasional jazz riffs. The group's first hit, Alex Bradford's "Too Close to Heaven," was released in 1953 shortly after Bradford's own version. The Davis' version was overshadowed by the composer's performance, even though Baby Sister brought a genuine sanctified approach to her determination to complete the journey to heaven, despite innumerable problems. In their "Twelve Gates to the City," Baby Sister delved into the Book of Revelations and began her journey with such lines as "twelve gates to the city and twenty-four elders to the kingdom" so that the Negro spiritual was transformed into a gospel song.

Many songs of the Davis Sisters were taken directly from the church services they attended and experienced while growing up, and hence a number of so-called congregational songs were staples in their repertoire. Some of these songs were "In the Morning when I Rise," "Get Right with God," and "God Rode in a Wind Storm." They were not unfamiliar, however, with other music. One of their most popular recordings was a gospel version of the Christmas carol "The First Noël."

The Davis Sisters became a force in gospel when they recorded Lucie Campbell's "He Understands, He'll Say 'Well Done'." By the time they recorded this song in 1955, it had been recorded by more than a dozen gospel singers, including Sister Rosetta Tharpe, whose recording was a popular hit. The difference in the Davis Sisters' interpretation and all the other recorded versions of the song was attitude. While Lucie Campbell envisioned a contemplative and meditative interpretation of the song—and indeed all recordings to the time of the Davis Sisters followed this idea—the Sisters came to the song with an aggressive pronouncement of joy, and even victory. "The battle was won and though I have not yet received the prize, I have overcome" was the attitude that Baby Sister conveyed when, in the tempo of a sprightly jubilee song, she declared:

> *Oh, when I come to the end of my journey,*
> *Weary of life and the battle is won;*
> *Carrying the staff and the cross of redemption,*
> *He'll understand, and say "Well done."*

The Davis Sisters

This affirmation of faith and conviction would never be heard with the same prayerful ears after Baby Sister squalled victory in those famous words.

The song that cemented the Davis Sisters in the minds of gospel music lovers, however, was their 1952 recording of Kenneth Morris' "Jesus Steps Right in When I Need Him Most." Set again in a jubilee (moderately fast) tempo, Baby Sister wailed on the line "Jesus Is with Me when I Need Him Most." As the chorus ended, she repeated the word "steps." Her recasting of the line came out as:

Don't you know the man steps, steps, steps

When she was particularly excited, she would deliver the line as:

Don't you know the man steps, yeah! yeah!
Can't you see Him come stepping, stepping, stepping

stating each syllable with a choreographed step forward by the group.

With Baby Sister in the lead—although Thelma, as second lead, could illuminate a gospel ballad and bring energy to one of the Pentecostal shout songs—the Davis Sisters emerged as the first female group to sing "hard" gospel. Hard gospel, which made its appearance in the early 1950s, was totally different from the Baptist style of singing, which emphasized beauty of tone, precise rhythm, and occasional ornamentation. Hard gospel, first introduced by the saints of the sanctified church, is characterized by straining the voice during periods of spiritual ecstacy for spiritual and dramatic expression, singing at the extremes of the range, delivering perpetual text, in some cases repeating words or syllables or developing the text through the employment of wandering couplets or quatrains or stock interjections ("Yes, Lord," "Don't You Know," "Listen to Me," and so on), and "acting out" songs with scrubbing motions for washing, stooping shoulders for "bearing the cross," and a military-like precision march for "walking up the King's highway." This style would soon be adopted by Dorothy Love Coates and Shirley Caesar and make another distinction between Baptist and Pentecostal gospel.

During the 1960s, the Davis Sisters added nonfamily members Imogene Green (1930–86), a Chicago-born singer with a leaning toward hard gospel, and Jacqui Verdell, who had a special talent for essaying the gospel ballad. As the sisters passed away, their deaths, averaging one a decade, were considered tragic losses in the African American church community.

Mary Johnson Davis

There were few pure soprano gospel soloists during the Golden Age. The ideal gospel sound was one of authority, symbolized by the alto voice. To be sure, Marion Williams and Delois Barrett were sopranos but in moments of high intensity each of these singers would reach into the bottom of their registers and growl. The only soprano who retained her soprano register and quality at all times—and yet evoked the spirit as easily as Mahalia Jackson—was Mary Johnson Davis (1899–1982), a native of Pittsburgh, Pennsylvania. Known for her ability to rouse any church with her Baptist lining hymn renditions of such favorites as "Come, Ye Disconsolate" and "I Need Thee Every Hour," Davis could also generate foot tapping and hand clapping with her rhythmic rendition of jubilee songs.

From age six she was a local singing celebrity in Pittsburgh and continued singing into adulthood, specializing in classical, Negro spiritual, and hymn interpretations. Upon hearing the songs of Thomas A. Dorsey in the late 1930s, she changed her style to that of the new gospel music, and in 1937, when the National Baptist Convention met in Los Angeles, she was accorded the title of "National Gospel Singer" for her spirited rendition of "Holy Spirit Surely Is My Comforter."

In the late 1930s she married an aspiring gospel songwriter, E. Clifford Davis, composer of "Holy Spirit." In order to help his career, she organized the Mary Johnson Davis Gospel Singers and in the 1940s secured a recording contract with Atlantic Records. Among the members of her group were the Banks Brothers—Jeff (pianist) and Charles—her sister Bernice Johnson, and Lucie Banks.

A longtime friend and colleague of Gertrude Ward, Davis moved to Philadelphia in the 1950s after the death of her husband. Remarried to the Reverend B. J. Small, she renamed her group the Mary J. Small Singers. She and Gertrude Ward were instrumental in developing young gospel groups throughout Philadelphia and the surrounding area. Davis retired from traveling in the 1970s but continued to sing in the Philadelphia area until shortly before her death. She is best known for her recordings of "These Are They" and "Walk in the Light."

The Dixie Hummingbirds

Like Chicago before it, Philadelphia was a piano-accompanied gospel town. Charles Albert Tindley used organ and piano for his gospel hymns (although at "Prayer Meeting" gospel hymns occasionally turned into gospel songs). Orzo Thurston Jones and the Dabneys used piano for sanctified singing, as did the congregation at the Mount Zion Fire Baptized Holiness Church. Clara Ward played piano for the Ward Singers, and Margaret Wells Allison played piano for the Spiritual Echoes choir. Philadelphia was indeed a piano-accompanied gospel town until the Dixie Hummingbirds moved there in 1942.

The Birds were unique in gospel: they could shout with the best of the shouters, but they always cherished and developed what quartets called the "minors." The Birds were one of many quartets that, according to Ray Allen in a 1984 study of Philadelphia quartets, subscribed to four song types:

> Sentimentals—*moderate to slow tempo; smooth, extended vocal phrasing; most major harmonies.*
>
> Minors—*slow tempo; smooth, extended vocal phrasing; generous use of minor, diminished, and augmented harmonies [called "off chords"].*
>
> Jubilees—*moderate to rapid tempo; short vocal phrasing; major harmonies.*
>
> Chop Jubilees—*very rapid tempo; short vocal phrasing; chopped, staccato-like attack on lyrics; major harmonies.*

While the piano-accompanied gospel singers called sentimentals "gospel ballads"; minors, "Baptist lining hymns"; and chop jubilees, "shout songs"; by any name the Dixie Hummingbirds could sing them all, and with the spirit. What the Birds brought to Philadelphia gospel was variety—and that variety would bring two Philadelphia male gospel quartets to the forefront (the other group would be the Nightingales).

The Birds were organized by James Davis in Greenville, South Carolina, and drew its original members from the junior chorus at the Bethel Church of God in Greenville, calling itself the Sterling High School Quartet after the high school they attended. When Fred Owens replaced the short-term J. B. Matterson shortly after the group's organization, Davis changed their name to the Dixie Hummingbirds (they had decided to leave school and sing professionally). The members were Davis, tenor; Barney Gipson, lead; Barney Parks, baritone; and Fred Owens, bass. After gaining a local reputation as a "smooth" singing group (specializing in sentimentals,

The Dixie Hummingbirds

minors, and jubilees), the Birds, like other quartets in their area, made their way to the National Baptist Convention in Atlanta where they met with only modest success but garnered enough engagements to keep them singing in and around the South Carolina area.

By the 1930s the Birds were popular enough to be invited to participate in "battles of song," a favorite church and entertainment activity throughout the South. During one such battle in 1939 in their hometown, they competed against the Heavenly Gospel Singers, whom they had met at the National Baptist Convention, and the Carriers, a group from Spartanburg, South Carolina, led by Ira Tucker (b. 1923). The battle was monumental, for not only did the Dixie Hummingbirds win (determined by applause from the congregation), they also gained two new members: Willie Bobo, bass of the Heavenly Gospel Singers, and Tucker.

Tucker, who had been heavily influenced by the Norfolk Jubilee (Jazz) Quartet and the Golden Gate Quartet, quickly became the major musical force in the group. They began to meld the jubilee quartet style with that of the jubilee jazz quartets (some of the Tidewater gospel quartets had switched to jazz singing). For the next fifty years the Dixie Hummingbirds' style would be characterized by a genuine gospel sound, but one with a nod toward jazz and show tunes.

The Birds' style was actually not unlike the quartets of the day: well-modulated tones between the head (lyrical quality) and chest (church-style), tight and sweet harmonies, explosive releases, and slight body movements. After the group moved to Philadelphia and came in contact with local church groups who possessed the same abilities, Tucker took on additional musical and show business attributes. There was no melodic or harmonic device that he could not execute: his lyric tenor voice was capable of cascading up and down not only the diatonic (seven-note) scale but the chromatic as well. Not only did he put his voice and vocal technique to use, he also became the model for the "activity" singer. He ran up and down aisles, jumped from the stage, and spun around without sacrificing one iota of the pure musical sound that he first brought to the quartet. Indeed, he served as the model for many of the rhythm and blues and soul singers from Jackie Wilson and Clyde McPhatter to Bobby "Blue" Bland and the Temptations.

Throughout the first fifteen years, the group went through several personnel changes, but by the late 1940s it had settled into a quartet with Tucker on lead,

Beachy Thompson (from the Five Gospel Singers and the Willing Four) as first/second tenor, Davis as second/first tenor, and Bobo as bass. Second to Tucker in significance to gospel was Bobo, who early on helped move the bass from its ungrateful position at the bottom of the harmony to that of co-soloist, thumping bass in each song at every opportunity. James Walker joined the group in the early 1950s, alternating lead with Tucker, and his semihard gospel technique helped the Birds move to the forefront of gospel quartets.

Ira Tucker, with William Bobo on guitar, leading the Dixie Hummingbirds to the pinnacle of gospel

The artistry of their first twenty-five years is magnificently illustrated in their recordings of "Lord, Come See About Me" (1949), on which Tucker takes the lead but at the end of each chorus Bobo interpolates a deep velvety bass anticipated note that gives the song its real character, and "Search Me, Lord" (1950) on which Tucker shows the full range of his vocal beauty and pyrotechniques.

Beginning in 1951 the Birds toured with the Angelic Gospel Singers in the first pairing of an all male quartet with an all female piano-accompanied gospel group. They toured at intervals during 1951 to 1953 in a series of highly successful gospel concerts. Their most popular joint recordings were "Jesus Will Answer Prayer" and "Dear Lord, Look Down upon Me," both recorded in 1950.

When the popularity of the gospel quartet movement began to fade in the mid-1960s, the Birds found a home on the folk music circuit and performed in major folk music festivals, including an appearance at the Newport Jazz Festival in 1966. When pop singer Paul Simon (b. 1941) wanted a gospel quartet to sing background on his 1973 recording of "Loves Me Like a Rock," the Birds were chosen. Their contribution to the popularity of the recording was so great that they later recorded the song on their own and it became a hit for them. The Birds went on to appear on such television shows as "The Merv Griffin Show" and "Soul Train," and by the late 1970s they had revived their career. Their popularity was still growing in the 1990s in large part because of the continuing popularity of their 1953 recording of "Let's Go Out to the Program" on which Tucker leads the group through imitations of the Soul Stirrers singing "Jesus Gave Me Water," the Blind Boys of Mississippi singing "Our Father," the Pilgrim Travelers version of "Mother Bowed," and the Bells of Joy singing "Talk about Jesus."

The Philadelphia gospel sound was helped in no small way by the fact that the Gotham, Savoy, and Imperial record companies had major studios in Philadelphia and Mary Mason, Walter Stewart, Louis Williams, and Charles Williams were extremely powerful DJs who favored a hometown sound. When the African American DJs around the country met with each other, they encouraged their friends to play the recordings of their hometown artists. The Philadelphia gospel singers were aware of this fact and treated their DJs accordingly.

GOSPEL IN DETROIT

While Philadelphia was the first major city to follow Dorsey in gospelizing the music of the African American church, cities much closer to Chicago were also responding, although not with the speed and power of the City of Brotherly Love. Pentecostal congregations had begun planting churches in Detroit as early as the mid-1920s, and Dorsey had established a chapter of his convention there in the mid-1930s. However, gospel in Detroit existed primarily in the Pentecostal/sanctified churches until the mid-1940s. Because of Detroit's proximity to Chicago, gospel musicians from Detroit moved easily between the two cities. But in the 1940s three people who were to shepherd the gospel movement in Detroit moved to that city.

Anna Broy Crockett Ford

The first to arrive was Anna Broy Crockett Ford (b. 1916), who moved there in 1942 from her native Lexington, Mississippi. She affiliated with COGIC, pastored by John Seth Bailey (c.1891–c.1986), and because of her natural talent for singing and her training at Chicago's American Conservatory of Music (1935–36), she was able to identify herself early on as one who would champion gospel music. While Ford was a powerful singer, possessing a strong but light alto voice, her greatest contribution came through her organization of gospel groups. Elder Bailey, later Bishop Bailey, recognized this strength in her and commissioned her to organize a gospel choir in his church in 1945. Her success with this choir inspired her in 1949 to organize the Music Department for the national Church of God in Christ. Additionally, Ford has served as the director of music for the Women's International Convention of the COGIC since 1951. Ford later moved to Chicago and continued her musical activities.

Reverend C. L. Franklin

C. L. Franklin

On the first Sunday in 1946, Clarence LaVaughn Franklin (1915–84), known as C. L. Franklin, preached his first sermon as the pastor of the Bethlehem Baptist Church in Detroit and thus began a thirty-five-year promotion of gospel music. And while Tabernacle Baptist Church, pastored by Charles Craig (flourished 1950–70), and a number of Pentecostal congregations, including Bailey's, were major venues for gospel in Detroit, Franklin was clearly the major force.

Born in a rural area of Mississippi near Indianola (the birthplace of legendary blues singer B. B. King), Franklin grew up near the village of Doddsville. When he was very small, his father served in World War I and returned only to abandon the family. His mother remarried, and her second husband's name is the name Franklin carried throughout his life. His mother and stepfather had one child, Aretha, and Franklin passed this name on to his own daughter. That name has since become famous.

In tenth grade, Franklin quit school and became a "season worker," that is, a migrant farm laborer who follows the planting and harvesting season throughout the United States. He became a preacher at age seventeen. Eventually he was able to relinquish the season work for the ministry, pastoring churches in Clarksdale, where he married Barbara, the mother of his children, and Greenville, as well as several other small parishes. He eventually moved to Memphis, where he pastored, then to Buffalo, New York, and finally to Detroit. The latter moves were not happy ones for before he moved north, Barbara died and he was left to care for his four children. In Detroit, female members of the church looked after the children, leaving Franklin free to care for his church flock.

Franklin was a singer, and while his singing was first rate, it did not match his "gospel" preaching. During Franklin's lifetime he recorded more than sixty of his sermons on double-sided LP records, each side lasting four or five minutes. On side one he would illustrate his oratorical ability, often being dramatically verbose. On side two he would shift into a musical key and virtually sing the remainder of the sermon. When his daughter Aretha began to sing, she mimicked the Franklin style of preaching in her singing.

Mattie Moss Clark

Although there is no doubt that James Cleveland was to gospel in the 1960s and 1970s what Thomas A. Dorsey was to that genre in the 1930s and 1940s, he was not alone in the necessary shift from Golden Age gospel to a more modern interpretation. One other choir director, Mattie Moss Clark (1928–94), had a major impact on the gospel choir in its new form. And even after her death, Clark continues to influence the direction that the gospel of the 1990s is taking.

The importance of gospel singers appearing before audiences at the National Baptist Convention diminished after the death of Lucie Campbell (who had made the convention the most important venue for introducing new gospel singers for forty years). The principal denomination for the introduction of new gospel singers became COGIC through its Midnight Musicals at the annual convention, under the direction of Mattie Moss Clark. Some of the singers who came to prominence through these musicals include Rance Allen, the Hawkins Family (Edwin, Walter, and Tramaine), Andrae and Sandra Crouch, Beverly Glenn, Donald Vails, Keith Pringle, and gospel saxophonist Vernard Johnson. Though presented in a COGIC forum, the Midnight Musicals became a nondenominational showcase for new gospel talent deemed worthy of presentation by Clark. Such power and prestige testified to the hard work and long miles traveled from her meager beginning in Selma, Alabama, to that of the most powerful woman in black gospel in the last decade of the twentieth century.

Born the second of six boys and two girls to Edward and Mattie Moss, Moss was brought up in the Methodist church, in which her mother was a singer (she was also a guitarist) and a licensed minister. Two of her brothers played instruments, and all sang. Moss began piano lessons at age six (she was taught by her older brother), and by age ten she played for services at the three small parishes pastored by her mother.

In preparation for entering Fisk University as a music major, Moss sang and studied piano throughout high school. Between graduation from high school and the opening of the next college term—when she was to enter Fisk—her father died. Wary of leaving her mother during such a crucial period, she elected to remain at home and attend Selma University. After one year at Selma, she decided to relocate to Detroit to live with her sister.

Coming into a strange town with musical talent but no venue for exhibiting it frustrated Moss, and she looked for a congregation with which to affiliate. She first served as pianist for a Baptist church but did not find the religious and musical expressions she craved. Within one year of her arrival in Detroit, she discovered COGIC, sought and found the Holy Ghost, and became director of the choir at what is now the Bailey Temple Church of God in Christ, pastored by John Seth Bailey. Her ability to compose music, play piano and organ, and direct choirs quickly led to her appointment as director of music of the Southwest Michigan Jurisdiction (diocese) of COGIC, and then president and director of the music department of COGIC, International.

She married Elbert Clark, a native of Gary, Indiana, a guitarist and Pentecostal minister who had come to Detroit shortly before her arrival, and bore him one son, Elbert Junior, and five daughters, Elbernita ("Twinkie"), Jackie, Denise, Dorinda, and Karen. In the 1970s the five sisters would become gospel superstars as the Clark Sisters. Elbernita, the leader of the group, became one of the leading organists and composers of the 1970s and 1980s and official organist for her mother's Midnight Musicals.

As the composer of more than one hundred songs, Clark was able to insinuate her musical ideas on a whole denomination of musicians. She eschewed a choir with a vibrant and aggressive sound with a fully opened throat—sometimes resulting in volume that destroyed purity of tone—for a choir with close harmonies and crisp rhythms. She began recording in 1963 with the Southwest Michigan State Choir of the Churches of God in Christ, and their first recording of her composition "Save Hallelujah" was enthusiastically received. This was followed by her most popular recording, "Salvation Is Free." She also recorded with the 1,500–member Church of God in Christ Convocation Choir, and through her recordings introduced such singers as Esther Smith, Betty Nelson, the Clark Sisters, and Douglas Miller. Her brother Bill Moss leads the gospel group known as Bill Moss and the Celestials.

Moss was not without the certain temperamental qualities known in people of such extraordinary talent. She was as well known for her temper tantrums as she was for her music. It was not unusual for Moss to throw books or musical scores—even during concerts—at singers who displeased her. Unfortunately, her name can hardly be mentioned without a discussion of the tantrum that resulted in her physical assault on Twinkie during a performance. And yet, she is remembered today as one of the most talented and innovative women in music, and singers flocked to her for training and guidance until her death.

Della Reese, Earnestine Rundless, and the Meditations

C. L. Franklin's influence on gospel in Detroit was great. Among those he influenced were Delloreese Patricia Early, popularly known as Della Reese (b. 1932), who was the second lead for a female group from Detroit known as the Meditation Singers. The Meditations were organized by Earnestine Rundless in 1947 and quickly became to Detroit what the Ward Singers and the Davis Sisters were to Philadelphia, what the Caravans were to Chicago, and what the Original Gospel Harmonettes would become to Birmingham: singers who made cities into gospel centers.

Indeed, between 1953 and 1959 in Detroit and the surrounding area, the Meditations personified the gospel sound. While their influence has not been generally acknowledged, within gospel circles it is commonly held that the Meditations had a great influence on the Motown Sound. Earnestine Rundless notes that in the early days of the group "a young fan named Diana Ross" got the front seat at most of their concerts.

Rundless came to Detroit from the historic Mount Bayou, Mississippi, but was reared in Chicago. After marrying E. A. Rundless, who relinquished his position as a singer in the Soul Stirrers to enter the ministry and move north, she formed a group of singers from her husband's Detroit church. These singers included Rundless, Della

Reese, her sister Marie Waters, and Lillian Mitchell. The Meditations were indistinguishable from other female groups of the time except in its lead singers Rundless and Reese.

Della Reese, one of the major popular music entertainers from the 1960s on, was born in Detroit. She attended high school there and studied at Wayne State University until she was recruited by Rundless to join the Meditations. She brought a great deal of gospel-singing experience to this group: she had been singing in church choirs since age six and toured with Mahalia Jackson during the summers of 1945 to 1949. She sang for short periods with Beatrice Brown, Roberta Martin, and Clara Ward before she left gospel in 1954 to pursue a career in popular music. In 1955 she began recording, showing the influence of Dinah Washington, who also began as a gospel singer. While Rundless leaned toward the sanctified style of singing, Reese, with her brassy yet crystal clear alto, always maintained a Baptist style with a solid melody line. Essaying myriad colors, she sustained tones while resorting to a drum-like sound when she delivered a song in the declaratory style. Her style is eloquently illustrated on her 1953 recording of "Jesus Is Always There." With unabashed homage to the style of the Ward Singers and W. Herbert Brewster's multimetered songs, this rendition begins in the tempo of a gospel waltz, during which Reese shows her ability to paint pictures with a gospel ballad. As she nears the end of the verse, however, she picks up the tempo and suddenly the group is singing in the jubilee style, prompting Reese to do a little preaching. She handles this like the old gospel hand that she is.

The Meditations were later accompanied and coached by James Cleveland, during which time they adopted the style for which the Caravans would later become famous. Despite all their changes of personnel and song styles, the Meditations remain one of the premier female gospel groups of Detroit.

Harold Smith and the Majestics

Harold Eugene Smith (1934–93), like Della Reese, was born in Detroit. As a teenager he came under the influence of Mattie Moss Clark and sang with her in choirs and small groups in the Detroit area. In August 1963 he organized the Majestics, a gospel choir of fifty voices, which made its debut the following year at the Henry and Edsel Ford Auditorium in Detroit. In addition to giving concerts, the group presented gospel music dramas in the style of those of W. Herbert Brewster, which incorporated dance.

The group appeared in concerts or rallies with Martin Luther King, Jr., Mahalia Jackson, and Duke Ellington and performed in Buffalo, New York, Boston, Philadelphia, and Chicago. Smith was a founder-member with James Cleveland of the Gospel Music Workshop of America in 1968 and was known for his flamboyant direction of choirs. His recording of Cleveland's "Lord, Help Me to Hold Out" is largely responsible for the song becoming a gospel standard.

Aretha Franklin

Like Sam Cooke, Della Reese, Lou Rawls, and Johnnie Taylor, Aretha Franklin (b. 1942) came to soul music after a distinguished career in gospel. Born in Memphis, Tennessee, to the Reverend C. L. Franklin and his wife, Barbara, Franklin grew up in Detroit and learned everything she knew about music in her father's church. While Franklin is known worldwide as the "Queen of Soul," the church still refers to her as "Aretha, Reverend Franklin's daughter." By connecting her with her father, the church registers a deep-seated hesitancy to dismiss Franklin from the church as it had done with Sister Rosetta Tharpe, Sam Cooke, and Lou Rawls. And part of this hesitancy is due to Franklin's attitude and behavior since she made the move to popular music.

Franklin never pretended to be anything other than a gospel singer, as clearly exhibited in early 1994 when she was given a Grammy Award for "Lifetime Achievement in the Recording Industry." She began her acceptance speech for the award with "I want to first give thanks to God Almighty, and then to my father, the Reverend C. L. Franklin, for you all know where I'm from." Only four years old when her father became pastor of New Bethel Baptist in Detroit, she literally sat at the feet of such gospel luminaries as Mahalia Jackson, Clara Ward and the Ward Singers, Rebert H. Harris, and James Cleveland. Her idol was Clara Ward.

She reacted like a sponge to gospel, and out of this wellspring of talent, she created a style that has influenced an overwhelmingly large number of African American female popular and soul music vocalists as well as a respectable number of non-African American female popular music singers. Only Bessie Smith, Dinah Washington, and Ella Fitzgerald can claim as many musical "daughters and granddaughters" as Aretha, and as late as the early 1990s she was still the Queen of Soul. Despite these accolades, none of her singing matches the pure and unadulterated soul of her gospel recordings at age sixteen when she poured forth with heartfelt renditions of "Never Grow Old" and "There Is a Fountain Filled with Blood." Her 1972 gospel album with James Cleveland entitled "Amazing Grace" has become the best-selling gospel album in history, and yet it does not capture a glimpse of the sound that Aretha gave when she sang gospel at her father's church during gospel's Golden Age.

Wynona Carr

By a strange twist of circumstances one of the greatest gospel composers and singers from Detroit spent only a short time there, although the tours and recordings she made while in Detroit certified her celebrity. Sister Wynona Carr (1924–76), born the same year as Clara Ward, was an enigma in gospel, as was Sister Rosetta Tharpe, after whom Carr's record producers patterned her and with whom she appeared in concert later in her career. During the early and mid-1950s, Carr served as one of the choir directors at C. L. Franklin's Bethlehem Baptist Church in Detroit. It was during her tenure there that she recorded her most popular hit, "The Ball Game," and her other "sports" song, "15 Rounds with Jesus."

With a progressive sound in the same category as Sister Rosetta Tharpe, though much more refined and hence less assaulting, Carr was too far ahead of the gospel world in which she lived. The major emphasis of her songs dealt not with Jesus and thanks, but with the metaphors and similes of the Christian religion. Additionally, her singing style did not evoke tears and sighs at her expression of heartfelt passion, but hand clapping and cheers at the sophisticated beauty of her jazzy singing style. Nowhere is this more eloquently illustrated than in her composition "The Ball Game" (1952):

> The first base is temptation (you know) the second base is sin,
> (The) third base tribulation, if you pass you can make it in;
> (Old man) Solomon is the umpire, and Satan's pitching the game,
> He'll do his best to strike you out, keep playing just the same.

Unlike most of the gospel singers of the Golden Age, Wynona Carr was not born in the Deep South but in Cleveland, Ohio, of Beulah and Jess Carr who had recently moved from the South. Her mother remarried when Carr was quite young, and she was brought up in the household of her mother and her stepfather, Arthur Summers, who encouraged the musically talented child to begin piano lessons at age four. At age thirteen she entered Cleveland Music College where she studied voice, harmony, and arranging. During her teens she played for several Baptist church choirs and at age twenty began to commute between Cleveland and Detroit, directing church choirs in both cities.

After serving a tenure as a member of the famed Wings Over Jordan Choir in Cleveland, she organized her own group, the Carr Singers, in 1945 and toured throughout the Midwest. Her life changed when the group served as the opening act for J. W. Alexander and the Pilgrim Travelers at one of their concerts in Cleveland. While Carr only directed the choir and served as an occasional soloist, Alexander was impressed enough to pay for a demonstration tape, which he took back to Art Rupe, the owner of Specialty Records, for which his group recorded. The demonstration tape landed a contract for Carr and through her ten-year affiliation with the recording company, she became a popular star. The Five Blind Boys of Mississippi made her "Our Father" a national hit. Her recordings of duets with Brother Joe May and her own compositions secured her place in gospel history.

Always attracted to popular music, rhythm and blues, and jazz as much as she was to gospel, Carr combined a career of the church and the club for a number of years. However, in 1955, with a letter to Rupe stating that "I've tried singing spirituals [gospel] for fourteen years when all the time my real thoughts were in the show world," Carr left gospel. She had one hit in secular music, "Should I Ever Love Again" in 1957, but by that time she knew that she had contracted tuberculosis. She retired to her family's home in Cleveland for two years and took to the road afterward as a rhythm and blues singer. She never regained the popularity she had won while with Specialty Records, which she left in 1959. She signed with Reprise Records. They released only one of her albums during her lifetime; others were released after her death. During the 1960s she appeared at several plush nightclubs, but was always plagued by ill health. She finally retired in 1970 and died in May 1976.

It is ironic that Carr's music made more money after her death. In the 1980s her composition "Operator, Operator" was recorded by Manhattan Transfer, the pop jazz group of the decade, and became a major hit. Had Carr been alive during that time she would no doubt have been a major star in either jazz or gospel.

The Gospel Quartets in Detroit: Flying Clouds and Evangelist Singers

Despite the fact that Detroit did not produce a male gospel quartet that achieved a national impression during the Golden Age of black gospel quartets, they have thrived in the city since the 1930s. As in most American cities, black gospel quartets abound, but like New York City, many of these groups elect to become community-based, singing more for pleasure than for money and limiting their performances to their hometown and traveling no more than two hundred miles for weekend engagements. This was the situation in Detroit except for two groups: the Flying Clouds and the Evangelist Singers.

FLYING CLOUDS

Like the Fairfield Four of Nashville, the Flying Clouds began as a teenage quartet in 1929. They were originally called the Russell Street Usher Board Four for their bene-factors, the Usher Board of the Russell Street Baptist Church. Personnel changed so often in the early days that few remember the original membership of the group. By 1942 they had changed their name to the Flying Clouds, after a popular automobile that had recently been introduced. During the 1940s membership included original member Horace Simmons, John Evans, Joe Union, and Elmer Stallworth, former lead singer of the Friendly Brothers of Houston, Texas. Until the middle 1940s the Flying Clouds were considered a sweet gospel group, emphasizing tight harmonies, controlled voices, and little physicality in stage decorum. Then, in order to compete with such famous singers as the Soul Stirrers and the Dixie Hummingbirds, the Flying Clouds recruited Joe Union, formerly of the Loving Brothers of Omaha, Nebraska. Union brought an aggressive lead to the group, providing a startling contrast to the understated lead of John Evans.

Even though the group had a weekly broadcast for more than a decade at Detroit's WJR and later sang over CLLW in Windsor, Ontario, and recorded for several Detroit labels, a national reputation eluded them. Two of their popular recordings of the 1940s are "Savior Don't Pass Me By" and Lucie Campbell's "Something within Me."

EVANGELIST SINGERS

Oliver Green, an experienced quartet singer by 1938, organized his own group that year, basing their style on quartets he had heard and sung with in his hometown of Dennison, Texas. After several changes, membership in the Evangelist Singers came to include Green, Jimmie Bryant, Bob Thomas, and Larry Barnes. Receiving their greatest popularity as the Detroiters, a change of name suggested by a talent scout for radio personality Horace Heidt who felt that the name Evangelist Singers was too spiritual, the group recorded several sides for the Specialty label. Their style combined both the sweet singing of the Alabama quartets and the shouting songs of the Pentecostal church. "Don't Drive Your Children Away," featuring the growling bass lead of Jimmie Bryant, is one of their most popular recordings.

Other Detroit Singers

Among other singers from Detroit who made an impression on gospel during its Golden Age were Cissy Houston, mother of the 1990s popular music star Whitney, who was a member of the Drinkard Singers, along with Mancel Warwick, the father of Dionne and DeeDee Warwick. Both Dionne Warwick and Whitney Houston sang gospel at one time but switched to popular music through which they gained fame. The partially blind Princess Stewart, who had trained for concert and opera but who eventually succumbed to gospel, and Sammie Bryant were also well-known singers. "Prophet" Jones, coming from Bessemer, Alabama, as did Alex Bradford, gave up playing the piano and singing to become one of the most flamboyant gospel preachers of all time.

Detroit Pianists and Organists

Detroit produced several esteemed keyboard artists, the most outstanding of whom was Herbert "Pee Wee" Picard (b. 1933), who served as pianist and organist for Dorothy Love Coates and the Original Gospel Harmonettes when Evelyn Starks, the original pianist, returned to public school teaching. Thomas Shelby (1900–72) served as minister of music for C. L. Franklin's Bethlehem Baptist Church for over forty-five years. This Memphis, Tennessee, native came to the attention of the Reverend Franklin during his tenure as pianist for E. W. D. Isaac and Lucie Campbell's Good Will Singers of the National Baptist Convention. Also, Shelby was the first pianist to teach Aretha Franklin gospel. Alfred Bolden (1937–70), a classically trained organist who was able to turn that technique into gospel, recorded several albums of organ gospel, hoping to identify that instrument as a solo voice in gospel.

GOSPEL IN ST. LOUIS

Records of the Pentecostal church show no strong influence in the introduction of gospel music in St. Louis, Missouri. Nonetheless, the 1920s, the period of the introduction of gospel music through the Pentecostal churches, also saw the rise of gospel in St. Louis. It is therefore noteworthy that by the early 1950s, when St. Louis was recognized as a gospel center, it was the Pentecostal singers who brought this recognition. Willie Mae Ford Smith, brought up in the Baptist church, had joined the sanctified church; Joe May was from the Church of God, one of several Pentecostal denominations; and in the middle 1950s the O'Neal Twins of COGIC joined other duos of gospel (although the twins, like Brother Joe May, were from East St. Louis, Illinois, they were considered part of the St. Louis, Missouri, school—as Robert Anderson of Gary, Indiana, was considered part of the Chicago school). In the last ten years of the Golden Age, when gospel was the most arresting music in the African American community, Tennessean Cleophus Robinson, a COGIC singer, joined the St. Louis school.

The National Baptist Convention influenced several of its St. Louis members to sing and compose gospel. Two of the most outstanding were A. B. Windom, composer, and Martha Bass, singer. But regardless of the denomination, all gospel singers sooner or later wanted to get to know a woman who was as strong as she was gentle: Willie Mae Ford Smith.

Willie Mae Ford Smith

The leader of gospel music in St. Louis and the surrounding area was Willie Mae Ford Smith (1904–94), who later earned the title of "Mother." She was born in Rolling Fork, Mississippi, but as a child moved with her family to Memphis. Piano-accompanied gospel was resonating throughout what was to become Mason Temple Church of God in Christ in Memphis but received little attention from Smith, because at that time, as she was later to recall, she was: "Baptist bred, Baptist Born, and when I die it will be a Baptist gone." In the 1920s, when her father could no longer work in Memphis, he moved his family to St. Louis, where young Willie Mae served as the leader in a family group organized by her father. The Ford Sisters, as they were called, soon garnered a local and regional reputation as one of the finest female quartets of Missouri and Illinois.

The female quartet, patterned after the male quartet—even to the extent of using the male vocal designations of tenor, baritone, and bass—had been a part of the African American religious music scene since the 1930s. And while they were comparable with the male quartets, often competing against them in battles of song, the piano-accompanied female group was the *new* sound in gospel. The Ford Sisters compromised by rendering some of their songs with piano, while others they performed *a cappella*.

Smith was the most talented of the sisters, possessing a dark contralto and an easy style of delivery. She could have performed in opera as easily as gospel, which would have been gospel's loss. The Ford Sisters sang at the 1922 National Baptist Convention and created a sensation. Thereafter Willie Mae, because of her extraordinary voice, was sought after as a soloist at each convention.

In 1929 Smith married James Peter Smith, who owned a small moving company. Shortly after her marriage the stock market crashed, and in order to assist with family finances, she began traveling to other cities and conducting musical revivals.

Mother Willie Mae Ford Smith, with her adopted daughter Bertha at the piano

Dorsey heard her on one of these trips in 1931 and invited her to Chicago in 1932 to help him organize the NCGCC. In 1936 he appointed her director of the soloist bureau and the principal teacher of singing. In 1937 she set the standard for solo singing with her rendition of her own composition "If You Just Keep Still" at the National Baptist Convention. Smith joined the Church of God Apostolic, a Pentecostal denomination in 1939, and her singing thereafter had the added elements of rhythm, bounce, and the percussive attacks of the sanctified singers.

Although her fame began to spread she made very few recordings, and those that she made met with little success. Without the recording success of Mahalia Jackson and Roberta Martin, both of whom considered her a superior singer, Smith could concentrate on preaching and singing at revivals. As she traveled she would also teach gospel singing and in this capacity met Edna Gallmon Cooke, Martha Bass (the mother of soul singer Fontella Bass,) Myrtle Scott, the O'Neal Twins, and her most famous student, Brother Joe May, who was the first to call her "Mother."

Mother Smith, as she was affectionately called, possessed a chameleon-like personality, and could be alternately sweet or sour. From years of traveling on buses and trains (most often alone) to teach gospel soloists, attempting to make a community of gospel singers in the St. Louis area, and continuously working to express her sanctification through song—as well as preaching—without the support of the "brethren of the church," Smith had built up defenses that could be volatile. She had to, in her words, "beat down" pastors of churches who would not permit her to sing from the pulpit, deacons who objected to her moving her body as she sang, and, most important, those who gave her little money for her singing. While she was, in the language of the church, "saved, sanctified, and filled with the Holy Ghost," she did not like to be crossed. Sallie Martin, with whom she worked for over sixty years in Dorsey's convention, was one of the few people who could disturb her sanctification, perhaps because they both saw themselves as the first assistant to Dorsey. Their on-again, off-again relationship was documented in the 1983 documentary *Say Amen, Somebody.*

Her most notable contribution to gospel, however, was the introduction of the "song and sermonette" into gospel music whereby a singer delivers a five- or ten-minute sermon before, during, or after the performance of a song. This device was later brought into standard gospel practice by Edna Gallmon Cooke and Shirley Caesar. Smith appeared at the Newport Jazz Festival and Radio City Music Hall, was celebrated in *Say Amen, Somebody,* and was featured in Brian Lanker's 1989 book of photographs called *I Dream a World: Portraits of Black Women Who Changed America.*

Brother Joe May

Mother Smith's most famous student, Brother Joe May (1912–72), was born, like her, in Mississippi. Hailing from the small village of Macon, May was brought up in the Church of God. He began singing at age nine and soon became a member of the Church of God Quartet, which traveled throughout Mississippi and Alabama. After marriage he and his wife and the first two of their seven children moved to East St. Louis, Illinois, in 1941 to be closer to Mother Smith and to find work.

As director of the soloist bureau of Dorsey's convention, Smith had run a revival (not of preaching but of singing) in Macon and had met May during that visit. Not only did she encourage May to sing, but mentioned to him that there was a great deal of work in the St. Louis area that would help him care for his family. May found work in St. Louis—he worked as a janitor but at a much higher salary than he was drawing in Mississippi—and visited Smith nightly to learn new songs. This led to concert appearances with her. Knowing that May was, at that time, extremely shy about his singing, Smith had to use all her powers to persuade him to accompany her to the National Baptist Convention and audition to sing a solo at the concert of new singers.

Trusting Smith, May auditioned at the National Baptist Convention in Los Angeles, was accepted, and became an immediate hit. He impressed J. W. Alexander, who was instrumental in securing a recording contract for him with Specialty Records. His first recording, Dorsey's "Search Me, Lord," became an instant hit. The popularity of the recording was due as much to May's voice as to Dorsey's song. May possessed a huge and powerful tenor with the agility of an Ira Tucker. Although he had been brought up singing the shout songs of the sanctified church he had learned to moan on an Isaac Watts hymn as well as any Baptist preacher. His powerful voice and Dorsey's songs, which he favored, made him a popular singer on the gospel circuit, and in 1950 he quit his job as a janitor at the Monsanto Chemical plant in St. Louis to go on the road as a professional singer. He was often paired in concert with Mahalia Jackson because of the similarity in their singing styles. Such concerts, often billed as a battle of song between the "World's Greatest Gospel Singer," a title then held by Jackson, and the "Thunderbolt of the Middle West," a title given to May by Smith, always generated huge crowds and powerful singing.

Although May presented solo concerts, he was most often part of a package of singers, among whom were the Pilgrim Travelers, the Sallie Martin Singers, Wynona Carr (all part of the Specialty stable), and May's son and daughter, Annette and Charles. While May never became the crossover artist that Jackson was—his singing style was considered too churchy for white audiences in the 1950s and 1960s— he was one of the most financially successful gospel singers of his day, often earning up to $50,000 a year. In 1957 May moved to Nashboro Records, a company that distributed mainly in the South. Without recordings in the West, Midwest, and Northeast, his popularity waned. Concerts became fewer, but May continued to travel and sing until 1972 when he suffered a fatal stroke. His recordings resurfaced in the late 1980s, and May became once again one of the most popular soloists in gospel.

Other St. Louis Singers

Two other St. Louis natives who were important figures in gospel between 1945 and 1955 were Martha Bass and A. B. Windom. Bass, who possessed a dark contralto, was known as a "house shouter" because of her ability to rouse a church into pandemonium. She sang with Clara Ward and the Ward Singers for several years. Windom, a one-time accompanist for Mother Smith, composed several gospel songs; her "I'm Bound for Canaan Land" and "I've Got the River of Jordan to Cross" became gospel standards.

GOSPEL IN TENNESSEE

Memphis was the city selected by Charles Harrison Mason as the headquarters of his Church of God in Christ, one of the congregations in which gospel was developed. Not only was there congregational singing of gospel during Sunday and weekday services, but special concerts of this music were presented during the annual convocation held in the city each November. Mason's church quickly became one of the places visitors to Memphis insisted upon frequenting, and word of the music spread throughout the state. Tennessee produced several important figures in gospel's Golden Age, none more important than Lucie Eddie Campbell.

Lucie E. Campbell

Lucie E. Campbell (1885–1963) has the unenviable distinction of having been born on a train just outside of Duck Hill, Mississippi. Her father, Burrell, worked on the railroad, and her mother, Isabella Wilkerson Campbell, would deliver him his lunch each day on the train that carried workers back and forth. While Isabella was returning from this lunch delivery one day, Lucie decided to enter this world. Miss Lucie, as she was called by members of the National Baptist Convention, delighted in telling this story, because it testified to her uniqueness.

Shortly after Lucie was born her father was killed in a railroad accident, leaving Mrs. Campbell to bring up nine children. Hoping to find work in a large city she moved her family to Memphis. Lucie attended elementary school in Memphis and graduated from Kortrecht High School in 1899. Her high school record was so extraordinary that she was named valedictorian of her class, and after graduation she was immediately hired by the Carnes Grammar School. She taught there from 1899 until 1911 when she was hired as teacher at Kortrecht, by then renamed the Booker T. Washington High School, where she taught for the next thirty-three years.

Campbell was just as dedicated to the Baptist church as she was to teaching and served as a national officer for the National Baptist Convention from 1916 when she was elected music director of the Sunday School and Baptist Training Union (BTU) until her death in 1963. In this capacity she arranged pre-convention musicals and directed the choir during the one-week series of services. From 1919 until 1960 Campbell wrote a song each year for the choir of the convention. Within weeks of the introduction of each new song, choirs around the country added the song to their repertoires. Several of the more than fifty songs written by Campbell have become gospel standards—quite a singular feat for a woman who never studied music.

Campbell's interest in music began in the 1890s when she listened to her elder sister's piano lessons. Campbell would go to the piano as soon as her sister was finished and play the pieces she had heard. She not only taught herself to play but taught herself to write out songs in music manuscript. As a college student at Rust College in Holly Springs, Mississippi, from which she graduated with a major in liberal arts in the summer of 1927, Campbell sang in the choir and was occasionally assisted in her composition by the choral director.

She was a lyricist who chose simple words to express her great Christian conviction. With melodies of simple beauty transporting lyrics of deep sincerity, Campbell was able to write songs that struck at the very heart of gospel music lovers. It is commonly acknowledged that "Amazing Grace" by John Newton is the most favored song among African American Christians and Thomas A. Dorsey's "Take My Hand, Precious Lord" is the second most popular song. There is little doubt then that Campbell's "He Understands, He'll Say 'Well Done'" comes in third:

> *If when you give the best of your service*
> *Telling the world that the Savior is come;*
> *Be not dismayed if men don't believe you*

He understands; He'll say, "Well done."
Oh, when I come to the end of my journey
Wearied of life and the battle is won;
Carrying the staff and the cross of redemption
He understands; He'll say, "Well done."

This 1933 composition was long a favorite for funerals but gradually moved into the gospel mainstream where it has been performed both as a gospel ballad at a slow tempo and as a fast shout song. Campbell's most famous shout song, "Jesus Gave Me Water," equally as effective when performed in the slightly slower jubilee tempo, tells the story of the woman who met Jesus at the well:

The woman from Samaria once came to get some water
And there she met a stranger who did her story tell;
He spoke, she dropped the pitcher, she drank and was made richer,
When Jesus gave her water that was not from the well.

Campbell was known as a feisty and authoritative woman who exercised a great deal of power in the National Baptist Convention. Mahalia Jackson could always inspire howls of laughter when she recounted how, during her audition before Miss Lucie for a spot on a concert during the National Baptist Convention, Miss Lucie interrupted her with great ceremony only to say very curtly, "Stand up straight, young woman." J. Robert Bradley, who succeeded Miss Lucie as director of music for the National Baptist Convention, could be equally hilarious when he reminded singers that Miss Lucie was so powerful that ministers' wives would give her the front passenger seat of the family car (with their husbands driving) while they sat in the back. Miss Lucie never refused such honors, thinking rather that the women were behaving properly. She maintained her high spirit until the end of her life, as evidenced by her marriage at age seventy-five.

W. Herbert Brewster

Memphis boasted a second important Golden Age composer, William Herbert Brewster (c.1898–1987). Brewster was the first gospel music composer to write songs that, when recorded, sold a million copies. Often called the "eloquent poet," he was born in the small village of Sommerville, Tennessee. After graduating from high school he entered Roger Williams College, from which he graduated in 1922. He moved to Memphis that year to become the dean of a proposed African American seminary sponsored by the National Baptist Convention. When the school did not materialize he accepted the pastorate of the East Trigg Baptist Church in Memphis and remained its pastor until his death. In addition to pastoring, he founded and directed the Brewster Theological Clinic, which had branches in twenty-five cities. His greatest joys, however, were writing biblical dramas, for which he also wrote the music, and composing gospel songs. During the 1940s Brewster wrote a drama each year and presented it at one of the auditoriums in the city. These presentations became sacred highlights of the year. It was for such a drama that the song "Our God Is Able" was composed. His *From Auction to Glory*, written in 1941, was the first nationally staged black religious play to feature gospel music written for the production. Previously, Negro spirituals had been used in religious plays.

Brewster composed his first song, "I'm Leaning and Depending on the Lord," in 1939, but it was not published until 1941. From this first composition it was obvious that Brewster was a learned and eloquent person with an extraordinary knowledge of the Bible. He drew on these attributes for his songs. In fact, much of what the African American community heard about the Old Testament in music during the Golden Age of Gospel might very well have come from Dr. Brewster (he was awarded an honorary doctorate by Bennett College of Greensboro, North Carolina). In addition to serving as a tour guide through the Old Testament in "Move On Up a Little Higher," Brewster provided a mini-atlas of the cities of God in "I Never Heard of a City Like the New Jerusalem":

> *I have heard of Babylon, with its walls and towers grand,*
> *With its temples and its gardens, palaces that once did stand;*
> *Where the three Hebrew children won over wicked men,*
> *And where Daniel held his own in a lion's den.*
>
> *I have heard of mighty Sodom, Ninevah and Jericho*
> *How they reveled in their splendor till their sins brought them low;*
> *I have heard of Tyre, Sidon and wicked old Gomorrha and*
> *How God snatched away their glory.*

While lyrics were the most outstanding feature of Brewster's songs, his sense of gospel tempos ushered in a new sense of foot patting and hand clapping. Growing up during the era of the "Dr. Watts" hymns and the Baptist lining hymn, he had a keen sense of emotion brought about through wringing each syllable and tone through several rhythmic variations. He combined the slow nineteenth-century hymn with the more rhythmic gospel song by dividing many of his songs into two parts. Like the operatic combination known as recitative and aria, the slow and unmetered section of the song unfolded the serious part of the song, while the rhythmic portion commented on or gave the moral of the whole. "Just over the Hill" begins with a slow and unmetered section:

> *There is a land of fateless day*
> > ***Just over the hill***
> *Beyond the rainbow and the sky*
> > ***Just over the hill;***
> *It's a land beyond compare, free from sorrows, pain or care*
> *And they tell me there's no night there*
> > ***Just over the hill.***

He then moves into a sprightly gospel tempo with the refrain:

> *Just over the hill, just over the hill,*
> *I'm on my way to the land of day just over the hill;*
> *Soon below I'll cease to roam, for I shall outrun the storm,*
> *And make my way to my happy home, just over the hill.*

During the slow section, the singer would embellish and elaborate at will, while during the faster sections rhythmic devices such as syncopation and double time (singing twice as fast) became outstanding features. These devices became all the more sensational when Brewster assigned a song three different tempos, as he did with "Faith Can Move Mountains" in which the verse is sung at a very slow and unmetered tempo, while the refrain is delivered in a lively tempo, and a special chorus is sung at the fast tempo of a shout song.

The vamp, a section of a song based on repetition, was Brewster's most popular compositional device. The vamp serves as the basis for "Our God Is Able" and "Move on up a Little Higher" but is most ingeniously employed in "Let Us All Go Back to the Old Landmark." Not only does Brewster show his skill at repetition, but his sense of rhyming is at its best in this composition of a chorus and three stanzas, each stanza ending with a four-line vamp:

Verse I	Vamp
He will	*hear us*
And be	*near us*
We'll be	*given*
Bread from	*heaven*

He will feed us until we want no more.

When the vamp from each of the three stanzas was sung successively, it provided an extended vamp of sophisticated gospel.

Brewster was honored at a weekend seminar at the Smithsonian Institution in December 1982, where his songs were presented in several concerts and he was the star of his own biblical drama *Sowing in Tears, Reaping in Joy*.

Queen Candice Anderson

Brewster was fortunate to find the precise voice he wanted to interpret his songs. That voice belonged to a young member of his singing group, the Brewster Ensemble. While still in her early teens the young girl, whose original name seems to have been forgotten, joined Brewster's church, and he heard her sing. (During the 1982 seminar in his honor at the Smithsonian Institution, Brewster told the audience that once he accepted Anderson as one of his singers, she literally divorced her family and spent most of her time at the church and with his singers. Her family appeared to have no problem with this and until her death Anderson was considered part of the Brewster family.) Because she was so beautiful and so talented Brewster decided that she should bear the name of a queen. He chose Queen Candice of Ethiopia, mentioned in the Bible in Acts 8:27–39, who was the queen of the eunuch converted to Christianity by Philip. He retained her last name and most of his published compositions bear the note: "As Performed by Queen C. Anderson."

Anderson (1913–59) had a light but powerful alto voice and appeared to have had an affinity for Brewster songs. According to Brewster, he could begin teaching her a song and before he could finish she would take over and complete that which she had never heard before. She was responsible for introducing such Brewster songs as "Move on up a Little Higher" (Mahalia Jackson learned the song from her); "Our God Is Able," as it was called when she sang it; and "Lord, I've Tried," made famous by the Soul Stirrers. Although she recorded with the Brewster Ensemble in 1950, none of the records have been located as of this writing. Queen Candice traveled little, and so only those around Memphis can speak with any authority about the voice that the "eloquent poet" chose to sing his songs.

J. Robert Bradley

At Lucie E. Campbell's death in 1963, John Robert Lee Bradley (b. 1920), known as J. Robert, became director of music for the National Baptist Convention. Bradley seemed destined for this position; he was discovered by Ms. Campbell when he was twelve years old, sang principal lead in a quartet organized by her for the National Baptist Convention in the 1930s, was selected by English composer Roger Quilter (1877–1953) during the late 1940s to introduce his new songs, and garnered a worldwide reputation as "Mr. Baptist," the most renowned singer within the Baptist denomination, both black and white.

Bradley was born to—in his words—"one of the poorer families in North Memphis." He attended elementary school there, but he disliked formal education and missed classes on a regular basis in third grade. Thereafter he attended school intermittently, never graduating from high school. At age twelve he was standing outside the city auditorium in Memphis on Christmas Eve when the area Baptists were holding their annual musicale. Bradley began to sing along with them. A policeman who was monitoring the crowd heard this lovely voice and took him inside to the director of the musicale, who happened to be Lucie E. Campbell. In one of those strange strokes of circumstance, Miss Campbell decided to have Bradley sing on the program. She was so impressed that she took the young singer under her wing and began to teach him her songs (among the Campbell songs dedicated to Bradley are "Even a Child Can Open the Gate," "Signed and Sealed with His Blood," and "Heavenly Sunshine"). Under Campbell's tutelage Bradley not only developed a voice that would be compared with the great Russian bass Chaliapin, but also learned how to sing a gospel song with all the fire of a sanctified preacher and delivered with all the care and cunning of an opera singer.

During the 1930s the Reverend E. W. D. Isaac, Jr.—who brought Campbell into the Baptist Training Union in 1916—and Campbell organized a male gospel quartet (with piano accompaniment) to travel around the country and appear at the National Baptist Convention singing songs that Campbell and others composed for the denomination. The Good Will Singers, one of the most popular gospel groups of the 1930s and 1940s, was composed of Bradley; Odie Hoover of Cleveland, Ohio; J. Earle Hines of Atlanta; and Charles Simms of Nashville. Thomas Shelby of Memphis served as the first pianist, and Elmer Ruffner (1913–88) followed him in this position.

Always interested in European art music as much as gospel, Bradley was encouraged by Dr. A. M. Townsend of the National Baptist Convention to study voice seriously in New York. He left the Good Will Singers in the early 1940s and began studying with Madame Edyth Walker (1870–1950), the famous Wagnerian mezzo-soprano, at her studio in New York. He later moved to London where he remained for six years studying and singing throughout Europe. He made his debut at London's Albert Hall in 1946 in a concert of German, French, and Italian songs; Negro spirituals; and Lucie Campbell's "Heavenly Sunshine."

Bradley has been praised for his controlled intensity, evenness of tone, and the sheer beauty of his voice. His earthy bass has a power unheard of in gospel. While some gospel singers decry him for his penchant for singing the slow gospel hymn and ballad, in 1975 his singing so inspired President William Richard Tolbert, Jr., of Liberia that he knighted him "Sir" Robert. Both Lucie Campbell and Mahalia Jackson requested that he sing at their funerals. In his quiet but extremely moving singing style, Bradley honored their requests.

Spirit Of Memphis

Quartet singing in Memphis has been a pastime and vocation for men and women since the early 1920s. Groups organized in the 1920s include the I. C. Glee Club, the Harmony Four, and the Mount Olive Wonders. Along with Jefferson County, Alabama, Memphis shares the record for having the most female gospel quartets.

Among the female *a cappella* quartets in Memphis were the Golden Stars, the Southern Junior Girls, and the Songbirds of the South, whose leader, Cassietta George, later became famous as a member of Albertina Walker's Caravans.

The most outstanding quartet from Memphis, however, was the long-lived Spirit of Memphis Quartette (by the early 1950s they dropped "Quartette"). The seeds of the group were planted in 1927 or 1928 when several members of different quartets would get together informally and sing. In 1930 James Darling, A. C. Harris, Forrest Terrel, and Arthur Wright formed a quartet but gave themselves no name. One evening when they were to appear on a program and had to be introduced, the group was discussing a name when Darling began to wipe his face with a handkerchief that had written in the corner "The Spirit of St. Louis" (in honor of Lindbergh's 1927 flight across the Atlantic in an airplane of the same name). Darling changed "St. Louis" to "Memphis," and this group was born.

Heavily influenced by the Famous Blue Jay Singers, the first professional quartet the group saw, they featured precise attacks and releases with harmony reminiscent of the university jubilee quartets. Their strength lay in the several leaders they had over the next thirty years.

Memphis was the home of Sam Phillips' Sun Records and Hallelujah Spiritual, a local label. Galatin, Tennessee, was home to Dot Records, and Excello Records was located in Nashville. Only the Hallelujah Spiritual label appeared interested in the Spirit of Memphis. Their first recording was released in fall 1949, and, although recorded in Memphis on Hallelujah Spiritual, it was immediately leased to Deluxe, a regional label. "I'm Happy in the Service of the Lord," backed with "My Life Is in His Hands," became regional hits.

The success of this recording inspired the group to leave their day jobs and go on the road as professionals. When the group became full-time singers, their membership included Early Malone, Jethroe "Jet" Bledsoe, Theo Wade, James Darling, Robert Reed, and the Reverend Robert Crenshaw. With the release of their recording they began to accept invitations to appear throughout Alabama, Arkansas, Mississippi, and Tennessee. Silas Steele from the Famous Blue Jay Singers and William Broadnax, known as "Little Ax," soon joined the group, and the Spirits boasted two of the greatest leaders in gospel quartets. Gospel music historian Anthony Heilbut described the Spirits during their heyday:

The group's powerhouse was the ever dependable Alabaman, Silas Steele, late of the Blue Jays and Bright Stars. Steele's thunderous baritone could shake a church, the subdued lead of Jet Bledsoe and the ringing tenor of Willie "Little Ax" Broadnax blended gloriously with his roars. Often James Darling, the group's baritone, would improvise a melodic counterpoint to Steele's lead, while the bass "boom-de-boomed" in accustomed style.

This description captures, in ringing sonority, the Spirits' singing of Wynona Carr's "Lord Jesus" in a live performance at Memphis' seven-thousand-seat Mason Temple in October 1952. While the quartet provides a solid harmonic and rhythmic background to compete with the solo—a beloved competition in gospel—Jet Bledsoe literally preaches his solo. The delight at this exchange is apparent from the shouts, encouragements, and screams of the audience (captured on the recording), providing an indication of the kind of ecstacy apparent at live performances of beloved gospel groups. Jet Bledsoe, the manager of the Spirits during the 1950s, took the group off the road in 1960, but they appeared locally for the next several years. In 1980, the group celebrated its fiftieth anniversary.

Samuel McCrary and the Fairfield Four

In April 1991 the Fairfield Four performed in concert at Carnegie Hall, helping to celebrate the one hundredth anniversary of the finest performance house in the United States. Two months later this group celebrated an anniversary of its own—its seventieth—as one of the world's leading male *a cappella* gospel quartets.

In late 1921 the Reverend J. R. Carrethers, assistant pastor of Nashville's Fairfield Missionary Baptist Church and a well-known musician, organized and trained a trio of young boys from the Sunday School to sing during services and special programs held at the church. When the trio became a quartet in 1925, the Reverend Stratton, then pastor of the church, and Mrs. Annie Clay, mother of the church, gave them the name Fairfield Four. The group sang "in their home church, at local churches and at teas and social gatherings for friends and acquaintances." Samuel McCrary (1911–91) joined the group in the mid-1930s and by the late 1930s the group had secured its first radio broadcast over WSIX. Doug Seroff, their biographer, comments on the addition of tenor McCrary to the group:

His silver-toned tenor voice, a marvel of projection and control, set the Fairfield
Four apart from other local gospel groups. Young Sam McCrary was the most
outstanding gospel quartet lead singer Nashville has ever produced.

In 1941 John W. Work III, the venerable composer and music educator from
Fisk University, came to the Fairfield church to record a sermon by the Reverend
Stratton for the Library of Congress. Work recorded the Fairfield Four as well, and
thus the group began a recording career that would last more than fifty years.

As the prize for winning a promotional contest held by the local Colonial Coffee
Company, the Fairfield Four began broadcasting over Nashville's 50,000–watt
WLAC in 1942 and continued their broadcasts for almost a decade. During their
broadcasting years, the members of the group were Samuel McCrary, first tenor and
lead; John H. Battle, alternate first tenor; George Gracey, second tenor; Harold L.
Carrethers, baritone and pianist (like many other quartets during the late 1940s and
1950s the Fairfield Four occasionally used piano accompaniment); and Rufus L.
Carrethers, bass. Their repertoire consisted of Negro spirituals sung in the style of
the university jubilee singers, jubilee songs, and the newer gospel songs composed
by Dorsey, Campbell, and Brewster. In 1946 the group signed a recording contract
with Bullet Record Company, and over the next fifteen years recorded more than one
hundred titles on such labels as Bullet, Delta, Dot, Champion, and Old Town.

The Fairfield Four, like the hundreds of black male *a cappella* quartets of the late
1940s and early 1950s, thought and spoke of their singing groups as "clubs." As
such, although a great deal of time was spent socializing and having fun with other
men who were all nearly the same age and had the same interests, they were ruled
by strict bylaws and, in some cases, a constitution. Doug Seroff published the following document of the Fairfield Four for a 1988 Gospel Arts Festival Day, held at
Fisk University in Nashville:

BYLAWS OF THE FAIRFIELD FOUR (c.1943)

1. *Business meeting and rehearsal twice weekly—Tuesday and Friday, 10:00*
   o'clock until. All not present on time will be fined 50 cents, absent—$1.00.
2. *All discussions be made in meeting and not in public. Anyone caught*
   arguing with anyone in public—$2.00.

3. *Members of quartet must be in church at all programs at 8:15 or be fined $1.00 without a lawful excuse.*

4. *For members caught drinking within 8 hours of program—be fined $5.00.*

5. *When in church any time during program no member should look at others, argue on stage or appear to look angry. Stage etiquette—no unnecessary talk, sitting out of order—if any clause be disobeyed— fined $1.50.*

6. *Any member caught with alcohol on breath while on duty—be fined $2.50.*

7. *When program is out of town make special place to meet at a certain time. If not present without lawful excuse—fined $1.00.*

8. *When money is in treasury after weekly division, no money will be given to any member unless necessary.*

9. *Any member accepting drinks from any strangers—be fined $5.00.*

10. *Any member that doesn't respect members of group or any outside person— saints or sinners—be fined $5.00.*

11. *Any member that tries to arrange or fix a song for the group and the others don't assist will be fined $1.00.*

12. *Any member caught with chewing gum while in service—be fined $1.00 upon entering church.*

13. *All fines must be paid at the end of week and divided among other members.*

14. *All members be in studio 30 minutes before going on air or be fined $1.00—absent $2.50.*

15. *Each member fined $2.50 for the word G. D. and $1.00 additional for each offense.*

16. *Any member that argues when fine is presented to be fined double.*

The Fairfield Four's fame spread throughout the United States, and they were in great demand. A split following a dispute within the group in the late 1940s resulted in two different quartets using the same name. By 1950 McCrary had pulled together a single group of singers that continued to sing into the 1990s. One of the newer members was bass Isaac "Dickie" Freeman from Johns, Alabama. While McCrary reigned as the supreme lead of the group, with the Reverend W. L. Richardson (1913–93) succeeding him in the 1980s, much of the Fairfield Four's reputation was based on the booming voice and skill of Dickie Freeman, often described as the "thumpingest bass in all of gospel."

A 1952 recording of the group, whose membership at that time included Samuel McCrary as first tenor and lead, Willie Love as second tenor, Willie Frank Lewis as baritone, and Isaac "Dickie" Freeman as bass, captures and illustrates their sound and style. The title of the song, "Tree of Level," bears the misunderstanding of the word "Lebanon" as it was pronounced on the original recording by the Dixie Hummingbirds. Despite this mispronunciation, the rendition shows McCrary at the height of his powers and provides an indication of how Freeman can "thump" bass.

Under Freeman's leadership the Fairfield Four continued to sing into the 1990s at folk music festivals, country fairs, and on the European folk and gospel circuits.

Cleavant Derricks

A new gospel song burst on the scene in the late 1930s and by 1945 had become such a popular favorite of gospel singers and Christian denominations that it was regarded as a folk song. The song was "Just a Little Talk with Jesus," composed in 1937 by Cleavant Derricks (c.1900–76), a pianist and choir director from Chattanooga, Tennessee. The phrase "a little talk with Jesus makes it right" has been one of the popular folk sayings in the African American community since the turn of the century. Because the phrase is used in the song, few people realized that there was, in fact, a Negro spiritual called "A Little Talk with Jesus Makes It Right." James Weldon and J. Rosamond Johnson published an arrangement of the spiritual in their 1927 *Volume Two of American Negro Spirituals*. The words, as contained in that arrangement, are:

> CHORUS
> *O, a little talk wid Jesus, makes it right, all right;*
> *Little talk wid Jesus makes it right, all right.*
> *Lord, troubles of ev'ry kind, thank God, I'll always find,*
> *Dat a little talk wid Jesus makes it right.*

While there are minor similarities between the harmonic structure of the Negro spiritual and Derrick's composition, the melody is totally different and the lyrics bear no relationship save the title:

(Basses)   *(Choir)*

Now let us   **have a little talk with Jesus**

Let us   **tell Him all about our troubles**

He will   **hear our faintest cry**

And He will   **answer by and by;**

Now when you   **feel a little prayer wheel turning**

And you   **know a little fire is burning,**

You will   **find a little talk with Jesus makes it right.**

VERSE

I once was lost in sin but Jesus took me in,
And then a little light from heaven filled my soul;
It bathed my heart in love and wrote my name above,
And just a little talk with Jesus made me whole.

Derrick placed the song in a jubilee—sprightly walking—tempo, assigned the bass lyrics to the triadic tones of a doorbell answered by the choir in a melody that alternates an ascending portion with a descending portion, and found that he had composed a song that was one of the first gospel songs to cross over into the jazz repertoire.

W. Herbert Brewster reported that in the early 1930s before Derrick began composing he came to Memphis and worked with him for a short time. Derrick's style of lyric writing attests to this association. Moreover, he borrowed one of Brewster's rhythmic devices in "Just a Little Talk with Jesus"—every syllable is set to a single tone, creating the kind of "patter song" made famous in Gilbert and Sullivan operettas.

Derrick was born in Chattanooga and grew up singing in the Orchard Knob Baptist Church. As a young man he and his wife, Cecelia, directed the choir at Orchard Knob. In his early thirties he was called to the ministry and moved first to Knoxville and then to Beloit, Wisconsin, founding a church in each place. He later settled in Washington, D.C., pastoring a church there until illness forced his retirement in the early 1970s.

Derrick continued to compose throughout his life, writing more than three hundred gospel songs. Others of his songs that have become gospel standards are "When God Dips His Love in My Heart," "I Trust Him on My Journey All the Way," and "We'll Soon Be Done with Troubles and Trials." Derrick realized a long-held desire when in 1975, after the song was more than forty years old, he recorded "Just a Little Talk with Jesus."

GOSPEL IN NEW YORK

Despite its prominence as an African American world cultural center and its role in the development of African American secular music after the 1920s, New York City has a less-than-illustrious place in the development of gospel music. It is ironic that this mecca of talent has not produced that major star, group, composer, publishing house, pianist, or organist who would set the standard in gospel and therefore entice gospel performers to the city because "things were happening there." The one exception was the Selah Jubilee Singers led by southern-born and musically initiated Thurmon Ruth. And while New York has always been considered a gospel city—every gospel singer must eventually appear there—during the Golden Age it was not a gospel center where the music was created and produced. However, New York City, like the other cities, began to participate in the same way as a "center."

Charlie Storey, who has sung with both the Jubilee Stars and the Brooklyn All Stars, witnessed the gospel movement in New York City from the late 1920s. He observed that when he moved to the city, he started on the road to gospel the same way his brothers and sisters had in the South. Born in Camake, Georgia, he moved with his family to Brooklyn in 1928. His father, a Holiness preacher, "set up a church in the family's small house at 711 Gates Avenue." Soon after their arrival Storey and his sisters formed a vocal "spiritual" group and began singing in neighborhood churches.

The Storey family arrived in New York at about the same time as Otha M. Kelly (c.1897–1986). Kelly, a Mississippi native, was saved under the Elder I. E. MacFadden in Hattiesburg, Mississippi, in 1914 and shortly thereafter moved to Chicago, coming under the tutelage of Williams Roberts, who later became the first Overseer (then Bishop) of the Chicago Jurisdiction of COGIC. After working fourteen years with Roberts, Kelly relocated to New York, eventually becoming Overseer and then Bishop of the New York Jurisdiction. Like other ministers in the Pentecostal denomination, Kelly brought this sanctified style of singing to New York.

This sanctified music filled homes, small churches, and storefronts throughout

New York, but it was not the only sacred music to make an impression on the city. The jubilee quartet movement had entered the city in the mid-1920s. Before that the original Golden Gate Quartet had been inspired by the Fisk Jubilee Singers to present concerts of Negro spirituals and folk songs before nonchurch audiences. College-trained quartets began settling in the city in 1927 when the Utica Jubilee Quartet, originally students from the Utica Normal and Industrial Institute in Utica, Mississippi, relocated to New York City. Ray Allen, in his study of New York quartets, reported that "in 1927 they began broadcasting over WJZ of the National Broadcasting Company, becoming the first African American quartet to be featured on a nationally syndicated radio program." While many of the jubilee quartets relocated to New York City—including the Virginia-based Golden Gate Quartet, the Dinwiddie Singers, and the Norfolk Jubilee Singers—few elected to make the switch from jubilee to gospel.

One of the first quartets to do so was the Southernaires. Representing the several southern colleges where they had been trained in the jubilee tradition, the Southernaires were formed in New York City and made their first appearance at the Williams International CME Church in Harlem that same year. The original membership included first tenor Homer Smith of Florence, Alabama; lead soloist and second tenor Lowell Peters of Cleveland, Tennessee; baritone Jay Stone Toney from Kentucky; and bass William Edmondson from Spokane, Washington. Although they sang the traditional jubilee songs, they were also able to make a house "shout" with the newer gospel songs. In the late 1950s this group made another switch—to popular songs and rhythm and blues—and stopped singing religious songs.

Soloists and groups who had nourished their talent in their southern hometowns, however, began to move into New York City in the 1930s. This second group of transplanted southerners were thoroughly steeped in the gospel tradition. The first of these was also the first superstar in gospel, Sister Rosetta Tharpe. Sister Tharpe was also the first of the sanctified saints who kept one foot in the church and one foot in the clubs.

Sister Rosetta Tharpe
At age four in her hometown of Cotton Plant, Arkansas, Rosetta Nubin (1915–73) stood on boxes playing a guitar only slightly smaller than herself and singing "Jesus

on the Main Line, Tell Him What You Want." While there was no doubt that she had an extraordinary voice—bright and clear, sonorous, warm, slightly brassy—and an easy delivery, she also knew at that tender age how to sing. Her pitch was solid; she knew the melody and could even add extra notes of her own. Her rhythm was as accented, syncopated, and intricate as any of the blues singers "in the bottoms."

None of these vocal qualities, however, matched her guitar playing. To be sure, she played her share of strummed chords, as most amateurs do, but she also played individual tones creating motives, runs, riffs, and melodies. This was all the more interesting because before the mid-1920s very few African American women played the guitar, opting instead for the piano, which was considered the appropriate instrument for women. Only one other African American woman gained prominence as a guitarist before the 1930s: "Memphis" Minnie Douglas (1896–1973), who began on the banjo but switched to guitar by age fifteen. The guitar family was not strange to Rosetta Nubin, for one of the first sounds she heard was her mother, Katie Bell Nubin (1880–1969), strumming the mandolin and singing sanctified songs, but Rosetta's string technique had surpassed her mother's even at age four.

Clearly, Rosetta Nubin was a prodigy, exactly what Katie Bell Nubin needed to do her work: carry the word of the Lord. As a woman preacher in the sanctified church, she was not able to call herself "Elder," the title used by ministers, nor was she able to oversee a congregation as the senior spiritual officer. Yet she felt that she was "called to preach." The one avenue left open for her was to teach. A female preacher who taught was called a missionary or an evangelist and could teach in any sanctified church and even conduct revivals. Unable to acquire the status of elder, Katie Bell Nubin became a missionary who, in traveling from church to church and town to town, acquired the status of evangelist. Her hook for drawing people to her services was "Little Rosetta Nubin, the singing and guitar-playing miracle." This duo—Katie Bell Nubin, woman preacher, singer, and mandolin player, and her daughter, Little Rosetta, singing and playing guitar—as members of the tent-meeting troupe of male evangelist P. W. McGhee, preached and sang their way through Arkansas, Mississippi, Florida, Georgia, and Tennessee before settling in Chicago in the late 1920s.

In Chicago the Nubins became participants in the growing Holiness movement and Rosetta earned a reputation as a "sweetly saved" young woman. Opportunities to demonstrate her talent abounded, and she accepted every opportunity offered. She began appearing in multiact concerts with performers of blues, jazz, and folk. Her close association with the sanctified church had mellowed her interest in secular music, but she could not deny that her guitar playing and certain aspects of her singing style had been strongly influenced by the blues singers she heard in Arkansas and the jazz she heard on every corner in Chicago, where both King Oliver and Louis Armstrong were holding forth. While she sang and played blues and jazz in the privacy of her home and at the homes of friends, she performed only gospel music in public.

On the advice of several Chicago promoters, Rosetta moved to New York in the mid-1930s and settled in Harlem, once again affiliating with the sanctified church. She soon married a minister from that denomination. This marriage did not last long however, because, like the sanctified church, her husband did not realize she had to be a free spirit. In 1934 Nubin married Wilbur Thorpe—he later changed the name to Tharpe—in Chicago, and he seemed to approve of her career. Upon arriving in New York, however, he began to publicly object to some of her professional action in public, perhaps in an effort to control this great talent. For example, he objected to her appearing without a hat (a necessity within the black church tradition).

Encouraged by her fellow singers in the sanctified church, Rosetta made a demonstration tape for Decca Records in their New York studio in mid-1938. Although she sang her usual repertoire of gospel songs, the producers felt that she could have a wider audience if her songs were less gospel and more worldly. While Katie Bell Nubin, now called "Mother Nubin," objected to any change in her daughter's style, Tharpe agreed to a four-record session in which the producers were free to record her according to their desires. On October 31, 1938, Tharpe recorded four sides for Decca: Thomas A. Dorsey's "Hide Me in Thy Bosom," but with the title "Rock Me"; "That's All"; "My Man and I"; and "Lonesome Road." The record company immediately released "Rock Me," billing the performer as "Sister Rosetta Tharpe." In addition to her own guitar accompaniment, she was backed up on the record by the full Lucius "Lucky" Millinder (1900–66) jazz orchestra.

The members of the sanctified church were shocked, but the record-buying public went into a frenzy for this new singer with the new sound. Her popularity was so great in New York City that she was included in John Hammond's first extravaganza of African American music, "From Spirituals to Swing," staged at Carnegie Hall on December 23, 1938. The concert was a sensation and was reported in newspapers throughout the United States. Sister Tharpe took advantage of this publicity and concertized throughout the Northeast but was not yet able to make the impact on her beloved South that she desired. This problem was erased with her second recording session for Decca in 1944.

The uproar over her accompaniment by a jazz orchestra was so strong that Sister Tharpe requested that Decca permit her to record with only her guitar. They refused this request but agreed to have her accompanied by a trio of piano, bass, and drum. The house boogie-woogie pianist for Decca during the 1940s and 1950s was Samuel "Sammie" Blythe Price (1908–92).

Price was born in Texas and as a child played alto horn in a boys' band in Waco. When he was ten his family moved to Dallas, where he began studying piano with Portia Washington Pittman (1883–1978), the celebrated musician daughter of Booker T. Washington (1856–1915), the educator and statesman. Price settled in New York in 1935 and in 1937 became staff pianist and arranger for Decca. Sammie Price was Tharpe's accompanist and arranger from her September 26, 1944, session with Decca until 1951.

The Rosetta Tharpe-Sammie Price sound blanketed juke boxes, victrolas, and turntables throughout the nation. Every skill that Sister Tharpe had honed since age four shone brightly with the bouncy boogie-woogie and pure blues accompaniments set up by Price on piano, Billy Taylor on bass, and either Wallace Bishop or Henry Cowans on drums. Other such drummers were Ed Burns, Kenny Clarke, and Kansas Fields. She was at her most illustrious on medium fast and fast songs. "Strange Things Happening Everyday" was set to a medium tempo and became the song that made Sister Tharpe famous. Her rendition begins with a few strumming chords on the guitar to solidify the harmony; she then follows with elongated phrasing of single tones. The unique element in this solo is not the single tones in themselves, but that in places where one single tone would normally suffice, Tharpe uses four. For each beat then, she plays four notes, giving each bar sixteen different tones. This is no easy task for any guitarist.

She begins the song with a line directed at the membership of the sanctified church that attempted to scandalize her name because she mixed blues and jazz with gospel. She asserts that they are committing what could be considered greater sins:

> *Oh, we hear church people say*
> *They are in the "Holy way,"*

and inserts an internal refrain:

> *There are strange things happening everyday.*

She pronounces "every" as "ev-vuh-ree" for rhythmic division. She follows with:

> *On that last great judgment day when they drive them all away,*

followed by the internal refrain:

> *There are strange things happening everyday.*

The independent refrain of the song with its call-and-response delivery follows. Surprising to some, Tharpe did not choose one of the established gospel quartets such as the Soul Stirrers or the Dixie Hummingbirds to serve as the congregation to her preaching. Instead, she used the trio accompanying her, which sang in voices suggestive of cynicism, satire, and levity. In the final analysis it was a perfect mixing, because "Strange Things Happening Everyday" was on the borderline between African American sacred music and secular music. This state of near ambivalence was noted by the people of the church, yet Sister Tharpe became the biggest star of gospel to that time, surpassing the Golden Gate Quartet in popularity.

Unfortunately, among church folk, Tharpe's talent could not be separated from her lifestyle. She would attend services with COGIC saints and within a few weeks or a month appear in concerts with such jazz stars as Cab Calloway, Benny Goodman, and Count Basie and at such establishments as Cafe Society. Her popularity became greater among nonsaints than with saints. And then Sister Tharpe received a boost to her gospel career.

On July 3, 1951, she married Russell Morrison, a former manager of the Ink Spots, in an extravagant ceremony at Griffin Stadium in Washington, D.C., for which she charged admission (since the marriage ceremony was to end with a concert). Before and after the ceremony, Sister Tharpe not only sang, but presented as her guests her new backup group, the Rosette Gospel Singers (four female singers); soloist Vivian Cooper; the Sunset Harmonizers; the Harmonizing Four; and a trio of bass, drums, and piano. The Bishop Wyoming Wells (1909–74) and the Reverend Samuel Kelsey, both ministers in COGIC, officiated during the ceremony. (Marie Knight, Tharpe's frequent partner, was not invited to sing because Morrison wanted to present Tharpe again as a soloist, a move that caused a breakdown in an almost sisterly relationship between Tharpe and Knight.) *Ebony* magazine published a photo layout of the wedding.

Given a new career through the wedding publicity, Sister Tharpe began another series of concerts. It was during this time, however, that the "anniversaries" and "extravaganzas" became popular. These multi-starred concerts sometimes had as many as twenty different singing groups on the same bill. When Sister Tharpe, with what was now called "secular-style" gospel, was pitted against such singers as Dorothy Love Coates and the Original Gospel Harmonettes, the Davis Sisters, and the Pilgrim Travelers, she appeared to be out of her league. Not only was her singing jazz inflected, her stage decorum was more reminiscent of a nightclub than of a church service. Her concert dates dropped off, and she lost her recording contract. In 1970 she suffered a debilitating stroke. Her attempts to concertize from a wheelchair after a slight recovery garnered more sympathy than cheers.

Marie Knight

Although Tharpe's fame as a solo artist was secure in 1947, Decca decided to pair Tharpe in duets with Marie Roach Knight (b. 1918). The two recorded and concertized together from 1947 to 1952. Knight, who became known as Madame Marie Knight, was born in Sanford, Florida, to a sanctified deacon and his wife and grew up in Newark, New Jersey, singing and playing piano. After establishing a local reputation in New Jersey as a gospel singer who possessed a solid and strong contralto and a delivery close to the one that Della Reese would make famous twenty years later, Knight went to New York. After singing with local groups for a number of years, she auditioned at Decca Records. Rather than offering her a solo contract they arranged duets for Knight and Tharpe.

Their most outstanding recording was "Up above My Head" from a November 1947 session in which Tharpe provides the call and Knight the response. Although Knight's voice is darker than Tharpe's, they made the perfect gospel duet, even on the chorus after Tharpe's solo interlude where Knight assumes the role of the male bass from gospel quartets, essaying her range from the top to the bottom.

Sister Rosetta Tharpe and Madame Marie Knight became the rage of the nation. They were able to provide variety in their concerts through several exchanges: Knight would play the piano while Tharpe sang; Tharpe would play the piano while Knight sang; they both stood and sang while Tharpe played the guitar; and Knight would stand as still as a concert artist while Tharpe treated every song as if it were an activity song for small children.

The Georgia Peach: Clara Hudman Gholston

The year after John Hammond presented his first Carnegie Hall "From Spirituals to Swing" concert, Radio City Music Hall, the recognized bastion of movies and music in the United States, presented a similar show. The gospel star for this presentation was "The Georgia Peach."

It was a long route from Atlanta's Mount Moriah Baptist Church to Radio City Music Hall for Clara Hudman Gholston (1903–66), and she made the trip against what appeared to be insurmountable odds. There is apparently no record of a Mr. Hudman, but her mother Esther was always known as the

Clara Hudman Gholston, The Georgia Peach.

devout woman who brought up three children in Mount Moriah. According to the Reverend C. J. Johnson (1913–90), the venerable singer of lining hymns and other congregational songs, he and Clara Hudman were brought up in the same church and often sang together, although Clara was about ten years older than Johnson. She began singing as a teenager and was known throughout Atlanta as the girl who could sing "Daniel in the Lion's Den." She and her brothers Luther and Ralph, both younger, formed a trio and would deliver stirring renditions of this missionary hymn (a Baptist song patterned after such Pentecostal songs as "I'm a Soldier" but performed at a slower tempo) on local programs:

Clara: It was Daniel in the den
    Brothers: In the den
Clara: Daniel in the den
    Brothers: In the den
Clara: And He locked
    Brothers: He locked
Clara: The lion's
    Brothers: The lion's
All: He locked the lion's jaw.

It was not unusual for ministers to see Hudman in the audience at a concert and ask her to come to the choir loft and sing. These invitations were more like pronouncements, and Hudman always obliged, singing "Daniel in the Lion's Den" or "What a Friend We Have in Jesus."

When Hudman was sixteen years old, the wife of the Reverend T. T. Gholston, pastor of Mount Moriah, became ill, and upon the request of Gholston and the deacons of the church, Mrs. Hudman gave permission for Clara, who no longer attended school, to take care of Mrs. Gholston and her two young boys during the day while the pastor cared for his flock. Clara cared for Mrs. Gholston until the pastor's wife died two years later. She then stayed on to care for the pastor's young children and prepare his meals. Six months after Mrs. Gholston's death, the minister married Hudman and moved her permanently into his home. Mount Moriah was split apart by the marriage; the deacons and older church members objected to such an early marriage, and the middle-aged women of the church were angry because the minister became a lost "catch" and his new wife was only eighteen years old and had "lived in the house with his wife." Gholston preached a sermon addressing all the public concerns about this marriage, but forgiveness did not seem forthcoming from his congregation. Within a few years he became an alcoholic, and on one Sunday when he was too inebriated to complete his sermon, the congregation "voted" him out of the pulpit. According to the Reverend C. J. Johnson who witnessed the episode, Hudman felt that she was a vehicle for the Lord's work and therefore stood by her husband. It would be several years before her youthful loyalty would wear thin.

Gholston accepted an appointment at a church in Detroit and after a few years there decided to move to New York City. Shortly after their arrival in New York City, Gholston and his wife separated, and she left the Baptist church and affiliated with Bishop Lawson's Refuge Church of Our Lord (a Pentecostal denomination). It was with this congregation that she found her "new voice" in gospel.

She began recording as early as 1930, and judging from one of her first recordings, "Lordy, Won't You Come by Here," she sang superbly in the Baptist tradition with conviction, clear delivery, and beauty of tone in a light contralto capable of smooth runs and explosive attacks. Her 1942 recording of Kenneth Morris's "Does Jesus Care," however, shows a matured, "tried and true" gospel singer with a fully developed dark contralto, filling empty spaces in musical time and making not only a sincere appeal to the listener to "accept Jesus because He cares," but showing herself to be one of the early great gospel singers.

Although she came to New York City from Detroit, her audience heard her Georgia roots in her singing and therefore dubbed her the "Georgia Peach," not only because of that popular name for southern women but because her style gave the title meaning: sweet, smooth, melodious singing fueled by the same intensity that the sanctified singers brought to their shout. She recorded extensively and traveled throughout the United States as a soloist and leader of a quartet. She made several appearances in New York on the same bill as Mahalia Jackson and Ernestine B. Washington. The three were the leading soloists in New York in the 1940s (Willie Mae Ford Smith was not well known in that city). She is regarded as a pioneer in gospel music.

Madame Ernestine B. Washington

Like so many of her compatriots, the "Songbird of the East," Ernestine Washington, was actually from the South. Although the program for her funeral in Washington Temple Church of God in Christ in Brooklyn on July 5, 1983, bore the caption:

Service of Victory for the late
Mrs. Ernestine B. Washington
The First Lady of Washington Temple
& Eastern New York Jurisdiction
Church of God in Christ

what was really being celebrated was a life of music and good deeds that had been nurtured in Arkansas and by the music of Arizona Dranes.

Ernestine Beatrice Thomas Washington was born in 1914 in Little Rock. She attended school in Arkansas and began singing at age four. Her mother was a popular sanctified singer in the Little Rock community, and she and little Ernestine were known for their duet of "I Come to the Garden Alone." Ernestine completed high school in Little Rock and was engaged in domestic work while singing at the annual Convocation of the Church of God in Christ, where she met and married the Reverend Frederick D. Washington (1913–88). Washington, who attended the Moody Bible Institute and later was awarded an honorary Doctorate of Humanities from Trinity Hall College and Seminary, traveled with his new wife to Montclair, New Jersey, where he founded the Trinity Temple Church of God in Christ. In the early 1940s the couple moved to Brooklyn, New York, where Washington founded the Brooklyn Church of God in Christ, which was later named Washington Temple in his honor, where he pastored until his death. He also served as Auxiliary Bishop of the Jurisdiction of New York.

Madame Washington had been strongly influenced by Arizona Dranes, and the resemblance in their singing style was uncanny. Dranes possessed a high-pitched mezzo-soprano-alto voice with a fast vibrato that would soar in the upper register; in the lower register she would adopt a soft growl. She approached her attacks with a percussive bent that set beginning words in phrases apart from other words, and she had a sense of melody and rhythm that was so secure that she simply rode on the meter that had been established, setting a rhythm to fit the text and mood of the song. The same description applied to the style of Ernestine B. Washington. If there was a difference between her style and Dranes', it was that Madame Washington lived in an age when singing at range extremes was accepted and expected, and she indulged the expectation. This style is evident in her 1946 recording of "Does Jesus Care" with the legendary William Geary "Bunk" Johnson (1872–1949) and his jazz band. Despite the traditional New Orleans-style jazz band, complete with an active drummer, behind her, Washington begins the song in a contemplative move, controlling voice and range while delivering a meditative soliloquy of questions and answers regarding the love of God. When she reaches the chorus, however, she spins forth the full range and power of her voice in a statement of affirmation: "Oh yes, I know He cares."

By 1946 the Reverend Washington had become a fixture in Brooklyn, one of the most respected ministers in COGIC, and Madame Washington was the official soloist of the denomination, singing the solo before the sermon of the presiding bishop in the flagship service of the annual November convocation in Memphis. Yet, she recorded with a "sinner" like Bunk Johnson. Unlike Sister Rosetta Tharpe, Madame Washington was not subjected to the contempt of the church membership for working with secular musicians. However, Madame Washington only recorded with Bunk Johnson and did not seek a relationship with him or his musicians (who played secular music) outside the studio. Also, the people of the church somehow felt complimented that such a star as Bunk Johnson was called upon to accompany one of their own.

Her 1957 recording of W. Herbert Brewster's "I Thank You, Lord" shows Washington in her sanctified style. Accompanied by her longtime pianist and organist Alfred Miller (b. 1920) and the members of her church choir, she unleashes the full power of her voice and the style that made her famous. This type of performance brought Washington fame as she toured throughout the United States, often appearing in concerts with the Roberta Martin Singers, Mahalia Jackson, and the Selah Jubilee Singers from her own neighborhood. At her death she was mourned in two crowded, overflowing services at Washington Temple, complete with all of the dignitaries of COGIC. To this date, there has been no replacement for the "Songbird of the East."

Thurmond Ruth and the Selah Jubilee Singers

Only one quartet was able to break through the New York syndrome and become a major force in gospel during the Golden Age. That group was led by Thurmond Ruth (b. 1914), who moved to that city at age eight and by twelve had organized the group that he would lead for the next forty-five years. The Selahs started out as disciples of the Fisk Jubilee Quartet style; moved to the Jefferson County, Alabama style; and within ten years of their organization adopted the gospel music of Chicago and the sanctified churches of the New York area. During their first decade their home was St. Mark's Holiness Church and from there they performed throughout the five boroughs of New York, taking occasional trips to New Jersey, Pennsylvania, and as far south as Baltimore. Inspired by the Soul Stirrers, the group approached J. Mayo Williams, a scout for Decca records, regarding a contract.

The Selah Jubilee Singers

By the time their first recordings were released in 1939, the group included Crip Harris and Melvin Coldten, both former members of the Norfolk Jubilee Quartet; Bill "High Pockets" Langford, formerly of the Golden Gate Quartet and the Southern Sons; Allen Bunn, who later gained recognition as a blues artist; Gene Mumford; and, of course, Ruth. Like many other groups of their time that began their recording career with an already recorded song, the Selahs' first recording was a "cover" of the Soul Stirrers' recording of a few months earlier, Rebert H. Harris' "Walk Around." The Selahs called their song "I Want Jesus to Walk around My Bedside." While the Selahs' version is interesting for its sophisticated editing of this southern testimony, it does not capture the sincerity, urgency, and old-time fire and brimstone of the original.

Once the Selahs came into their own, however, they were hard to beat. An example of their mature style is the 1958 recording of Thomas A. Dorsey's "Today." Rendered almost exclusively in the Baptist lining hymn tradition of unpulsed singing in which the highly embellished syllable created a phrase, the Selahs injected new life into this beloved song. True to tradition, they delivered the first line of the song in the Baptist lining hymn tempo, but beginning with the second line, they moved into a foot-patting jubilee tempo, complete with a call and response. The response was not merely a repetition of the call but a return to earlier days with the refined "oom-ma-lank-a-lank-a-lank" response of "Yes, my Lord" at every turn where rhythm was needed. The climax was a vamp at the end of the chorus, accompanied by guitar. The guitar accompaniment showed the influence of not only the Golden Gate Quartet, the major influence on Ruth, but the gospel style of the period, in which few quartets dared to sing *a cappella* at concerts where other gospel singers used piano or guitar accompaniment.

Other New York City Singers

New York City had a very active community of local singers who made a career of traveling from church to church within the five boroughs. Most of these groups never recorded, and few traveled farther from the city than Philadelphia. Yet they kept New York City gospel music lovers supplied with concerts, radio broadcasts, anniversary programs, and local representation on concerts when famous traveling singers appeared in the city. One of the local favorites was the Sunset Jubilee Singers, organized in 1940. According to Ray Allen, author of *Singing in the Spirit: African American Sacred Quartets in New York City*, they were among the most popular groups in the city in the early 1940s. Although the Sunsets made a few recordings for the Hub and Okeh labels, they were unable to garner a national reputation.

As children, sisters Fay (b. 1936) and Anna (b. 1938) Scruggs both sang piano-accompanied gospel in New York City. By age seventeen Fay had landed a contract with and cut two sides for Atlantic Records. Within a year she had gone to record producer Arnold Shaw, and under the name Fay Adams cut a song called "Shake a Hand." This song became one of the biggest hits of 1953. Her sister, Anna, known as Anna Tuell, remained with gospel and became one of the premier gospel soloists in New York City.

New York City's Daniels Singers, while not singing much outside of the city, was the favorite local group to open concerts for traveling gospel stars during the 1950s. Organized by leader-pianist-arranger Jackie Daniels (1910–56), the group was composed of leaders Evelyn Price and Anna Quick Griffin, and the husband-and-wife team of Connie and Becky Burruss. Daniels, a pianist and organist who also accompanied other singers, was well known as an organist throughout the Northeast. Along with Alfred Miller, James "Blind" Francis (b. 1914), and Herman Stevens, he was one of a handful of organists who truly could play gospel. In 1948 he organized the Daniels Singers and for the next decade they ruled the piano-accompanied gospel wing of New York City, often in direct competition with the Herman Stevens Singers. Two of their best-known recordings on the Savoy label are "Jesus," their theme song, and Thomas A. Dorsey's "Search Me, Lord."

James "Blind" Francis was the regular organist for the tent revivals of A. A. Childs in the early 1950s and accompanied Mahalia Jackson on several recordings. He also traveled with her while she concertized in the Northeast.

Alfred Miller, organist and choir director at Washington Temple Church of God in Christ in Brooklyn in the early 1950s, was the favorite organist of Madame Ernestine B. Washington, and traveled with her on occasion as her pianist and musical director. Miller organized the Miller Singers in the 1950s and recorded several songs that met with modest popularity. However, the group had a fluctuating membership—always dependent upon the engagement—and would often serve as the local group that opened for traveling singers. Miller was often called on to accompany, both on recordings and in concerts, such singers as Mahalia Jackson, Clara

Sunset Jubilee Singers

Fay Adams and Anna Tuell

Ward, the Davis Sisters, and Bishop F. D. Washington. He, along with Francis, Daniels, and Stevens, constituted the New York Gospel Organ Guild.

Gospel DJ Joe Bostic

By the early 1950s, gospel music was the music of the working-class African American Christian, and performers, producers, and promoters of gospel made an honest attempt to touch the religious mood of these people as rhythm and blues had touched the secular mood. Concerts were presented, recordings were made and sold, and gospel DJs became plentiful, although few were able to have a career outside the radio station, since most had no skill in concert production or artist management. Along with such luminaries as "Hoss" Allen, John Richburg, and Jean Noble, New York City's Joe Bostic could ensure a career by playing and commenting on certain recordings. While the other DJs ruled the South, Joe Bostic ruled New York City.

Joe William Bostic (b. 1909) was born in Mt. Holly, New Jersey, attended public schools in the city and graduated from Morgan State College (now University) in 1929. After conducting radio programs in Baltimore and serving as a sports correspondent for the *Afro-American*, he settled in New York in 1937. Working in both journalism and radio, he hosted "Tales from Harlem" for WMCA from 1937 to 1939 and was a DJ for WCMW from 1939 to 1942. He joined the staff of WLIB in 1942 where, in addition to his radio programs, he produced weekly talent shows with live performers. It was during this time that Bostic became aware of the gospel audience and devoted his energies to the new sacred music.

He began to produce concerts of gospel music in some of the most respected venues in New York City and created a sensation in 1950 when he presented his first "Negro Gospel and Religious Festival" at New York's Carnegie Hall. Among the guests were the Selah Jubilee Singers and the Herman Stevens Singers. The pièce de résistance, however, was the star attraction: Mahalia Jackson. While succeeding Carnegie Hall presentations were festive occasions, featuring such singers as the Roberta Martin Singers, James Cleveland, and Professor J. Earle Hines, none carried the significance of the first Mahalia Jackson concert, for Bostic had introduced pure gospel into Carnegie Hall. To be sure, John Hammond had introduced a kind of gospel with Sister Rosetta Tharpe and the Mitchell Christian Singers, but Bostic's was a different gospel. His was gospel for a primarily African American audience, and his audience wept, clapped, shouted, and fainted to a music that was not rendered for form and fashion, but for "soul salvation."

Bostic was considered the "Dean of Gospel Disk Jockeys," because he was among the first and the most successful of the DJs to use radio to gather large crowds for gospel singers. As late as 1959 he produced his "First Annual Gospel, Spiritual and Folk Musical Festival" in Madison Square Garden before an audience of eleven thousand, thereby opening up yet another venue for gospel.

GOSPEL SPREADS ACROSS THE NATION

As the 1940s came to an end, gospel had insinuated itself so strongly on the African American community that it was no longer necessary for aspiring gospel singers to move to major gospel music centers like Chicago and Philadelphia. Every major city wanted to be identified with gospel, and groups began to spring up in all areas, making such cities as Richmond, Birmingham, and Los Angeles as sonorously gospel as those called home by Roberta Martin and Clara Ward. The Tidewater area of Virginia, which had produced such groups as the Silver Leaf Jubilee Singers and the Golden Gate Quartet, contributed yet another group that would become one of the leaders of the quartet movement: "Gospel Joe" Williams and the Harmonizing Four.

Joseph Williams and the Harmonizing Four

Joseph "Gospel Joe" Williams (b. 1916) was born in Richmond, Virginia, into a musical family. His mother was a singer at the Second Baptist Church where the family worshipped, and his father was a singer with the Zion St. John Jubilee Singers, a local *a cappella* quartet. Williams remembered that as a very small boy, "I used to stand up beside him and sing the best I could." It was not long before Williams began to stand on his own; when he was eleven years old and attending Richmond's Dunbar Elementary School, he was invited by three school mates who had been gathering after school to sing jubilee songs to join with them in organizing a quartet. Thomas "Goat" Johnson, Levi Handly, Robert Simpkins, and Joseph Williams became the Harmonizing Four on September 27, 1927, and gave their first public performance on October 27, one month later, at the Dunbar School.

Like the Zion St. John Jubilee Singers, after whom they patterned themselves (along with other male *a cappella* quartets of the time), the Harmonizing Four specialized in singing Negro spirituals, hymns, and the new gospel songs of Charles Albert Tindley and Lucie Campbell. From the beginning the group emphasized what Kip Lornell called "a full, sweet vocal blend that became their hallmark." As they developed and experienced personnel changes over the years, they continued to give special prominence to close harmony, precise attacks and releases, and a smooth sound.

Jimmy Jones of The Harmonizing Four

They made their first recordings in 1943 for the Decca label, a contract probably secured for them by Sister Rosetta Tharpe, the label's principal gospel singer at that time. In addition to recordings of their own with Decca, the group recorded several sides with Sister Tharpe. Her close performance associates, they appeared with her on the "Ed Sullivan Show" in the 1950s and sang at her wedding to Russell Morrison in 1951. Their reputation as church singers was so secured that they, unlike Sister Tharpe, were not ostracized by church members.

By the time of their first recording, the group had acquired guitarist Lonnie Smith (the father of jazz pianist Lonnie Liston Smith), who joined the group in 1941. They recorded and traveled for the next decade as a solid, dependable group with a reputation based on close harmony and country-style singing. By 1957 when they began recording for the Vee-Jay label, their personnel consisted of original members Williams and Johnson, plus Smith and new member Jimmy Jones.

Jones, formerly of the Texas-based Southern Sons Quartet, provided a bass foundation for the Harmonizing Four that few other groups could claim. Not satisfied to simply support the group, Jones became a soloist and an obbligato bass, singing his part in the harmony and at the same time singing above, around, and outside the others. With a full, flat, virtuoso voice, Jones was one of that small group of basses who could compete with any lead, whether he was Joseph Williams, R. H. Harris, or Ira Tucker. Jones' skill and the style the Harmonizing Four had developed over thirty years were nowhere more thoroughly demonstrated than on the group's

1957 recording of "Farther Along," a standard in the African American church since its publication in 1937. The song is cast in a call-and-response arrangement, and in it Jones celebrates the basso profondo by singing the melody at the very bottom of his range but with the power of his middle register. He begins in a slow, almost contemplative mood, and by the end of the chorus, has moved the entire melody up an octave. While Jones thunders in and around the melody, the other singers set up a harmonic and rhythmic response that is constant in its movement, leaving Jones free to explore with his considerable talent.

There was no doubt, as gospel music historian Anthony Heilbut observed, that "Joseph Williams is one of the most sincere and subtle readers of a lyric this side of R. H. Harris," and the other members of the Harmonizing Four blended their considerable talents with his to produce memorable performances.

CBS Trumpeteers

A little to the north of the Tidewater region another gospel quartet was making history. Joseph Johnson, who learned his quartet skills as a member of the Golden Gate Quartet and the Willing Four Quartet, decided to organize a group that he could influence in both repertoire and style. In 1946 in Baltimore he formed a group called the Trumpeteers with Joe Armstrong, baritone; Raleigh Turnage, tenor; James Keels, bass; and himself on lead. The Trumpeteers were the personification of the jubilee quartet: tight and sweet harmony, tenor voice lead, and attacks and releases that were perfectly coordinated. Shortly after they were organized the Trumpeteers began singing over WCAO radio in Baltimore and were noticed by the Columbia Broadcasting System, whose executives signed them to a daily radio show. In honor of this collaboration, the group added CBS to their name. They, along with the Golden Gate Quartet and the Wings Over Jordan Choir, were among the few jubilee and gospel singers to have a network radio program.

Their contract with CBS lasted only two years, but the radio show gave the group national celebrity and helped them land a contract with Score Records. The first recording session on September 12, 1947, produced their greatest hit, Theodore R. Frye's arrangement of "Milky White Way," a gospel blues song like Tindley's "Stand by Me" and Eugene Smith's "I Know the Lord Will Make a Way, Oh Yes, He Will." Each of the three stanzas are sung to the same melody. Although the group often performed *a cappella*, this particular rendition begins with the guitar playing each note of the chord of the song. Johnson begins in a quiet mood, as if speaking to a neighbor, over a humming background by the group (one of the outstanding features of this rendition:

> STANZA 1: *I'm going to walk that milky white way some of the days*
> STANZA 2: *I'm gonna tell my mother howdy, howdy when I get home*
> STANZA 3: *I'm going to meet God the father, God the son.*

Like the lead singer of other jubilee quartets who were making the transition to gospel, Johnson sings with equal amounts of vigor and restraint, permitting the beauty of his voice and singing style to carry the message of the song. While the background voices maintain an even hum behind the soloist, at the second stanza the bass singer adds just enough interpolated thumps to give the performance the lilting rhythmic quality it needed to make listeners pat their feet. Not until 1952, when the Bells of Joy released their "Let's Talk about Jesus," would there be another quartet recording that commanded the attention of every gospel music lover as "Milky White Way" did in late 1947 and 1948.

Joseph Johnson kept the Trumpeteers together until shortly before his death in 1984. Since that time the group has been managed by Calvin Stewart, a native of South Carolina, who joined the group in 1949. They no longer sing in the jubilee quartet style but have succumbed to the hard gospel techniques of singing at the extreme ranges and seeking more to overpower than to soothe. But every so often the sweet style of the CBS Trumpeteers comes through again, reminding the listener of their sound from the first decade of the Golden Age of Gospel.

James "Woodie" Alexander and the Pilgrim Travelers

While the African American quartet movement began in Jefferson County, Alabama, just before the beginning of the second decade of the twentieth century, it was not long before Houston became the center of the Southwest for jubilee/gospel quartets. The Soul Stirrers had become the leading quartet in the Southwest, and young African American males who could only sing a chorus of "Mary Had a Little Lamb" were attempting to form groups and duplicate the success of Rebert H. Harris and the leading quartet from Houston. Of the many groups that were formed in Houston as a result of the success of the Soul Stirrers, the most popular was a group only a few years younger than their idols.

Joe Johnson gathered together a group of young men from Houston's Pleasant Grove Baptist Church and formed the Pilgrim Travelers in 1936. As a community-based group, personnel, style, and repertoire changed frequently as they appeared in the area, usually on weekends at church and quartet concerts. Their membership began to stabilize in 1944 when, after winning a quartet competition, they were given the opportunity to travel with the Soul Stirrers.

In 1947 Johnson decided to move the group to Los Angeles rather than to Chicago to avoid direct competition with the Soul Stirrers. When the group arrived in Los Angeles, James "Woodie" Alexander became the manager. Seldom featured as a song leader, Alexander selected the repertoire, composed several songs for the group, coordinated stage behavior, selected uniforms, replaced singers when needed, and booked the group. Alexander was born in 1916 and reared in Coffeyville, Kansas, home of the legendary African American choral director Eva Jessye (1895–1992) and sang both gospel and popular music during his youth. Before joining the Pilgrim Travelers in 1946 he played professional baseball in the Negro League and sang with the Southern Gospel Singers. With more than a bit of the "smooth operator" blood in his veins, Alexander was almost a dictator, but his style was so understated that, when in conversation or association with him, one was completely unaware that he was, with cultivated skill, directing the entire encounter. Because he did not appear to be malicious in the slightest way, singers and promoters forgave his understated dictatorship where his group was concerned. Alexander used this skill to push the Pilgrim Travelers into the forefront of gospel quartets.

By the time the group had their first recording session in late 1946, the membership was composed of Alexander, tenor; cousins Kylo Turner and Keith Barber, who until they joined the Pilgrim Travelers had worked as farmers in Cleveland, Texas, leads; Jesse Whitaker, who joined the group in California, baritone; and Rayford Taylor, bass. Their first recordings show the influence of the Golden Gate Quartet and the Soul Stirrers, the reigning quartets of the day. Tindley's "What Are They Doing in Heaven" and Kenneth Morris' "Dig a Little Deeper in God's Love" both show the precise attack, close harmony, rhythm execution, and even the timbre of the Gates and the Soul Stirrers.

In 1948 the Travelers scored successes in the gospel market with their two biggest hits. Brewster's "Thank You, Jesus" and Mary Lou Coleman's "Jesus" (with which the Ward Singers also scored a major success in 1949) showcased the group in two of their three styles: gospel jubilee and gospel ballad. While "Thank You, Jesus" sets up a toe-tapping tempo over which the group literally spits out their thanks to Jesus for bringing them "a mighty long way," "Jesus" is cast in somber colors and tempo—one of those instances where tempo and mood belie the text.

The text of "Jesus" is a rehearsal of the goodness of the Lord and could very well have been delivered as a jubilee or a shout. The ballad tempo, however, ensures strict attention to the lyrics; a more sprightly tempo might have drawn the listener to the beat. The song begins with an anticipation by Turner on the word "oh," to which he assigns nine different tones, followed by the entrance of the group on the word "Jesus." To give the fullest accentuation to the word, the group pronounces it as "Cheesus" and delivers it in dark and resonant harmony. Before continuing with the text, bass singer Raphael Taylor inserts a riff (bum-bum-bum-bum-bum) of five tones (which would become a standard gospel "lick"), as the group continues with "when troubles burden me down." A similar phrase is then delivered, including Taylor's insertion, with the words "I know your love's all around." The Travelers then deliver one of their signature melodic and harmonic devices on the word "oh." While the group holds a single tone, Turner begins his word an octave (eight tones) higher and shimmers down an octave where he will sing the remainder of the phrase. (This device would become associated with Ira Tucker in the early 1950s.) While Turner became much more vocally active during the two stanzas of the recorded version, the song remains a prime example of the mixture of jubilee and gospel, for which the group became famous. They scored several major hits in the next few years, including "Jesus Met the Woman at the Well," "Jesus Gave Me Water," and the immensely popular "Mother Bowed"; however, few of their recordings captured their talent and conviction as well as "Jesus."

In addition to his work with the Pilgrim Travelers, as talent scout for Specialty Records, Johnson secured recording contracts for Wynona Carr and Dorothy Love Coates and the Original Gospel Harmonettes. He also recommended singer-pianist Jessy Dixon (b. 1938) to Brother Joe May as his pianist.

Claude Jeter and the Swan Silvertones

Male falsetto singing, a cherished practice in African singing since ancient days, became associated with rhythm and blues and soul singing in the United States. Long before it became popular as a secular music device falsetto was thoroughly entrenched in gospel singing, and the credit for this all-important technique, which every male singer attempts at some point, can be attributed to two quartet singers, Rebert H. Harris and Claude Jeter (b. 1914). More striking than the beauty of his falsetto is Jeter's judicious use of the device. Not content to discard the natural voice altogether, like Eddie Kendricks and the Bee Gees, Jeter essays his beautiful and firm lyric tenor voice in most of his singing. But for special climaxes and emotion he turns to his falsetto, one of the purest and strongest among singers to date.

Claude Jeter (in white), the inspiration for many soul music singers, and the Swan Silvertones

Jeter was born in Montgomery, Alabama, to a middle-class family whose father was a lawyer and held a professional position for the Tennessee Coal and Iron Railroad. His interest in music was kindled early by his mother, who had a local reputation as a "singer of note." Unfortunately, his father died when Jeter was eight years old and his mother was left to rear the children. Shortly after his father's death, the family moved to Kentucky where Jeter completed high school and sang in the church choir and with informal quartets. He then began working in the coal mines across the border in West Virginia, and to provide entertainment he organized a quartet of his fellow mine workers and named them the Four Harmony Kings. In 1938, the Four Harmony Kings, consisting of Jeter, his brother, and two miners, began singing locally. Within a few months they had garnered a reputation as "some of the sweetest singing boys in the world." While they worked in the mines during the week their weekends were reserved for short singing trips throughout West Virginia and nearby Kentucky and North Carolina.

In the early 1940s the group relocated to Knoxville, Tennessee, and underwent some personnel changes, the most important of which was the addition of Solomon Womack as second lead. The group then was composed of Jeter, first tenor and lead;

Womack, second lead; John Myles, baritone; and Henry Bossard, bass, who would emerge, along with Jimmy Jones, Isaac "Dickie" Freeman, and Raphael Taylor, as one of the leading bass singers in gospel. They performed in the traditional barbershop style, in which Jeter's light and lyrical voice contrasted well with Womack's heavier tenor. *A cappella* singing was the rage at this time, although a few quartets used guitar, and the Four Harmony Kings were masters of the art. According to Jeter:

> When they [the Four Harmony Kings] sang ... it wasn't too emotional. They would just stand flat-footed and sing, because they tried to specialize in harmony. They wanted the music to be right.... In those days, it was more like barbershop harmony.

The group was offered a sustaining Sunday morning spot on WDIR, a 25,000-watt station that could be heard as far away as North Carolina and Florida. Just before they began broadcasting their name changed to the Silvertone Singers to avoid confusion with the more popular Four Kings of Harmony. The show was sponsored by Swans bakery and, in order to provide additional publicity for the company, the group again changed its name—this time to the Swan Silvertone Singers.

Through their radio broadcasts, the Swan Silvertones became one of the most popular quartets in the South, which led to a recording contract with King Records in 1946. Over the next five years the group recorded more than one hundred titles for the label. From these titles one of the most characteristic performances as well as one of their most popular songs was "All Alone." Kerrill Rubman, in her study of this group, describes their performance:

> In "All Alone" the group uses two other approaches. The verse is sung in barbershop-style blended harmony, without rhythm, with pauses to emphasize individual chords. In the chorus, Claude Jeter and later Solomon Womack exhibit "gospel"-style lead singing, improvising vocal flights with snatches of the lyrics as the group sings the chorus in a steady rhythm. Underneath, Henry Bossard adds bass runs.

The group relocated again in 1948, this time to Pittsburgh. With a new membership consisting of Jeter; Louis Johnson, second lead; Paul Owens, alternate lead and second tenor; Myles; and William "Pete" Connor, bass, they switched to the Specialty label in 1951 and to Vee-Jay Records in 1955. Their biggest hit, "Mary, Don't You Weep," was recorded on the Vee-Jay label in 1959. This gospel song underwent an almost complete change from its first incarnation as a Negro spiritual:

> *Oh Mary, don't you weep, don't you mourn,*
> *Oh Mary, don't you weep, don't you mourn;*
> *Pharaoh's army got drown(d)ed,*
> *Oh Mary, don't you weep.*

The Swans slowed the tempo down from a jubilee to a sprightly gospel ballad tempo, gave it a call-and-response arrangement, and opened up the form to include an extended vamp. Jeter begins the song contemplatively, singing the chorus and verse, each set to the same tune, to sixteen bars rather than the eight to which it was sung in the Negro spiritual:

> *Jeter: Oh, I'm singing Mary*
> > ***Group: Oh Mary don't you weep***
> *Jeter: Tell Martha not to mourn*
> > ***Group: Tell Martha not to mou—rn***
> *Jeter: Listen, Mary*
> > ***Group: Oh Mary don't you weep***
> *Jeter: Tell Martha not to mourn*
> > ***Group: Tell Martha not to mou—rn***
> *Jeter: Pharaoh's army*
> > ***Group: Pha—a—raoh's army***
> *Jeter: Got drowned in the sea one day*
> > ***Group: Drowned in the Red Sea***
> *Jeter: Listen, Mary*
> > ***Group: Oh Mary don't you weep***
> *Jeter: Tell Martha not to mourn*
> > ***Group: Tell Martha not to mou—-rn.***

After leading the verse, Jeter turns the remainder of the song over to Paul Owens who delivers the vamp (the "working out" section) during which he repeatedly sings the word "Mary." The song reaches its climax after Owens has raised the pitch and volume several notches, creating a vocal frenzy. "Mary, Don't You Weep" was accompanied by guitar, as were many other songs recorded after Linn Hargrove became guitarist for the group in 1955.

Jeter felt the call to the ministry and was ordained in Detroit's Church of Holiness Science in the mid-1960s. He then left the group and settled in New York City where he occasionally preaches and continues to sing both as a soloist (he had a successful recording of Brewster's "Lord, I've Tried" in 1972) and as a member of "reunion" quartet concerts. After his retirement from the Swans, the group continued singing with new leaders James Lewis and Carl Davis.

Other Early Golden Age Singers

THE RADIO FOUR

The Radio Four, a Nashville group, was so named because they, like many groups in the 1930s and 1940s, had weekly broadcasts over a hometown radio station. These five brothers probably sang over WBDL of Bowling Green, Kentucky, according to Chris Smith, annotator of the 1982 re-release of "There's Gonna Be Joy" by The Radio Four. Organized in the late 1940s, the group was composed of George, Ray, James, Claude, and Morgan Babb. While Morgan, probably the youngest, began as a substitute and guitarist, he became the principal singer in the group; later he switched to a solo career in the 1970s. Their first recordings were made in 1952 and show the group having a special ability to execute jubilee songs. Among their most popular recordings are "How Much I Owe" and "When He Calls."

THE SWANEE QUINTET

Like the Harmonizing Four, the Swanee Quintet was a prime example of the down-home unaffected quartet. Led by the Reverend Reuben W. Willingham, the group's membership remained constant for decades. Along with Willingham, members were Charlie Barnwell, James "Big Red" Anderson, Rufus Washington, and Johnny Jones, with guitarist William "Pee Wee" Crawford. Unlike most quartets who gained popularity in gospel, the Swanee Quintet kept Augusta, Georgia, as their home base. Although Augusta has been a metropolitan city for many years and the group was organized there, they consciously cultivated the rural sound of early quartets.

Their hard gospel style is demonstrated on their recording of "In My Savior's Care."

THE BELLS OF JOY

This group made their debut with what turned out to be the most popular recording of their career. "Let's Talk about Jesus," led by A. C. Littlefield, was the most popular gospel song during 1953. Alternating between jubilee and hard gospel techniques, the Bells personified the changing quartet. The jubilee style, with its emphasis on harmony, attacks, and releases, and time and tune, was replaced by much louder singing, extreme range investigation, and faster tempos.

SISTER O. M. TERRELL

A group of female vocalists made significant contributions to the development of gospel during 1945 through 1955. Among them was Sister O. M. Terrell, about whom little is known other than that when she began recording she was living in South Carolina and had a Sunday radio program at station WPAL in Charleston. Her affiliation with the First Baptized Holiness Church is apparent from her 1953 rendition of "God's Little Birds." Terrell shows a kinship to Sister Rosetta Tharpe: although her guitar is far less sophisticated than Tharpe's, her timbre and her Dranes-like delivery (also apparent in Tharpe's voice) are a testament to the influence of the early gospel singer.

SISTER JESSIE MAE RENFRO

Completely unlike the Arizona Dranes school of singers, Sister Jessie Mae Renfro is a product of modern gospel, complete with hard gospel techniques. Born in 1921 in Witchataxee, Texas, Sister Renfro was brought up in the COGIC in Dallas. Although attracted to secular music she chose to sing gospel and traveled with the Sallie Martin Singers during the mid-1940s. Although she began recording in 1946, it was not until the early 1950s that she found songs and a style that attracted public attention. While her voice is lighter in color than Clara Ward's, she possesses the same metallic hue and even has a delivery similar to Ward's, eschewing embellishments for sustained tones. Her rendition of the gospel blues (a 16–bar harmonically schematic composition) in "I've Had My Chance" demonstrates her fondness for resorting to the hard gospel technique of broadening tones as she enters her higher register. Her compatriot in COGIC, Emily Bram, was different from her in several ways.

MADAME EMILY BRAM

Emily Bram (c.1919) a Texan, began singing in her youth in COGIC and as a young adult began preaching. Evangelist Bram conducted revivals in which she alternated singing and preaching. Her voice, like that of traditional African American preachers, has the ability to stretch into a growl at will, and she has the power of a quartet. She is an aggressive singer who can build a climax in only three or four notes, as amply demonstrated on her 1951 recording of "Blessed Assurance," rendered in the style of the long-meter Baptist lining hymn.

ETHEL DAVENPORT BANNISTER

Jacksonville, Florida, produced a singer, who, with a wider audience, might well have rivaled Wynona Carr. Ethel Davenport Bannister (1910–85) possessed a brassy alto with a delivery halfway between the sanctified shouters and the Baptist moaners. Known principally as a soloist, Bannister often teamed with *a cappella* male quartets for the harmonic and rhythmic support they provided. Always delivering her lines halfway between the Baptist moaner that she was and the sassy declamations of a jazz singer, Bannister was as much show person as gospel singer. This style, however, did not prohibit her from settling into real gospel when the spirit or the competition demanded it, which was the case on July 22, 1955. On that day she appeared in concert at the Shrine Auditorium in Los Angeles on a bill with the Pilgrim Travelers, Dorothy Love Coates and the Original Gospel Harmonettes, the Soul Stirrers featuring Sam Cooke and Paul Foster, the Caravans with Albertina Walker and James Cleveland at the piano, and Brother Joe May with his children Annette and Charles. Anthony Heilbut, annotator for the recorded version of the concert, reported that Bannister rendered a "haunting version of 'My Troubles Are So Hard to Bear,' supported vocally by Brother Joe May and his children."

Bannister earned a national reputation through her recordings on the Coral, Gotham, and Herald labels and for many years hosted a Sunday evening gospel program over Jacksonville's radio station WJAX.

Herman James Ford

Herman James Ford (c.1898–c.1958) is considered the "mystery" composer in gospel, for although he wrote several of the most popular gospel songs of the 1950s, he was not a singer, pianist, or conductor, nor was he considered a part of any gospel community. It is known that he lived and copyrighted his songs from Washington, D.C.; that he was a member of the Vermont Avenue Baptist Church in that city; and that he lived on G Street. Almost thirty years after his death, the older members of Vermont Avenue Baptist remembered Ford as a quiet man who was regular in his attendance at services, but few remembered him from gospel concerts held at the church.

Nonetheless between 1946 and 1956 Ford published twenty-six songs through the publishing houses of Roberta Martin, Martin and Morris, and Andrea (New York). His songs were recorded and made famous by singers such as Mahalia Jackson, the Angelic Gospel Singers, and the Pilgrim Travelers. Three of his most popular compositions were the jubilee song "This Same Jesus," the gospel waltz "Somebody Save Me," and "In My Home over There." This last song was made famous by Mahalia Jackson in the tempo of a Baptist lining hymn:

> *When my work on earth is done at the setting of life's song*
> *I am going to my home over there;*
> *I shall walk the golden stairs free from sorrow, pain or care,*
> *I'll be happy in my home over there.*
>
> *In my home over there that the Lord has prepared,*
> *There will be peace, there will be joy everywhere;*
> *I shall see His face so fair and a starry crown I'll wear,*
> *I'll be happy in my home over there.*

Mysterious or not (it was possible to mail compositions into publishers), Ford ranked with Dorsey, Morris, and Brewster as a principal composer of the first part of gospel's Golden Age.

The Gospel Choir

Groups of four, five, or even six singers could travel by car, train, or bus around the country singing gospel, but groups of twenty-five or more found it too expensive to travel. The large groups—the relatively new gospel choirs—were, nonetheless, popping up throughout the United States. Very few choirs recorded during the first ten years of the Golden Age of gospel, and the better gospel choirs, those directed by the leaders of the gospel movement, could be heard only at the National Baptist Convention, when singers from all over the United States were formed into a mass choir, or at one of the Dorsey conventions. There were, however, three choirs that recorded, and one had a national weekly radio program heard by a large part of African American society each week.

Wings Over Jordan was unique in the annals of gospel, for as William Talmadge reported in his study *From Jubilee to Gospel*, this choir was "neither a trained nor folk-style" group. They performed each song in the style in which it was composed. While the choir was a group of very talented singers, the soloists in particular "projected a sophisticated awareness of all of the elements of black music from folk through popular." They sang Dorsey's and Campbell's compositions as if they were members of the National Baptist Convention, as indeed many were.

A choir of thirty to forty voices, Wings Over Jordan was organized by the Reverend Glenn T. Settle (1895–1952) in 1937, shortly after he was assigned to the Gethsemane Baptist Church in Cleveland. Upon discovering that the church had no choir with any degree of excellence, Settle studied music and served as the first director of the group. Within a few months the choir auditioned for local radio station WGAR. Their popularity became so great that they were picked up by the CBS radio network for whom they presented a Sunday morning program entitled "Wings Over Jordan" from 1937 to 1947. Under the direction of Worth Kramer, their second director, the choir featured a repertoire of "skillfully arranged" Negro spirituals, hymns, and gospel songs ("He Understands, He'll Say 'Well Done'," recorded in 1948; "When I've Done The Best I Can," recorded in 1953; and "Somebody Touched Me," recorded in 1960). The Wings sang in a gospel style reminiscent of that of Mother Willie Mae Ford Smith, in which beauty of tone, extension of breath, and clarity of diction were all combined with passion and flair.

The most fully developed gospel choir of the first decade of the Golden Age was the St. Paul Baptist Church Choir of Los Angeles. Like the Reverend Settle in Cleveland, when the Reverend John L. Branham was assigned to the St. Paul Baptist Church in Los Angeles, he found no choir that could sing the music to which he had become accustomed in his native Chicago. In 1947 he organized the Echoes of Eden Choir with J. Earle Hines as director and Gwendolyn Cooper Lightener as pianist.

Hines had served as baritone soloist for the National Baptist Convention's Good Will Singers, and Lightener had been pianist for Emma L. Jackson, composer of the gospel blues "I'm Going to Die with the Staff in My Hand" and with whom she composed "I Can See Everybody's Mother, but I Can't See Mine" (1945). These were gospel musicians who knew the tradition, and together they developed the Echoes of Eden into the premier gospel choir in the nation.

Drawing from the compositions of the Chicago school of composers—Dorsey, Roberta Martin, Sallie Martin, and Emma L. Jackson, and Lucie Campbell of Memphis—and augmented by the budding California school of composers, Hines and Lightener developed a choir that sang with "open" throats (a necessity in gospel singing), that could learn parts, and that was not afraid to get "happy" as they sang. Shortly after its organization the choir was featured on a Sunday evening broadcast from St. Paul Baptist Church that could be heard in "seventeen states with an audience of one million people (the largest audience on the West Coast)." Their early 1946 recordings sold regionally, but at their second session in April 1947 they recorded Thomas A. Dorsey's "God Be with You" and the missionary hymn turned gospel song "I'm So Glad Jesus Lifted Me," both of which became gospel standards. "God Be with You" by Dorsey and Artelia Hutchins replaced the beloved "God Be with You Till We Meet Again" by Jeremiah E. Ranks and William G. Tomer (1832–96) as a benediction song. The choir had several other popular recordings, among them Kenneth Morris's "What Could I Do if It Wasn't for the Lord?" and Dorsey's "If We Never Needed the Lord Before, We Sure Do Need Him Now."

The choir of C. H. Cobb's First Church of Deliverance in Chicago was perceived as a laboratory for composers in Chicago; as soon as a song was published it was featured by this choir. Ralph Goodpastor was a hard taskmaster with the choir and his strict directional manner resulted in a well-trained and ready choir for each Sunday's midnight radio broadcast from the church. The 50,000–watt station carried this choir throughout the Midwest and on clear evenings into New York City. Many of Dorsey's, Morris', and Roberta Martin's songs were introduced over this broadcast, but none was as popular as Goodpastor's semigospel rendering of Albert Hay Malotte's (1895–1964) arrangement of "The Lord's Prayer."

Like jazz lovers visiting New York and working a night at Small's Paradise, a premier jazz spot of the 1940s and 1950s, when gospel music lovers traveled around the country, they included in their activities a church service where they could hear one of the several choirs who had developed national reputations, some even without the benefit of recordings. Among these were services at Chicago's Greater Harvest Baptist and Salem Baptist churches, New York's now Childs Memorial Church of God in Christ, and Mason Temple Church of God in Christ in Memphis.

The Gospel Band

As if the introduction of gospel music into the Azusa Street Movement were not enough to shock the conservative Christian, the Pentecostalists went one step further and accompanied this music with tambourines, drums, and cymbals (the piano was not introduced into gospel until the early 1920s). Basing their practice on Psalms 150, the Pentecostalists felt that all instruments belong to God and were made for the expressed purpose of serving Him. The use of instruments other than the organ provided further fodder for those who felt that the preaching and singing in the Pentecostal church was primitive. The Pentecostalists were undaunted; in fact, they encouraged the playing of all instruments in their service. This practice resulted in the organization of gospel bands in the 1920s. These bands were unique for two reasons: very few, if any, of the players could read music and were therefore taught their parts by rote, with the leader playing a part over and over until the student eventually learned to play the tune as it was played for him. Also, the bands did not play in the style of Duke Ellington's or Count Basie's bands where the trumpets had one part while the saxophones had another and the two parts were put together to make an arrangement. The gospel band played like a choir with one instrument acting as soloist and the other instruments acting like the choir. The result was a band that played like a choir sang.

While gospel bands occasionally accompanied the congregation during praise services, they were at their best when they played alone. It was common during the 1940s for larger Pentecostal congregations to have a gospel choir and a gospel band. As the Hammond organ with powerful Leslie B-3 speakers became popular in Pentecostal churches, the gospel band gradually lost its popularity. The one denomination that continued to cultivate the gospel band was the United House of Prayer for All People, Church on the Rock of the Apostolic Faith, Incorporated.

This congregation was founded by Bishop Marcelino Manoel de Graca, better known as "Sweet Daddy Grace" (1884–1960). Born in the Cape Verde Islands, Grace began preaching in 1925 after moving to the United States. He was a flamboyant and charismatic leader who demanded that his followers worship him as God, but was instrumental in feeding and lodging thousands of African Americans during the Depression. Like most Pentecostal services, Grace's services were heavily laden with music. Nick Spitzer, historian of the gospel bands of Daddy Grace, observed that in order "to propel his energetic services and attract a congregation, Daddy Grace established brass bands, modeled in part on the instrumental jazz of the era, to perform gospel hymns. Today [1992] there are more than 130 Houses of Prayer, each with one or more large brass bands."

Perhaps the best known of these bands is the Kings of Harmony of the national headquarters of the United House of Prayer. According to Nick Spitzer this band, like others, has a sound created by a lead trombone and a "choir of twelve trombones, a baritone horn, a sousaphone, and drums and tambourine." Two other popular bands are McCollough's Sons of Thunder of Brooklyn, New York, and the Sounds of the South of Savannah, Georgia. In addition to playing for services and presenting concerts, these gospel bands perform at funerals, parades, groundbreakings, and anniversary services.

Sam Cooke

And The Walls Came Tumbling Down: 1955–65

hereas the first ten years of the Golden Age of Gospel testified to the emergence and inclusion of gospel music in the African American Baptist and Methodist churches, the second decade of the Golden Age witnessed the crumbling of the firm walls that had kept gospel from the larger part of American society. During the first ten years of the Golden Age the gospel network comprised a comparably small group of churches and singers; the second decade was marked by a national gospel community that included not only most black churches, but also reached others through radio, recordings, television, and theater. Indeed, the second decade witnessed the crumbling of the wall that had forbidden performance in nonsacred venues.

Sister Rosetta Tharpe sang gospel at Carnegie Hall in 1938, the Georgia Peach and her quartet sang at Radio City Music Hall in 1939, and Sister Tharpe and the Dixie Hummingbirds sang at Cafe Society in the 1940s. But those appearances were looked upon with disdain, because at that time Christians were admonished to follow the dictum to be "in the world but not of the world." They believed that associating with non-Christians (much less going into a theater) would lead to temptation, and if Christians refrained from associating with the "unsaved," whether at work or elsewhere, the likelihood they would backslide was remote.

In the mid-1950s, however, black Christians, and especially gospel singers, began to feel an obligation to spread the word to the unsaved. The question was how to get the word to the unsaved if the unsaved would not come where the word is preached and sung? They solved this problem by taking gospel music into "nonsacred" places, turning these venues into sanctified, Baptist, and Methodist places of worship. Gospel singers developed a new attitude: it became a compliment to be invited to sing outside the church. Mahalia Jackson was one of the first gospel singers—with this new attitude—to step over the crumbling walls when, on October 1, 1950, she presented her first concert at Carnegie Hall.

In the mid-1950s, Jackson was persuaded to sing on Dinah Shore's television show. Jackson chose songs that captured the best in gospel, and her demeanor was consistent with that of the saints. The show included the obligatory duet with the hostess. The duet, while entertaining, was not a good mixture: Shore was trying too hard to sing gospel, and Jackson was visibly uncomfortable because of the restriction of singing gospel with a nongospel singer. But Jackson's appearance was viewed as a success and led to an appearance on the "Ed Sullivan Show." This time the audience was treated to pure gospel with only Jackson and her longtime accompanist, Mildred Falls.

In 1957 Clara Ward and the Ward Singers invaded the Newport Jazz Festival, which attracted jazz lovers and critics from all over the world. Richard Gehman, music critic for *Coronet* magazine (July 1957), offered this appraisal of the Ward Singers performance at the festival:

> *They seemed nervous as they arranged themselves around a microphone and the woman at the piano, Clara Ward, played a few bars of introduction. They glanced at each other as though to muster strength. And then with a smiling placidity—they sang.*
>
> *Rhythmic, high, clear, in perfect harmony they sang, the words in metered, driving cadence, underscored by piano. They began to clap their hands; and within seconds, hundreds in the audience were clapping with them. The singers*

threw back their heads and went into a second chorus, fervent and joyous. The voice of one, a young girl of ample girth [Marion Williams], soared above the others whose voices beat a counterpoint behind hers.

Mahalia Jackson sang at the festival in 1958 with equal success. Jackson's 1959 appearance at Carnegie Hall drew gospel aficionados as well as gospel novices. Marshall Sterns, critic for the August 1959 *High Fidelity*, must have held membership in the latter group:

The effect is something for which my rather Puritanical New England background never prepared me. Gentle old ladies on all sides start to "flip" like popcorn over a hot stove. Directly in front, an angular woman springs to her feet, raises her arms rigidly on high, and dances down the aisle shouting "Sweet Jesus!" A white-clad nurse, one of thirty in attendance, does her best to quiet her. This is a religious possession, as old as Africa itself.

Sterns could have written his description with only three words: they had church!

By the 1960s a completely new audience for gospel had developed. This was an audience composed of people who liked music, especially music with a beat. But this new audience's unfamiliarity with the music or with African American cultural traditions produced some interesting reactions. In 1963 business leaders, more concerned with making money than with cultural mores and folkways, began moving gospel to nightclubs. Gospel nightclubs soon opened in New York, Miami, and Los Angeles. The music critic for the May 24, 1963, issue of *Time* magazine visited such a club and wrote this review:

For months (and in the record business, months are decades), desperate music hustlers have been searching for the new groove. Exceptional huntsmen confined their attention to Negro music, which, with the single exception of country, has supplied them with every new idea since the blues. Last week, with appropriate fanfare, they proclaimed they had found the sound: pop gospel. Waving contracts and recording tape, Columbia Records moved into a new Manhattan night club, the Sweet Chariot, and began picking such devotional songs as "He's All Right" for the popular market. "It's the greatest groove since rock 'n roll," said Columbia pop A & R Director, David Kapralik. "In a month or two, it'll be all over the charts."

"TV Gospel Time," a one-hour national television show of gospel singers, lasted two seasons and attracted an African American audience. It also introduced gospel to a large white population that would not normally attend churches where it was performed. The format of the program was built around a guest host (soloist or group) and a group of gospel singers who appeared once or twice during the hour, offering sometimes as many as three songs. The studio audience was all black, and the sponsors were, in part, black-owned businesses. The program was treated like a church service with the host acting as the preacher and the audience as the congregation. Most of the major stars appeared on the program including Sister Rosetta Tharpe, the Soul Stirrers, and Alex Bradford and the Nightingales. But "TV Gospel Time" aired on Sunday mornings before noon when the largest part of the gospel-loving audience was in church. The ratings were low, and sponsors received little for their investment. Consequently, the program was dropped.

"Hootenanny" was a national radio program that aired in the late 1950s and 1960s. The Saturday afternoon broadcast had a format similar to that of "TV Gospel Time," but the host was permanent. During this part of the 1960s, gospel groups, especially *a cappella* male quartets, found a new audience. Male quartets, such as the Fairfield Four, Dixie Hummingbirds, Swan Silvertones, and the Soul Stirrers, and piano-accompanied gospel acts, such as Alex Bradford and the Caravans, appeared on this show.

In 1962 the Apollo Theater, a bastion of African American entertainment, began to book gospel acts. Around that time the Apollo had begun to lose its audience. This was partially the management's fault: the theater booked the same performers year after year, and the new talent it presented couldn't compare with such contest winners as Ella Fitzgerald or Sarah Vaughn. But the rest of the blame lay with integration. The days when a black entertainer in New York could only find work uptown were fading fast. Even though black entertainers had always worked downtown, there was always a certain indignity that accompanied downtown work. Even major stars felt so unwelcome in predominantly white venues that once they were off stage, they lived and socialized in Harlem. Black stars were not feted with the grand parties given to white stars, and many were paid less than white stars of comparable reputation and celebrity. But in the 1960s black entertainers approached their work downtown feeling, "I can perform here legally now, and if you want me you will have to treat me with the same dignity given to Patti Paige."

Considering the money that could be made by booking top black acts, downtown managers began according a new respect to black stars who appeared in their venues. While this was good for African Americans in general, it meant that the Apollo had lost its previous advantage in attracting quality acts. It was feared that all the music created by African Americans had been co-opted by the moneymen downtown. So the management of the Apollo decided to turn to one area still untouched by white entrepreneurs: gospel. They selected the summer months—when New Yorkers escape their apartments in whatever way they can and the city is overrun with tourists—as gospel months. At first gospel acts were paired with secular ones. When the management discovered that gospel acts could stand alone, the Apollo soon began to present entire gospel weekends. The Caravans were one of the first groups to be booked; then the Dixie Hummingbirds appeared; Clara Ward and the Ward Singers followed; and Dorothy Love Coates and the Original Gospel Harmonettes made an appearance.

These shows yielded great financial rewards for the Apollo for almost two years, until the market became saturated. But the appearance of gospel singers at the Apollo—between movies that often negated the very message of gospel—opened up new venues for gospel performance that could never be closed off again.

In the early 1950s, gospel music's popularity did not go unnoticed by singers aspiring to a career in rhythm and blues. The emotional singing of such groups as the Soul Stirrers, Pilgrim Travelers, and Dixie Hummingbirds, with their versatile and charismatic lead singers and tight harmony background singing, was the impetus behind early rhythm and blues vocal groups, many of whom sang gospel when they were first organized. The Larks were originally the Selah Jubilee Singers, who appeared in public as a gospel group but who also had a successful recording career as a secular group.

Billy Ward, the son of a preacher father and a choir-singing mother, began composing classical and gospel songs at age fourteen when the family relocated to Philadelphia from Los Angeles. When Ward organized the Dominoes in 1950, the group sang both gospel and rhythm and blues. The other leader of this group was Clyde McPhatter.

The Five Royales, led by the brothers Lowman and Clarence, started out as the Royal Sons Gospel Group of Winston-Salem, North Carolina, in 1945 and delighted churchgoers throughout the South until 1951, when they went to New York to develop an eastern following. There they recorded first as the Royal Sons Quintet, a gospel group, and also as the Five Royales, a secular group. By the mid-1950s they were so popular as a rhythm and blues group that they stopped recording gospel.

Both the Ravens, organized in New York City in 1945 and the first rhythm and blues group to incorporate dance steps into their act, and Sonny Til and the Orioles, organized in 1946 in Baltimore, Maryland, were not only inspired by gospel quartets but created their sound by combining jazz, blues, and gospel.

The early rhythm and blues soloist Jackie Wilson replaced Clyde McPhatter as lead singer of Billy Ward and the Dominoes and easily moved into the gospel/blues sound that this group had developed. Little Richard (Richard Penniman), one of twelve children, grew up in a devout Seventh Day Adventist family. While the Seventh Day Adventists did not sing gospel music at that time, Little Richard sang gospel while serving as the pianist for a Baptist church in his hometown of Macon, Georgia. He was particularly impressed with Clara Ward and the Ward Singers and adopted Marion Williams as a singing model, going as far as incorporating her "high who" into his own songs. Little Richard joined several other blues shouters, including Big Joe Turner, Big Bill Broonzy, and Jimmy Rushing, whose singing style was based on that of sanctified singers.

In the mid-1950s the influence of gospel quartets among secular singers began to decline. This decline coincided with the rising influence of piano-accompanied gospel. Nowhere was this influence exhibited more clearly than in the singing of Ray Charles, Aretha Franklin, and James Brown, all of whom came to prominence during the last decade of the Golden Age of Gospel. These three people literally created the style of music known as "soul," and they created it by borrowing from gospel music. Ray Charles (b. 1930) was brought up in a Baptist church in Albany, Georgia, and played for Sunday School and church. Although he did not play gospel, between 1945 and 1955 Charles became so inundated with gospel that he abandoned his desire to be the next Nat "King" Cole and found his calling by combining gospel style with the blues and popular music, delivering his songs in the voice and style of a sanctified preacher. Charles has acknowledged that Alex Bradford and the

Pilgrim Travelers had tremendous influence on his post-1950 music. James Brown (b. 1933), too, was reared in the Baptist church where gospel had found a home. Brown, like Charles, was not a gospel singer. But the emotional intensity and delivery of his "Please, Please, Please" (1956) sounds for all the world like a gospel singer pleading for the grace of God. And Aretha Franklin has never pretended to be anything other than what she is: a gospel singer. As late as 1994, when she was named to the Grammy's Hall of Fame, she declared "You know, I'm nothing but a gospel singer."

Jazz musicians also came under the influence of gospel. In the 1950s, when secular music began to return to its blues roots, gospel techniques and devices recreated the "feeling" (soul) that had been lost. Among the most famous jazz compositions in the gospel style were Horace Silver's "The Preacher," Bobby Timmons' "Moanin'," and Jimmy Smith's "The Sermon."

GOSPEL AND THE TRADITIONS
OF AFRICAN AMERICAN FOLK MUSIC

With the mixing of gospel and several kinds of secular music, it is clear that African American sensibilities about music changed radically during the second half of the Golden Age. Some critics have mistakenly judged African American sacred music by Western European standards: they try to find distinct differences in *sound* between what is considered secular and what is considered sacred. They find the melodies, harmonies, rhythms, instruments, timbre, and behavior of secular music unworthy of expression in the service of the Lord. When they apply these constrictions to what is sacred and secular in African American music, they create an artificial division. As with other cultural manifestations of African American society, it is not the medium in itself that carries the message but how that medium is used and the response it receives.

All African American folk music is drawn from the same wellspring of musical materials. This wellspring includes scales, melodies, harmonies, timbre, and rhythm, as well as a person's behavior during performance and while listening. If the wellspring offers "blue notes" for use in folk music, both secular and sacred music will employ blue notes. If rhythmic motives and riffs are the only folk elements in African American music, sacred music will use these motives and riffs. Otherwise the music would have to draw from outside the culture—and be less true to itself. The

African American musical wellspring is as important to its culture as material from the European wellspring is to the descendants of European culture. This does not mean that music making is limited only to materials from a single cultural source, but it does mean that musical traditions should not be judged by the standards of another culture's folk materials.

When people call gospel music spiritualized secular music, they usually are thinking of the blues. But only those ignorant of the fact that the Negro spiritual, the progenitor of gospel, was almost one hundred years old before the blues arrived make such a claim. Blues and jazz employ the same materials that spiritual music employs—and in most cases in the same way. Because they come from the same wellspring, they are sisters and brothers under the beat. The mood of the performer and the listener determines the effect that the music produces. Albert Murray, in his book *Stomping the Blues*, notes that:

> *Downhome church music [gospel] is not fundamentally less dance-beat-oriented, it simply inspires a different mode of dance, a sacred or holy as opposed to a secular or profane movement, a difference which is sometimes a matter of very delicate nuance.*

There is a difference nonetheless. As recognized by no less eminent a scholar than W. E. B. DuBois, there is a "twoness" that accompanies being an African American, and salvation is attained only by those who know which part of their culture to exhibit at which time. This problem of "twoness" was nowhere greater than in the mid-1950s when gospel invaded the African American church. Murray responded to this situation in this way:

> *There is, after all, a world of difference between the way you clap your hands and pat your feet in church and the way people snap their fingers in a ballroom, even when the rhythm, tempo, and even the beat are essentially the same.*

In the 1930s and 1940s, when African American parents were struggling to send their children to piano lessons, it was most likely so they could play in church, not in a juke joint. However, the person who played in the juke joint on Saturday night might also be the pianist for church on Sunday. Inevitably, the residue of Saturday evening's performance would drain out on Sunday morning, just as it was inevitable that Friday night's choir rehearsal would see its demise on the dance floor Saturday night. James Cone, in his book *Spirituals & the Blues*, goes as far as to say:

> The blues are "secular spirituals." They are secular in the sense that they confine their attention solely to the immediate and affirm the bodily expression of black soul, including its sexual manifestations. They are spirituals because they are impelled by the same search for the truth of black experience.

Thomas A. Dorsey is called the Father of Gospel Music and rightly so. Even if he had not composed more than five hundred gospel songs, traveled around the country teaching them, and opened the first publishing company for the express purpose of publishing African American gospel music, the fortitude with which he met the resistance of African American ministers when he sought to introduce gospel music into their congregations was sufficient to earn him that title. It should be remembered that Dorsey was not well received in the 1930s when he presented a kind of music that ministers termed "all jazzed up." Michael Harris, in his book on Dorsey, recounted the story of a minister who promised Dorsey a spot in the Sunday morning service to present his songs yet dismissed the congregation at the end of the service, all the while looking directly into Dorsey's eyes. There were ministers who permitted gospel in their services, but it had to be sung by the junior choir, a group that was more cute than musical or serious. Dorsey, undaunted, persevered.

THE NEW AND NEWLY REVISED GOSPEL QUARTETS

There was no doubt in 1955 that gospel music was here to stay and that it wanted the recognition that other American music enjoyed. Gospel musicians felt that they had earned and deserved the respect of the music world because they had paid their dues. They were as talented, musical, and well presented as any other musicians, and they felt they were as innovative as any music group in the country. In fact, gospel singers opened the last decade of the Golden Age with an innovation that at first met with great resistance in the gospel world: piano-accompanied male gospel quartets. The success of keyboard-accompanied quartets reached its peak with the advent of Sam Cooke as the leader of the Soul Stirrers, one of several groups that became prominent or was reborn during the years 1955 to 1965.

Sam Cooke and the Soul Stirrers

Sam Cooke appeared destined to lead the Soul Stirrers and make them once again the leading quartet in the country. Every musical activity from his early years until 1951 when he assumed the group's leadership pointed in that direction. One in a family of eight boys and two girls, Cooke (1931–64) was born to the Reverend Charles and Mrs. Anna Mae Cooke in Clarksdale, Mississippi. Shortly after his birth the family relocated to Chicago's South Side where the Reverend Cooke had accepted the pastorate of a church. The Cooke children all sang in the church choir and later formed a group consisting of Sam, his two sisters, and a brother. Calling themselves the Singing Children, they performed at their father's and other churches on the South Side.

Cooke received his musical education in Chicago's public schools, and sang in the glee club of Wendell Phillips High School. While still in high school he was invited to join the Highway QCs, a neighborhood quartet named after the Highway Baptist Church and Q.C. High School in Chicago. The quartet, prominent in its own right, had been organized by Soul Stirrer baritone R. B. Robinson and served as an unofficial training camp for the Soul Stirrers: not only did Sam Cooke and Johnnie Taylor come to the senior group from this neighborhood quartet, but Willie Rogers, who remained a gospel singer until his death, was the third leader to graduate to the Soul Stirrers.

Even as a teenager Cooke showed an unusual talent for gospel. He possessed a light lyrical tenor voice, an easy and smooth vocal delivery, and an ability to improvise that never overpowered the melody with its embellishments. Cooke was particularly adept at textual interpolations, adding or subtracting words from the original text of the song to fill in spaces occupied by rests in the melody or as a prefix to the text. In a performance of the song "What a Friend We Have in Jesus," Cooke would lead into the opening with a phrase such as, "Sometimes when I'm lonely I just say to myself 'What a Friend We Have In Jesus.'" When he switched to popular music he carried this device with him, and it was never more strategically employed than on his first hit, "You Send Me" when he led into the chorus of the song with "I know, I know, I know that YOU SEND ME." Cooke also wrote beautiful songs and knew how to "work" an audience without resorting to stage histrionics—the same qualities possessed by Rebert H. Harris, then leader of the Soul Stirrers.

The Soul Stirrers

As Cooke neared his twentieth birthday Harris noticed a change in gospel that went totally against his grain. In his paper "Sam Cooke: Soul Stirrer," Dave Law, a 1992 graduate student at New York's Brooklyn Conservatory of Music, elaborates:

> All the hysterical "carrying-on," gimmickry and showboating from the performers, which caused equally hysterical reactions from the female audience in particular, became too much for Harris to handle. In disagreement with this new direction in gospel performance, Harris took his high morals and gentlemanly ways and left the sinful temptations of the road and the Soul Stirrers in 1950.

Cooke inherited Harris's position in January 1951. At first sounding and acting like a clone of Harris, Cooke gradually evolved into a thoughtful and creative singer as well as a prolific songwriter. When Cooke had completed the creation of his new persona, he easily won the hearts of the congregation with his beautiful voice, extraordinary vocal technique, youthful good looks, and, as far as women were concerned, according to Law, "irresistible charm and sexuality." Cooke brought the Stirrers to the forefront again but with a difference: no longer were they the reverent semirural *a cappella* quartet of Harris's day, but a sophisticated, pop-oriented performing group, accompanied by guitar in concerts and by guitar, piano, and organ on recordings.

In March 1951 J. W. Alexander, the leader and manager of the Pilgrim Travelers and a talent scout for Specialty Records, brought the new Soul Stirrers to the Specialty label and from their first session produced a fine version of Campbell's "Jesus Gave Me Water." The recording met with immediate success. The Stirrers noted the success of Cooke's arrangement, and as he had matured musically and developed his own distinctive style, they agreed to his becoming the group's leading arranger and composer. One of the first songs Cooke wrote for the group was "That's Heaven to Me."

His most famous composition is "Nearer to Thee," in which Cooke's ability to write lyrical poetry is evident from the opening verse:

> *The minister was preaching*
> *And the crowd was standing near,*
> *The congregation was singing a tune*
> *In a voice that was loud and clear...*
> *They were singing "Nearer My God to Thee."*

With Cooke leading the song in his distinctive voice, complete with the repetition of words and singing the word "oh" on five or six tones, the Stirrers gave new life to quartet singing—and incidently brought the quartet several steps closer to the style of piano-accompanied groups.

Cooke's success with the Stirrers did not go unnoticed by record producers and popular music promoters. Alexander, hoping to leap ahead of other record labels that might attempt to entice Cooke into rhythm and blues, began recording Cooke singing secular music under the name Dale Cooke. One of these songs, "I'll Come Running Back to You," became a minor hit. It was about this time, in late 1956, that

Alexander's contract as talent scout for Specialty was sold by the gospel division to the rhythm and blues division. Specialty rhythm and blues producer Bumps Blackwell directed Cooke's second recording for the Keen label. Cooke soon moved to RCA and became an extremely successful crossover artist. His engagements moved from small clubs to theaters and eventually to the Copacabana in New York City. He even did a screen test on October 2, 1964, for a part in the movie *In the Heat of the Night*. The world will never know whether Sam Cooke the singer would have become Sam Cooke the actor, for he was shot and killed under mysterious circumstances in a Hollywood motel on December 10, 1964. Nonetheless, Cooke's contributions to gospel and the many soul singers who adopted his techniques and sang his songs, even thirty years after his death, are still recognized and applauded.

Archie Brownlee and the Five Blind Boys of Mississippi

One of the most familiar sights of gospel concerts in the 1950s was five or six blind men, each with his hand on the shoulder of the man in front, being led by a sighted man to the performance space. And the most familiar sounds at gospel concerts in the 1950s were the wails, shrieks, and hard gospel singing of Archie Brownlee and the Original Five Blind Boys of Mississippi.

Archie Brownlee (1921–60) holds the title of the "hardest singing" man in gospel. This title is due in part to the hard gospel techniques he adopted after his group left Mississippi and moved to Chicago. In Mississippi the group was, like most other quartets at that time, practiced in the cardinal rules of jubilee singing—time, tune, and tenor—and gave special emphasis to blending and nuances. After moving to Chicago and noting the excitement generated when fellow singer J. T. Clinkscale interjected strident moans and wails into his singing, Brownlee adopted this technique and took it to a higher level that was enjoyed by many. Others, however, thought it overly exaggerated: it was not uncommon for Brownlee to insert wails, shrieks, screams, strident falsettos, yells, and grunts all into one song. In most cases these devices brought a certain excitement to a rendition; at other times, they appeared to disrupt what had been a beautifully developed vocal line. There was never full agreement on Brownlee's singing style, but that lack of consensus did not hinder the group from becoming one of the most popular quartets of the 1950s.

In 1932, while attending the Piney Wood School for the Blind in Piney Wood,

Archie Brownlee and the Five Blind Boys of Mississippi

Mississippi, Brownlee formed a gospel group, the Cotton Blossom Singers, from among his classmates. The original members of the group were Brownlee, Sam Lewis, Lloyd Woodard, Lawrence Abrams, and Joseph Ford. When the group began to earn enough money from singing in local churches and at parties to pay their own tuition (they were originally scholarship students), they changed their name to the Jackson Harmoneers, after the largest city in Mississippi. During this time they traveled with the International Sweethearts of Rhythm, an all-female orchestra from the Piney Wood Country Life School, a school for sighted students, and sang Negro spirituals and novelty songs.

In 1944 the group turned professional, changed their name to the Original Five Blind Boys of Mississippi, and relocated to Chicago where Brownlee could be closer to Rebert H. Harris, his idol and mentor. The membership at this time consisted of Brownlee, Abrams, Woodard, J. T. Clinkscale, and the Reverend Percell Perkins. The group began recording around 1951 and had many hits during the next decade. Among their popular recordings are "I'm Willing to Run" and "Will Jesus Be Waiting," in both of which Brownlee sings solidly but uses hard gospel techniques; "I'm Going to Tell God," in which he modulates his voice and gives a simple and refined

How Sweet the Sound

reading to the lyrics; and "I'm Going to Leave You in the Hands of the Lord," a "mother" song. Mother songs invariably recounted the story of ungrateful children who had mistreated or disappointed their mothers. Such songs usually ended with no remorse being shown by the children. In "Leave You," Brownlee wonders if he treated his mother right during her life, because as she was dying she told him she was "leaving him in the hands of the Lord," a black church statement meaning "I can do no more with you."

The Blind Boys' most popular hit was a 1952 recording of Wynona Carr's "Our Father." This rendition finds the Blind Boys at their very best and illustrates a blending of the jubilee and gospel styles. The background voices repeat the words "Our Father" as constant as the ticking of a clock throughout the rendition in deep vocal colors with tight harmonies and crisp attacks and releases, not unlike that of the better jubilee quartets of the 1930s. Over this drumlike accompaniment Brown delivers two verses separated by a chorus. In a full fleshy voice Brown sings the Lord's Prayer as the first verse using minor, but attractive, ornamentation. However, when he reaches the chorus he cannot resist inserting one of his signature screams and delivers two more during the second verse. Screams notwithstanding, "Our Father" illustrates the singing of one of the finest male quartets.

Clarence Fountain and the Five Blind Boys of Alabama

At about the time that the Blind Boys of Mississippi were organized, a group of blind students in Alabama were also organizing a gospel quartet. In 1937 Clarence Fountain (b. 1929) was an elementary school student singing in the Talladega Institute for the Deaf and Blind Glee Club. Fountain and a friend, Johnny Fields (b. 1927), selected George Scott (b. 1929), Olice Thomas (b. 1926), and Velma Bozman Traylor (1923–47) from the Glee Club and formed the Happy Land Jubilee Singers.

Their early style was influenced by the Golden Gate Quartet, to whom they would listen during the Gates' national broadcasts. They borrowed the Gates' repertoire as well. As soon as they learned enough songs, they began to sing at churches and social functions in Talladega, Tuskegee, and Birmingham, and because they could hear people say "there go the blind boys," they changed their name to accommodate their audience. The name change caused many problems for the group: sometimes they were advertised as the Blind Boys and other times as the Happy

Clarence Fountain and the Five Blind Boys of Alabama

Land Singers. Further, in the 1940s they heard Brownlee's group that was also called the Blind Boys. When the two groups toured together in the early 1950s, they each added the name of their home state to their names.

The Alabama Blind Boys left Talladega in 1944 and became professionals. Fountain, the leader of the group, had a strong high baritone voice with a slow vibrato, which he used to color slow Negro spirituals and hymns. The background singers supported Fountain with a resonant barbershop harmonic foundation. The Blind Boys brought this sound to Coleman Records when they began to record in 1948. By 1949 they had their first hit record with Emma L. Jackson and Gwendolyn Cooper Lightener's "I Can See Everybody's Mother, but I Can't See Mine." Their being blind added additional meaning to the song. The success of this "mother" record consciously or unconsciously affected their repertoire, because during the next decade they would record a number of mother songs, all of which became popular. Among them were "Living on Mother's Prayers" and "When I Lost My Mother." Fountain, after hearing that Brownlee was "tearing up churches" with his screams and shrieks, adopted the technique with the same results. In the mid-1950s, when the two blind groups toured together, all their concerts were characterized by extremely hard singing.

Because of misunderstandings and anger, Fountain left the group twice but returned each time. He first left in 1969 and toured as a solo act until he returned to the group in 1975. In 1983 the Alabama Five Blind Boys and J. J. Farley and the Soul Stirrers starred on Broadway in a musical version of Sophocles' drama *Oedipus*.

Julius "June" Cheeks and the Sensational Nightingales

Julius "June" Cheeks (1929–81), who later became the Reverend Julius Cheeks, was the personification of the hard gospel singer. By the time of his death he had very little voice left, but he could still "bring a house down."

Cheeks was born in Spartanburg, South Carolina, and was attracted to gospel as a child by the recordings of the Dixie Hummingbirds, the Fairfield Four, and the Soul Stirrers. He began to sing in the second grade, at which time he also left school permanently to work in the cotton fields and at service stations. He spent his leisure time singing with a local quartet, the Baronets. He was singing with this group when the Reverend B. L. Parks, a former member of the Dixie Hummingbirds, approached him to sing with a new group he was forming, the Nightingales. (The original group called the Nightingales was formed in 1942 in Philadelphia with members Howard Carroll of the Hummingbirds, Paul Owens of the Swan Silvertones, Ben Joiner, and William Henry. At the height of their popularity they cut several sides for Decca Records but disbanded shortly after the session.

The Reverend Julius "June" Cheeks and the Sensational Nightingales

Gospel Quartets of the Golden Age

In the early 1950s gospel quartets were known as much by their leaders as by their repertoire and harmony. Within a few years these leaders wove their groups into a sweet (close harmony, precise attacks and releases, and understated—yet firm—rhythmic accentuation) or hard (energetic and extremely intense solo and background singing, a preaching style of delivery, and exaggerated physical gestures) gospel group.

Sweet Gospel	Hard Gospel
CBS Trumpeteers	Blind Boys of Alabama
Dixie Hummingbirds	Blind Boys of Mississippi
Harmonizing Four	Mighty Clouds of Joy
Pilgrim Travelers	Sensational Nightingales
Soul Stirrers	Spirit of Memphis
Swan Silvertones	Swanee Quintet

Sweet and Hard Gospel
Fairfield Four

In 1946 Parks changed the personnel to Cheeks, Joseph "JoJo" Wallace of Wilmington, North Carolina, and Carl Coates, a Washington, D.C., native living in Birmingham. (His wife was Dorothy Love Coates of the Original Gospel Harmonettes.) The group went to Goldsboro, North Carolina, where they spent a month in rehearsal for their first appearance. The Nightingales were an immediate sensation. In fact, they were called sensational so often that they added the word to their name. Much of their success was due to Cheeks' overpowering vocal style. Possessing a thick baritone voice, he approached singing as he did preaching (to which he turned in 1954). Like Archie Brownlee, he employed falsetto, growls, and screams in his singing, much to the delight of the audience. Two of his most popular recordings are "Somewhere to Lay My Head" (1955) and "The Last Mile of the Way," recorded in the last year of his life when his voice was ragged, his breath was short, and he had difficulty reaching the notes he heard in his head. And yet, "The Last Mile of the Way" shows Cheeks at his most poignant, sincere, and, considering what little voice he had left, his most versatile:

> *If I walk in the pathway of duty,*
> *If I work till the close of the day;*
> *I shall see the great King in His beauty*
> *When I've gone the last mile of the way.*

Cheeks left and returned to the group several times. In 1960 he formed his own group, the Knights, with which he recorded "The Last Mile of the Way." In the late 1960s he disbanded this group and sang for a while with the Mighty Clouds of Joy. After 1970 he spent his time preaching in Baltimore, Newark, and Miami. The Nightingales continued to sing into the 1990s under the leadership of Calvert McNair, Jr.

THE CALIFORNIA SCHOOL OF GOSPEL

African American gospel music developed in the South and Midwest despite its start in Los Angeles. After the close of the Azusa Street Revival in 1909, the people who had moved to Los Angeles disbanded and returned to their hometowns or staked out new territories in Mississippi, Tennessee, Arkansas, Texas, and other southern states where they could plant churches. Since only the people who had attended the revival services knew of the new sanctified singing, the old-line churches of Los Angeles continued to sing the hymns, Negro spirituals, and anthems they had sung before the revival. Even the Apostolic Fifth Gospel Mission, Seymour's church, returned to singing "spirited" hymns and Negro spirituals. Not until the 1930s did gospel (as it was known on the East Coast) return to California, and Los Angeles was its most receptive city. Dorsey, Sallie Martin, the Roberta Martin Singers, Robert Anderson, and Thomas Shelby made frequent visits, sometimes remaining in the city for five weeks at a time, while ordering sheet music from Chicago. In the 1940s, when a coterie of California gospel composers developed, several opened publishing companies. These were local and regional companies that lacked the distribution of Dorsey or Martin and Morris, so California continued to seek the latest gospel songs from the East Coast and the Midwest.

J. Earle Hines

The first important gospel singer from the East Coast to settle in Los Angeles was James Earle Hines (1916–60), a native of Atlanta, Georgia. He attended Atlanta public schools and participated in the musical activities of the churches, the city, and the college community of Atlanta University, and Spelman, Morehouse, Clark, and Morris Brown colleges. Most of these activities featured Western European art and music. After high school he moved to Cincinnati where he attended the Cosmopolitan School of Music and later matriculated at Columbia University in New York City. After two years at Columbia he returned to Cincinnati and began directing local church choirs.

During the 1930s Hines was recruited by Dr. L. K. Williams, president of the National Baptist Convention, to sing in a male quartet that Lucie Campbell and E. W. D. Isaac were putting together to travel to National Baptist Convention churches and represent the convention in song. Hines accepted the invitation and for several years sang with the Good Will Singers along with J. Robert Bradley and Thomas Shelby, among others. He received a thorough grounding in the African American sacred music tradition at the annual National Baptist Convention as a member of the convention choir during the early 1940s.

In 1947 Hines was hired as the director of the newly founded Echoes of Eden Choir at St. Paul Baptist Church in Los Angeles. The choir quickly became the most outstanding gospel choir in the city and was the first black church choir to have a weekly radio broadcast. The choir also has the distinction of being the first true gospel choir to make records. In the late 1940s and early 1950s, they produced several hits, among them Kenneth Morris' "He's a Friend of Mine," Dorsey's "God Be with You," and the two songs that made them famous, "Yield Not to Temptation" and "Just Look for Me in Heaven."

With a baritone voice that sounded as if it were made of steel, Hines was an aggressive singer, at times literally shouting out lyrics. He was particularly adept at realizing older hymns in the Baptist lining hymn tradition. His flamboyant stage mannerisms helped, rather than hindered, his ability to "upset" a church; the sisters would execute a holy dance or faint, while the men attempted to inconspicuously wipe the tears from their eyes.

Cora Martin-Moore

Singer, pianist, and choir director Cora Juanita Brewer Martin-Moore was born in 1927 in Chicago. She was the oldest child of Lucius and Annie Claude James Moore, but as a youngster she was adopted by gospel pioneer Sallie Martin and thereafter used the name Cora Martin. She attended public schools in Chicago and began her musical career as a child at that city's Mount Pleasant Baptist Church. She joined her adopted mother's group, the Sallie Martin Singers, as a teenager and toured with them throughout the United States, even after 1947 when she made her home in Los Angeles and affiliated with the St. Paul Baptist Church. As a soloist in the Sallie Martin Singers, Martin-Moore gained fame through a recording of Robert Anderson's "Eyes Hath Not Seen" on which she displays an alto voice of even tone, highly developed breath control, and restraint in embellishments. She was equally at home with jubilee music, illustrated when she sang the Alex Bradford part in "He'll Wash You Whiter than Snow" while on tour with the Sallie Martin Singers.

After moving to California, Martin-Moore attended California State University at Dominquez Hills and earned a bachelor's degree. She served as minister of music and director of the Echoes of Eden Choir and worked as a religious music DJ, in addition to owning a music studio and record shop.

Eugene Douglass Smallwood

Until the arrival of Doris Akers in Los Angeles, Eugene Douglass Smallwood (b. 1920), born in Guthrie, Oklahoma, was the principal gospel music composer in Los Angeles. He began composing and publishing his music in 1939, the year he came to Los Angeles City College as a music major. While attending college, he served as the minister of music at the Zion Hill Baptist Church and sang tenor with the Three Sons of Thunder. Smallwood also organized, along with Earl A. Pleasant, the Interdenominational Chorus, the venerable Smallwood Singers, and a music school with James Lewis Elkins, a former member of the Wings Over Jordan Choir. His crowning achievement was the founding of Opportunity Baptist Church, where he has served as senior minister since 1946. Gospel musicians who have worked with him at his church include Albert A. Goodson, Robert Anderson, the Simmons-Akers Singers, Thurston G. Frazier, and Raymond Rasberry.

The composer of more than one hundred gospel songs, Smallwood is most famous for his composition "When He Spoke," which has been recorded by Mahalia Jackson, the Davis Sisters, the Robert Anderson Singers, and the Clara Ward Singers. Smallwood, who still possesses a bright tenor voice, was honored in February 1994 at the Smithsonian Institution for his contributions to gospel music. During the ceremony, Smallwood sang several impassioned renditions of his own songs.

Doris Akers

By the 1990s several Christian hymnals (including the United Methodist and the African Methodist Episcopal) contained either "Sweet, Sweet Spirit" or "Lead Me, Guide Me." Both songs were composed by the most prolific composer in gospel music since the days of Dorsey, Campbell, Brewster, Morris, and Roberta Martin: Doris Mae Akers.

When she arrived in Los Angeles in 1945, Doris Akers (b. 1922) was not only a seasoned singer, pianist, and choir director, but a composer as well, having written her first composition at age ten. Akers was born in Brookfield, Missouri, but her family moved to Kirksville, Missouri, when she was five. She studied piano, sang in her high school glee club, and while still a teenager, organized a five-piece band called Dot Akers and Her Swingsters that featured swing jazz and other popular music of the 1930s and 1940s.

In Los Angeles she sang and played for the Sallie Martin Singers and later organized her own group with Dorothy Simmons, the Simmons-Akers Singers, which concertized throughout the United States. Akers won special prominence in the late 1950s and 1960s when she became the soloist and director of the Sky Pilot Choir, one of the first racially mixed choirs in Los Angeles, which featured African American gospel music.

Akers'1947 composition "I Want a Double Portion of God's Love" became the first of many hit songs that she would write. Others are "Lord, Don't Move the Mountain," which was made famous by Inez Andrews, "You Can't Beat God Giving," "Grow Closer," and "God Is So Good to Me." Akers' compositions are unique for their elegant and sophisticated lyrics and for their melodies, which draw less from Negro spiritual and gospel characteristics and more from European art music and American popular music. Her most famous composition, "Lead Me, Guide Me," is a gospel song set as a lullaby:

I am weak and I need Thy strength and power
To help me over my weakest hour;
Help me through the darkness Thy face to see,
Lead me, oh Lord, lead me.

Chorus

Lead me, guide me, along the way
For if you lead me, I cannot stray;
Lord, let me walk each day with Thee,
Lead me, oh Lord, lead me.

The title of this song was chosen as the title of the African American Catholic Hymnal in 1987.

Dorothy Vernell Simmons

For many years Akers' singing partner was Dorothy Vernell Simmons (b. 1910), a gospel singer and choir director. A native of Louisiana, Simmons moved with her family to Chicago when she was seven years old. After high school she worked in the Martin and Morris Music, Inc. where she came into contact with gospel music. Martin discovered Simmons was a singer and engaged her as a member of the Sallie Martin Singers when they were organized in 1940. Simmons visited California in 1944 with the Sallie Martin Singers and in 1947 decided to move there. Her association with Akers began in 1948. Her lyric soprano, agile and with a high range, blended sonorously with the mezzo-soprano-alto of Akers. Akers' compositions and the singing of the Simmons-Akers Duo were the inspiration for Edwin Hawkins' arrangement of "O Happy Day" and the new gospel sound from Los Angeles.

Thurston Frazier

The most important California gospel choral conductor after J. Earle Hines was Thurston Gilbert Frazier (1930–74). Frazier was born in Houston, Texas, and moved to Los Angeles in the late 1930s. His introduction to gospel music came when he met J. Earle Hines and sang in one of his choirs. He studied repertoire and conducting with Hines and found gospel more demanding and more inspiring than, and just as difficult as, the music he studied as a music major at Los Angeles City College.

Frazier gained fame as the director of the Voices of Hope Choir, a community gospel chorus that he and Gwendolyn Cooper Lightener, former pianist for Mahalia Jackson, organized in 1957. Their first album, released in the early 1960s, included Frazier's composition "We've Come This Far by Faith." The song became extremely popular and was soon being sung by choirs throughout the United States. Frazier's choral style, much closer to James Cleveland's than Thomas A. Dorsey's, anticipated the style of the 1970s and 1980s, with its three rather than four parts, a full bright sound, and rhythms closer to those of rhythm and blues than to those of Negro spirituals.

Frazier served as director of music at Phillips Temple Christian Methodist Church and Opportunity Baptist Church. His most popular compositions are "Come Holy Spirit" and "Let Us Sing Praise," both of which show traces of the Western European art music that he studied in college. Frazier was widely praised for his ability to direct and command gospel choirs of five hundred voices.

Albert A. Goodson

Albert A. Goodson was born in Los Angeles in 1933 and acquired his musical education in the church. Although he was raised in the Pentecostal church, he joined St. Paul Baptist Church at age twelve to learn the music and technique of J. Earle Hines and Gwendolyn Cooper Lightener. While studying with Hines, he served as assistant pianist for the Echoes of Eden Choir and the Hines Good Will Singers. He later served as choir director at Grace Memorial Church of God in Christ and Opportunity Baptist Church. During the early 1950s he toured and recorded with the Sallie Martin Singers, as well as served as their pianist. He moved to Chicago in 1955 where he was engaged as minister of music at Fellowship Baptist Church, pastored by the Reverend Clay Evans. At the invitation of Thomas Wyatt, director of the Wings of Healing Ministry, he returned to Los Angeles in 1961 to direct the interdenominational Wings of Healing Gospel Choir.

While living in Chicago he composed the song that would catapult him to fame within a few short months of its release. "We've Come This Far by Faith," recorded by the Voices of Hope, became as popular a processional for the gospel choir as Dorsey's "God Be with You" was a benediction song for congregations:

We've come this far by faith, leaning on the Lord,
Trusting in His holy work, He's never failed me yet;
Oh, oh, oh, can't turn around,
We've come this far by faith.

Arthur Atlas Peters and Dave Carl Weston

Two important but lesser-known gospel musicians from the California school are Arthur Atlas Peters and Dave Carl Weston. Peters (c.1907–75), born in Slidell, Louisiana, began playing piano at age seven and studied piano with the local school teacher. He attended Southern University and after graduating taught school in Mississippi for several years before moving to Los Angeles in 1936. He immediately immersed himself in music, singing spirituals, anthems, gospel, and Western art music. Later he served as director of the choir at Phillips Temple Christian Methodist Church and simultaneously opened a music store where he taught gospel singing. In 1939 along with Eugene Smallwood and Amos Pleasant, he organized the Three Sons of Thunder, a gospel trio.

Victory Baptist Church, a prominent church in Los Angeles, was founded by Peters in 1943, and in 1949 he began "Voices of Victory," a weekly radio broadcast. The first television broadcast of his church services began on April 5, 1953, and continued for a number of years. Victory Baptist Church was among the first to welcome gospel into its sanctuary.

David Carl Weston was born in Lufkin, Texas, in 1923. After attending Prairie View A & M College (now University) for one year, he relocated to Santa Monica in 1942 where he joined Calvary Baptist Church. At the same time he entered the University of California, Los Angeles, from which he graduated in 1947 with a major in English and a minor in music.

He served as pianist for the gospel and youth choirs at Calvary and organized the Merri-Tones, a community gospel choir. His own group, the Dave Weston Singers, toured with the Jordanaires, the Sallie Martin Singers, and Brother Joe May. Between 1951 and 1955 Weston lived in Chicago and directed the choir at the First Church of Deliverance. In 1955 he returned to California where he became Calvary's first minister of music.

PIANO-ACCOMPANIED GROUPS

Piano-accompanied gospel demanded virtuoso piano playing. The gospel piano style of the 1950s, with its heavy chords played in the center of the keyboard, rolling bass, and punctuated riffs in the upper part of the keyboard, was so distinctive that one had to be grounded in gospel in order to execute the style. Quartet gospel, older than piano-accompanied gospel, was at the peak of its popularity during the early 1950s. Gospel supported by piano emerged as the public's favorite, and singers took great pains in selecting pianists, because no group could be strong if its pianist was weak. Having worked at developing a style since the 1926 recordings of Arizona Dranes, by 1955 gospel pianists were as popular as the groups they were with. Some groups even mentioned the pianist in their name, such as the Davis Sisters and Curtis Dublin and the Original Gospel Harmonettes and Herbert "Pee Wee" Pickard. Several pianists were considered phenomenal. In addition to Dublin and Pickard, Mildred Falls, Mildred Gay, Jessy Dixon, and James Herndon were sought-after pianists. Most pianists in gospel during the 1950s were also the leaders of their group and created piano styles to fit the singers. The most outstanding among these were Clara Ward, Roberta Martin, Alex Bradford, James Cleveland, Edgar O'Neal, Raymond Rasberry, Charles Taylor, and Lucy Smith. The art of gospel piano and pianists developed to such a degree that quartets, heretofore accompanied by guitar (and before that singing *a cappella*) began using piano accompaniment at first for recordings only and gradually in concerts. The Soul Stirrers with Sam Cooke was one of the first quartets to use piano; by the late 1950s, however, nearly all quartets used piano at one time or another. Piano gospel finally came into its own.

Dorothy Love Coates and the Original Gospel Harmonettes

The 1940 National Baptist Convention met in Birmingham, and a local pianist was called on to play for the convention choir. Her friends sang in the convention choir and when the convention was over she and those friends decided to form a group to sing some of the songs they had learned. The pianist was Evelyn Starks (b. 1922), who would serve also as composer and arranger; the singer who proposed the formation of the group was Mildred Madison Miller (b. 1923), who was a member of the William Belvin Singers as second soprano. The other singers were Odessa

Dorothy Love Coates and the Original Gospel Harmonettes performing live to a church audience

Glasgow Edwards (b. 1921), second alto; Vera Conner Kolb (b. 1924), first soprano; and Willie Mae Brooks Newberry (b. 1923), first alto.

They named themselves the Gospel Harmoneers, but later became the Original Gospel Harmonettes when a record producer suggested they find a more feminine name. Within a few months of their organization, they were approached by A. G. Gaston, the leading African American funeral director in Alabama, to sing for a half-hour weekly radio broadcast on station WSGN, with Gaston Funeral Homes as their sponsor. The Harmonettes sang on the weekly program for a year and became regional stars. They toured Alabama and several states in the East and West and served as the local group to open concerts when famous stars appeared in town.

The Original Gospel Harmonettes: Willie Mae Newberry, Vera Kolb, Mildred Miller, Odessa Edwards, and Dorothy Love Coates

Their first recording session took place in New York City in 1949. During this session they recorded, among other songs, "Move on up a Little Higher" and "In the Upper Room." The recordings from this and a second session yielded little results, but the group continued to travel, drawing huge crowds through word-of-mouth publicity. J. W. Alexander, of the Pilgrim Travelers and a talent scout for Specialty Records, became interested in the group and arranged an audition for them in California. The group decided they wanted Dorothy McGriff Love, who had substituted for individual members of the group on several occasions in the early 1940s, to join them for the recording session. They went to Nashville and persuaded Love, who was living there with her husband, Willie Love of the Fairfield Four, to make the trip with them.

Their first session for Specialty produced two songs, equal in popularity, that immediately placed the singers in the forefront of female gospel groups. Love was given the lead in "I'm Sealed," a gospel ballad set to a gospel-waltz tempo. From the first note it was apparent that this soloist was extraordinary: a singer with a sanctified timbre and a preacher's delivery. As the song unfolded, the passion became

Dorothy Love Coates and the Original Gospel Harmonettes

greater and by the end of the recording more than a few listeners would be weeping. The other side of the recording was a semishout song, "Get Away, Jordan," with the lead shared by Miller and Love. Miller proved to be a formidable singer and matched Love nuance for nuance. What was of particular interest was the minivamp inserted toward the end during which Love, using African American folk axioms and phrases, describes a peaceful death. The public soon discovered that Love had written the additional lyrics and music, and they were primed for more of her songs.

The Harmonettes followed this first release with a string of hits that were new to gospel. Most Love compositions bore a relationship to Brewster's songs, which were wordy and historical. Love's songs were wordy but bursting with well-known folk sayings that tugged at the hearts of listeners. Her compositions include "You Can't Hurry God," "That's Enough," and "I Won't Let Go." Perhaps her finest composition is "You Must Be Born Again," in which the chorus says:

> _You must have that fire and Holy Ghost, that_
> _Burning thing that keeps the prayer wheel turning;_
> _That kind of religion you cannot conceal, it makes_
> _You move, it makes you shout, it makes you cry when it's real;_
> _Keep your head right in the winding chain (till your)_

Soul's been anchored in my Jesus' name (you know I'm)
Filled with it, free from sin, don't you see, you must be born again.

With Love, who by this time had married Carl Coates of the Nightingales, improvising on the solo, the group delivered this chorus in short staccato punches. And the longer they sang, the more excited Love became. She would then add

Gospel Pianists

Combining ragtime, barrelhouse, and Protestant hymns, Arizona Dranes and those who followed her created one of the most distinctive piano styles in music: gospel. By the end of the Golden Age of gospel its piano style had been refined and had begun to permeate American popular music. While there were many more progressive gospel pianists than can be mentioned here, a few of the most prominent are listed below.

Early Period
(Development)
Estelle Allen
Thomas A. Dorsey
Arizona Dranes
Kenneth Morris
Bertha Wise

Middle Period
(Refinement)
Margaret Allison
Jeff Banks
Curtis Dublin
Mildred Falls
Evelyn Gay
Ruth Jones (Dinah Washington)
Gwendolyn Cooper Lightener
Roberta Martin

Evelyn Starks
Clara Ward

Late Period
(Virtuosity)
Doris Akers
James Boyer
Alex Bradford
James Cleveland
Jessy Dixon
James Herndon
Edgar O'Neal
Herbert "Pee Wee" Pickard
Raymond Rasberry
Lawrence Roberts
Charles Taylor
Eddie Williams

growls, shrieks, and grunts to match the rhythmic and perpetual motion of her body.

The Harmonettes brought a new intensity to gospel that could only be matched by the frenzy of a joyful sanctified shout. At the same time they brought a quiet dignity and simple elegance to gospel that belied its inherent emotional capabilities. They performed in pastel robes, and when they otherwise appeared in public, they were always clad in fashionably styled, tailored suits. They were soft spoken, exhibited a refinement not seen since the days when Roberta Martin traveled with her group, were always seen together, and comported themselves as the Original Gospel Harmonettes—but without the artificial pride they could have assumed.

When they hit the stage, however, they were something else. While the others maintained an almost subdued stage presence, when Coates began to reach back into her life's experience as one of God's disenfranchised children and recount "how she got over," the group's demeanor changed. Without acting like the sanctified saints and giving up their entire presence to God, the Harmonettes began to "have church." Often performing with only one microphone, that microphone would be right in front of Coates' mouth, and the other members of the group would huddle around it and answer Coates note for note. When overcome by the spirit, Coates' eyes would open wide and remain open without blinking for minutes on end. As she sang, jerked, jumped, shouted, waved her arms, and moved through an audience, the lyrics of the song she was singing sprang vividly to life. On several occasions at the end of a song, the group would have to lead Coates back to the stage because she was completely out of herself, having given herself over to the Master.

In fact, as the supreme hard gospel singer, Coates could "take a house" and have everybody standing up, swaying, shouting, crying, or fainting like no one else, including her near-equal, Ruth Davis of the Davis Sisters. She would leave in the dust such hard singers as Silas Steele, Archie Brownlee, Clarence Fountain, and Julius Cheeks. When the Harmonettes made their first appearances with Coates, the audience was unprepared for what they eventually came to love. Coates brought more than fifteen years of gospel singing and passion to the Harmonettes.

Born in 1928 in Birmingham, Alabama, into a musical family, by age ten Coates was playing piano for her church Evergreen Baptist. As a teenager she sang with the Royal Gospel Singers and the McGriff Singers, a family group composed of three sisters and one brother. The group had a weekly broadcast over WJLD, one of the first live radio gospel concerts in the city. It was for the McGriff Singers that Coates began to compose, but it was not until she was a Harmonette that her compositions began to rival those of her idol, W. Herbert Brewster. What Brewster was able to say in the eloquent language of a sage, Coates was able to say in the homespun language of a weary traveler. In her 1953 composition "You Can't Hurry God," she spoke like a deacon from the Amen Corner:

> You can't hurry God, oh no, you just have to wait.
> You have to trust Him and give Him time, no matter how long it takes;
> You know He's a God you just can't hurry, He'll be there, don't worry,
> You know He may not come when you want Him, but He's right on time.

The Harmonettes appeared at Carnegie Hall in 1953, then at the Apollo Theater, Madison Square Garden, and concert halls throughout the United States and the Bahamas. After the Original Gospel Harmonettes disbanded in the 1960s, Coates organized the Dorothy Love Coates Singers and made several tours of Europe and in the late 1960s appeared in concert at Harvard University.

Albertina Walker and the Caravans

The Roberta Martin Singers were fantastic in that each member was such a great soloist that a concert could have been built around them individually. Albertina Walker and the Caravans were also fantastic, because not only could concerts be built around each singer, they eventually were. The Caravans have produced more gospel superstars than any other group or choir. Among their alumnae are Bessie Griffin, Shirley Caesar, Inez Andrews, Cassietta George, and Dorothy Norwood. Each of these singers was given the opportunity to develop herself by the Caravans' leader, Albertina Walker, one of the finest gospel singers of all times.

ALBERTINA WALKER

Walker was born in Chicago in 1930 and began singing at West Point Baptist Church at age eleven. By the time she was seventeen, she had joined a group led by Robert Anderson. In 1952, with Ora Lee Hopkins, Elyse Yancey, and Nellie Grace Daniels, who were also members of Anderson's ensemble, she organized the Caravans. The original Caravans were timid singers in comparison to the group that would emerge

Albertina Walker and the Caravans

in three years, but they were good timid singers. Their recordings of "Think of His Goodness to You," "Blessed Assurance," and the Negro spiritual "All Night, All Day" bear witness to close, earthy harmony, percussive attacks, and a precise rhythm unlike any other female gospel group. Tina, as Walker is called, was responsible for most of the solos in the original group, and it was the beauty of her voice and singing style to which others were attracted. Her voice is a husky contralto with a characteristic crack of three or four descending tones as she moves through a melodic line, a feature also heard from soul singer Gladys Knight. The sincerity with which Walker sings can turn a dry Protestant hymn into a jubilant testimony of faith.

By 1953 and with the addition of Bessie Griffin, the Caravans began to change into an ensemble of soloists. Walker, who has always believed in a kind of musical democracy, began to share the spotlight with each new singer. Yet none matched the soulful Albertina Walker, as illustrated on her 1980 recording of "Please Be Patient with Me."

BESSIE GRIFFIN

Bessie Griffin (1927–90), like her more famous compatriot Mahalia Jackson, was born in New Orleans, and the rich musical heritage of her birthplace exuded from every note she sang. After her mother died, Griffin was brought up by her grandmother. This meant church all day every Sunday and one day during the week. Early on Bessie began singing the songs she heard in church, and by the time she reached high school she was considered to be one of the best soloists in New Orleans.

Griffin moved to Chicago in 1951 and became part of that city's musical scene. Comparisons were often made between Griffin and Mahalia Jackson, although few similarities, save power, existed between their style. Griffin possessed a contralto that was lighter in texture than Jackson's and much more fluid. Griffin was capable of executing pyrotechnics such as sustaining tones for long periods, inserting growls, essaying a coloratura-like run, and singing for long periods of time (it was not unusual for her to sing one song for twenty minutes). She brought these assets to the Caravans in 1953. Her special song with the group was an extended version of Alex Bradford's "Too Close to Heaven." Griffin sang the song in such a way that each stanza brought the listener closer to heaven as she increased pitch, embellishments, and volume. In 1954 Griffin left the Caravans and thereafter followed a solo career, concertizing in the United States, Europe, and Africa, and singing gospel in nightclubs on the West Coast.

SHIRLEY CAESAR

"Baby Shirley, the Gospel Singer," as she was called by age ten, was born in Durham, North Carolina, in 1938 to a mother who was a great church worker and a father, known as "Big Jim," who was a legendary quartet singer. One of her greatest joys as a young child was attending the rehearsals of the Just Come Four, the *a cappella* quartet in which her father sang lead. Her father died when she was twelve years old, and she was thereafter responsible for her invalid mother. To help with finances, she joined the traveling group of the "one-legged preacher," Leroy Johnson, and she appeared regularly on his television show out of Portsmouth, Virginia, in the early 1950s. She also cut several records for the Federal label.

After graduating from high school, she enrolled in North Carolina State College (now North Carolina State University) seeking a major in business education. In 1958 she attended a concert by the Caravans and was so mesmerized by their singing that she wanted to join the group. Through a strange set of circumstances, and with the assistance of Dorothy Love Coates, Caesar withdrew from college in 1958 and joined the Caravans whose members at that time included Walker, Cassietta George, and Inez Andrews.

Caesar has a light alto voice with a rapid vibrato marked by its agility. She possesses an extensive range, the upper part of which she uses at the climax of a song. Her songs are delivered in a style not unlike that of a preacher (which she is), and she can energize an audience. Indeed, most audiences are on their feet several times during a Caesar concert. She first demonstrated her ability to completely mesmerize an audience in 1961 with her rendition of "Hallelujah, It's Done." During the choruses of the song she ad-libs in the style of African American folk preaching tantamount to a short sermon or sermonette. This song and sermonette form was also

Gospel Organists

From its introduction into gospel in 1939 by Kenneth Morris, the percussive sound and myriad colors of the Hammond organ were eventually adopted by rhythm and blues and jazz performers. Among the several prominent gospel organists performing during the Golden Age were Alfred Bolden who, in addition to gospel, played European art music, and Billy Preston, who became the premiere soul music organist.

Alfred Bolden	"Little" Lucy Smith
James "Blind" Francis	Gerald Spraggins
Ralph Jones	Herman Stevens
Alfred Miller	Louise Overall Weaver
Kenneth Morris	Willie Webb
Billy Preston	Maceo Woods

practiced by Mother Willie Mae Ford Smith and Edna Gallmon Cooke. In later years Caesar would perfect this practice to such a degree that she had no peer.

Her other special talent was the dramatization of songs, as first demonstrated in 1958 with "I've Been Running for Jesus a Long Time" and "I'm Not Tired Yet." Each time the word "running" appeared in the lyrics, Caesar would run up and down the aisles to the delight of the audience. She surpassed her dramatization of that song in 1962 when, while singing "Sweeping through the City," she pantomimed sweeping, moving through the auditorium and giving special energy to the corners of the hall.

Caesar left the Caravans in 1966 and organized her own group, the Caesar Singers. While in this group she developed a repertoire of mother songs, the first of which was "Don't Drive Your Mama Away" in 1969. Other such songs recorded by Caesar are "No Charge" and "Faded Roses," her first crossover piece.

Caesar became an evangelist in 1961 while with the Caravans, and in the 1980s, upon her return to Durham, she established the Mount Calvary Work of Faith Church, of which she is the pastor and her husband, Harold I. Williamson, is the presiding bishop. She also returned to college and earned a degree in business education in 1984, served on the Durham City Council, and founded the Shirley Caesar Outreach Ministries. In 1972 Caesar was the first gospel singer to be nominated for a Grammy Award, which she won. In addition to awards from the Gospel Music Association and the NAACP, she has been inducted into the Gospel Music Hall of Fame. Caesar is the most popular gospel singer since Mahalia Jackson.

INEZ ANDREWS

Inez McConic Andrews (b. 1929), like Dorothy Love Coates, was born in Birmingham, Alabama, to a Baptist preacher father and a sanctified singing mother. Her mother died when she was two years old, and she was raised by her father. She received her education in Birmingham public schools and sang in the junior choir of her father's church. She sang locally as a soloist and joined the Carter Choral Ensemble, which traveled around the Alabama, Mississippi, and Georgia region. She also sang for a short period with the Raymond Rasberry Singers and intermittently substituted in the Original Gospel Harmonettes.

In 1957 James Cleveland, while serving as pianist and arranger for the Caravans, persuaded Andrews to move to Chicago and join the group. Her addition sparked new energy because Andrews, like Caesar, was a singer and "preacher." There the similarity ends. While Caesar was a light mezzo-soprano-alto, Andrews was a metallic contralto; while Caesar had the rapid-fire delivery of an impassioned sanctified preacher, Andrews chose a slower, majestic delivery characteristic of a presiding bishop. Yet they were equally fiery.

Andrews had her first hit with the Caravans singing Cleveland's "Soldiers in the Army," which develops the ideas contained in the sanctified congregational song "I'm a Soldier in the Army of the Lord":

> *We are soldiers in the army,*
> *We've got to fight although we have to cry;*
> *We've got to hold up the blood-stained banner,*
> *We've got to hold it up until we die.*

Andrews turned "Soldiers" into an order, sung with the authority of a commanding general. However, that emotion in no way matched her passionate pleading to Mary in the Claude Jeter arrangement of "Mary, Don't You Weep." After four or five stanzas of gently requesting Mary to cease weeping, Andrews turns the song into one of the most compelling vamps in all gospel. She begins to call Mary's name gently at first; the second time she calls with a louder and higher tone; and with the third call she ascends into the very top of her register and wails "Ma—a—a—ry!"

In the early 1960s Andrews left the Caravans and organized her own group, the Andrewettes. With this group she toured Europe in 1965. Since that time she has concertized and recorded as a solo artist. "Lord, Don't Move the Mountain" by Doris Akers was a big solo hit for Andrews in the late 1970s. Occasionally Andrews reunites with other former members of the Caravans for concerts.

DOROTHY NORWOOD

If Shirley Caesar and Inez Andrews are preachers, then Dorothy Norwood is the master storyteller. This Atlanta, Georgia, native (b. 1930) blanketed the 1960s with gospelized stories of ungrateful children, boys who have circuitous meetings with Jesus, and old ladies with houses.

Norwood grew up in the Baptist church and honed her singing skills in choirs and groups in Atlanta before moving to Chicago. By 1955 she was a member of the

Caravans. Norwood's voice is a burnished alto, capable of great warmth and yet elastic enough to produce a preacher's growl. Although outstanding with the Caravans, Norwood did not seem to come into her own until she left the group in the late 1950s. Then, she sang with a number of groups including James Cleveland's Gospel Chimes. It was as the leader of her own group, the Norwood Singers, that she became a superstar, not because of her singing but because she knew how to tell a story.

Her four most famous stories are "Johnny and Jesus," "The Boy and the Kite," "The Old Lady's House," and the overwhelmingly popular "The Denied Mother." On her recording of "The Denied Mother," perhaps the saddest of all mother songs, Norwood begins her story in this manner:

> *A mother who, having sent her daughter away to college, goes to the train station to meet her at the end of a year of school. Though the mother is standing at the station with her arms open wide to greet her daughter, her daughter looks right at the mother, turns in another direction and walks away. Though feeling rejected and hurt the mother runs after the daughter and asks her why she did not greet her as the other daughters did their mothers. The daughter answers that she didn't greet her because she didn't want anyone to know that the old lady with all the burns and scars on her face was her mother. Her mother told her that when she was a baby three months old, she left her in the house to go outside and hang up her washing. When she looked around she saw that the house was on fire, and though her neighbors tried to keep her from going inside, she could only think about her baby, went in the house and not only saved her baby, but put her hands over the baby's face so that the baby would not be scarred.*

At the end of the story the mother says "that's all right though; I know a man [Jesus] who sits high and looks low." In this live recording, the audience roars their approval for the mother's fail-safe salvation. Throughout the recording the audience has participated as if they were responding to a preacher, and that is the role Norwood takes in the performance. Like C. L. Franklin would, she begins the story in her normal speaking voice. As the story progresses and the spirit arises, she moves into the key of the organ and piano that accompany her with sustained and staccato chords and begins to chant the story. By the time she reaches the end, she has turned her narrative into song. She and her singers immediately begin Dorsey's famous prayer "Take My Hand, Precious Lord." Norwood moved to New Jersey and sang with a number of choirs but in the 1970s returned to her native Georgia.

CASSIETTA GEORGE

Cassietta George was born in 1928 in Memphis, Tennessee, and died in Los Angeles in 1995. She graduated from McKinley High School in Canton, Ohio, where she lived for a number of years. After she finished school, she returned to Memphis and sang for a while with the Songbirds of the South, one of the many female *a cappella* quartets in Memphis during the 1940s and early 1950s. She later sang with the Brewster Ensemble. In the early 1950s she moved to Chicago, and in 1954 became a member of the Caravans.

Short in stature and slight of build, George astounded audiences with her thin and clear but huge voice. Having been brought up in the *a cappella* tradition, she was particularly sensitive to attacks and releases. In public performances it was clear that despite piano accompaniment she marked the rhythm in her singing with physical gestures. Her most popular song with the Caravans was a spirited arrangement of "Somebody Bigger than You and I" that carried such a popular music character that it just missed becoming a crossover hit for the Caravans.

George began composing while with the Caravans and has composed more than twenty-five songs, including "To Whom Shall I Turn?" and "I Believe in Thee."

OTHER CARAVAN PERFORMERS

Several other singers made their own contributions to the Caravans. Imogene Green (b. 1931), a Chicago native and schoolmate of James Cleveland, began singing gospel in high school with Cleveland accompanying her on piano. During the course of her transition from a soprano to a robust sounding contralto, she sang with the Caravans (1955–57), Cleveland's Gospel Chimes, and the Davis Sisters. Delores Washington, Josephine Howard, and Louise McDonald each sang with the Caravans during the 1960s.

Among the pianists who played for the Caravans were James Cleveland, Eddie Williams, and James Herndon. Herndon wrote the group several compositions that became famous, among them "I Won't Be Back No More," "No Coward Soldier," and "He Sits High and Looks Low."

Professor Alex Bradford

Almost twenty years after his death, Alex Bradford (1927–78) is still considered one of the most talented singer-composers in gospel and certainly its most flamboyant. In a relatively short while, Bradford moved from his hometown of Bessemer, Alabama, to the front line of the national gospel scene to become the toast of Broadway and the "Darling of the Continent." This task would seem difficult for a "whiskey sounding" baritone who was "always on stage," but it came easy for Bradford.

Born to a father who was an ore miner and a mother who was a cook, seamstress, beautician, and stage mother, Bradford was given piano and dancing lessons at age four, even though this was during the Depression. Within a few short months of his dancing lessons, he was appearing on stage. The admiration and applause he received during his short-lived vaudeville career stayed with Bradford forever. The excitement of the theater, the overwhelming admiration of the audience, and the congeniality among the performers inspired six-year-old Bradford to join a sanctified church near him—the ambience seemed the same as vaudeville's to him. However, his Baptist mother brought him back to the family church in short order. At age thirteen Bradford joined a children's gospel group, the Protective Harmoneers, and within a year he had his own radio show on which he sang, played the piano, and presented other talented youth.

Bradford attended elementary and junior high school in Bessemer but after what was perceived as a racial altercation, he was sent to New York City to complete high school. He did not remain there long, and on his return to Bessemer, his mother enrolled him in a prestigious African American private school, Snow Hill Institute, approximately 160 miles from his hometown. Founded in 1893 by William James Edwards, the great-grandfather of film director Spike Lee, Snow Hill was comparable to such African American boarding schools as Palmer in North Carolina and Fessenden Academy in Ocala, Florida. Bradford was an extremely bright student, excelling in English, history, and music. Only slightly interested in European classical music, Bradford led jam sessions with other students in the latest blues hits. He would also lead them in the latest songs of the groups that visited Bessemer: the Kings of Harmony, the Swan Silvertones, the Famous Blue Jay Singers, and Arizona Dranes—who were singing sanctified gospel as early as 1926—and the Brewster Ensemble, featuring Queen Candice Anderson. Bradford's musical activities did not

Professor Alex Bradford and the Bradford Specials

deter his teachers from appointing him a teacher's assistant. As a result his classmates named him "Professor," a title he used throughout his career.

After graduating from high school Bradford served a tour in the armed services during World War II and upon his release in 1947 moved to Chicago, the center of gospel. His great desire was to join the Roberta Martin Singers. Although Martin welcomed him to Chicago and presented him at her concerts, she offered him no spot in her group. Robert Anderson presented him in concert with his group but made no attempt to make him a star. Bradford became friendly with Mahalia Jackson who hired him for a short period as her secretary and traveling companion. During one of their tours, he copied down the names of promoters from her address book for use at a later time. While traveling with Jackson, Bradford received a call from Willie Webb informing him of a vacancy in his group. Bradford joined the Willie Webb

Singers, and at their next recording session Webb permitted Bradford to sing the lead on Bradford's arrangement of the nineteenth-century white Protestant hymn "Every Day and Every Hour." While this recording was not a hit, in it devout gospel lovers recognized not only a new voice, but a new style. This recording opened the door for Bradford.

On the minor, but ultimately significant, success of "Every Day and Every Hour," Bradford organized a group called the Bradford Specials and recorded nine songs, all composed by Bradford, for Specialty Records' gospel division under the supervision of Art Rupe on July 19, 1953, in Chicago. On the advice of Rupe, "Too Close to Heaven" was selected as the first release. The gospel world—save the few who had noticed "Every Day and Every Hour"—was taken by surprise when this gigantic husky overseer-type voice stated that:

> *I'm too close to my journey's end,*
> *I'm too close to shaking hands with all my friends,*
> *And I wouldn't take nothing for my journey right now,*
> *Lord, you know I've got to make it somehow;*
> *I'm so close—almost reach my goal,*
> *(I said) I'm so close to finally saving my soul,*
> *I'm too close to heaven to turn around.*

If the beauty of Bradford's rough voice and his ability to make it toss and turn at will was not sufficient, halfway through the verse of the song he inserts a real high C in falsetto and immediately drops back to his gruff baritone.

Bradford was supported on "Too Close" by the Bradford Specials—James Brendon, Jonathan Jackson, Billy Harper, Louis Gibson, and Charles Campbell. Bradford was to have several hits during the next decade. Among them were "Lord, Lord, Lord," "I Won't Sell Out," and "He'll Wash You Whiter than Snow," a duet with Sallie Martin. By this time in Martin's career her voice had deepened almost to the range of Bradford's.

Just at the point at which Bradford's popularity began to wane, he was approached by Broadway producers to star in one of the earliest gospel musicals. *Black Nativity* opened in 1961. The play was highly successful and went on to have a run in London. Later he starred in the musical *Don't Bother Me, I Can't Cope*. He and

Vinette Carroll were preparing a new production, *Your Arm's Too Short to Box with God*, when he died.

Raymond Rasberry

Raymond Rasberry, pianist, composer, and choral director, was the first child of Gertrude and Raymond Rasberry, born in 1928 in Akron, Ohio. Learning to play the piano completely by ear at age eight, he became something of a sensation in his hometown because of his ability to hear songs only once and then duplicate them almost exactly. As a member of a Pentecostal church, Rasberry had ample opportunity to develop his talent by accompanying hymns and shout songs led by the congregation. (In Pentecostal churches the congregation begins the song; the pianist must find their key and create an accompaniment.)

Wynona Carr heard him play piano while he was still in his teens. Impressed with his virtuosity, she hired him as her pianist. Carr was her own best accompanist but wanted to stand and sing for greater contact with the audience. Rasberry traveled with Carr on weekends through high school, and after he graduated from East High in Akron, he moved to Cleveland to work with her and one of the choirs she was directing. His fame as a pianist spread, and he began accompanying other singers as well. He accompanied Mahalia Jackson on one of her tours and played piano for Clara Ward and the Ward Singers on several of their recordings.

In the mid-1950s, Rasberry organized the Rasberry Singers, a group of five men. His was the first major all male piano-accompanied group since Alex Bradford had formed the Bradford Specials. What made the Rasberry Singers unique, according to Anthony Heilbut, was that the group contained the finest male soprano in gospel, Carl Hall. The Rasberry Singers had several hit recordings, among them "No Tears in Heaven" and "We're Crossing over One by One," composed by Rasberry. His composition "Only What You Do for Christ Will Last" became a gospel standard and was recorded by several singers including Mahalia Jackson.

Marion Williams and the Stars Of Faith

Clara Ward and the Ward Singers had the perfect combination of voices and styles in Clara, Marion Williams, Henrietta Waddy, and Gertrude Ward and undoubtedly could have gone on singing as a group until they were too old to perform. However,

Marion Williams had come too far from scrubbing floors during the week and singing in local churches on weekends to take a back seat.

By the mid-1950s, Marion Williams had become gospel's leading lyric soprano and one of its greatest growlers. She had appeared at Carnegie Hall, Boston's Symphony Hall, and almost every Baptist church that had a piano, but she did not lead the Ward Singers, nor had she reaped the financial benefits that came to the group in large part because of her talent. She was, in the old vernacular, a "side man," and she needed either to go out as a soloist or to form her own group so that she could develop her ideas.

Kitty Parham leading the Stars of Faith in "Looking to Jesus"

In 1958 after being refused a raise and reimbursement for hotel expenses, Williams and Henrietta Waddy quit the group. Mrs. Ward was so certain that neither singer could make a living without her management that she gave little concern to their departure; she had organized a second group of singers who performed independently as the Clara Ward Specials, and she replaced Williams and Waddy with two singers from this group. But without Mrs. Ward's knowledge, Williams contacted the remaining members of the Clara Ward Specials—Kitty Parham, Frances Steadman, and Esther Ford—and invited them to become members of a group she was organizing. Like Williams and Waddy, the three felt Mrs. Ward was mistreating them. They immediately accepted Williams' invitation, and Mrs. Ward was left without the Clara Ward Specials. Williams never worked with the Ward Singers again. Audiences, however, delighted in witnessing the two groups during the same concert, especially since Williams' group now had the most exciting singers.

Kitty Parham (b. 1931), a native of Trenton, New Jersey, grew up in COGIC and was a leading soprano soloist in that denomination. From her experience as a song leader in congregational singing, Parham had cultivated every nuance of shout singing and could execute them all for long periods. Esther Ford (b. 1925) from Detroit, another COGIC singer, had long been an associate of Mattie Moss Clark and the na-

Marion Williams and Henrietta Waddy of the Stars of Faith

tional music scene. The gospel ballad, with which she could "paint a picture" and send audiences into hysteria, was her specialty. Frances Steadman (b. 1915) a native of Greensboro, North Carolina, who later lived in Baltimore, was brought up in both the Baptist and sanctified churches. She knew how to handle the shout and the Baptist lining hymn. Steadman, one of the most talented contraltos in gospel, when performing in the Baptist lining hymn tradition would, as Mahalia Jackson used to say, "take you back to slavery days."

Each of the five women was a powerful soloist, but none had the voice of Williams, and none could weave a musical spell like she could. One of their most successful recordings was a remake of the Ward Singers' song "Packing Up." The song deals with preparation for meeting Jesus, and in performance Williams would walk through the audience collecting as many as twenty purses. On her way back to the stage, she would return each purse to its rightful owner to the amazement and delight of the audience.

A special honor came to Williams in 1961 when she and the Stars of Faith were asked to appear on Broadway in Langston Hughes' *Black Nativity*. In 1971 Williams recorded Dorsey's "Standing Here Wondering Which Way to Go," which was selected as background music for the popular television commercial for the U.S Army "Down and Out," and in 1980 Barney Joseph, founder of the famous Cafe Society and owner of the New York nightclub The Cookery, called on Williams to substitute for the ailing Alberta Hunter. Two more great honors came to Williams in the early 1990s. She was selected as a MacArthur Fellow, an award that carries a $350,000 stipend, and she was the first gospel singer to receive a Kennedy Center Award for outstanding contribution in the arts.

The Lockhart Singers

One of the most popular gospel songs of 1954 and 1955 was "Own Me as a Child," composed, sung, and recorded by Esther Lockhart, two of her sisters, and one cousin who sang as the Lockhart Singers. Although their two recordings were popular, these teenagers seldom traveled out of their native Chicago. They became, instead, a fixture on many of the concerts of traveling singers in Chicago, and although they attempted to introduce other songs from their repertoire, audiences demanded that they sing their hit:

Oh Lord, hear my voice, a long time ago I made my choice
Trying to walk in this gospel way, you said you'd hear me whenever I pray;
You know that Satan has set a trap for me but when I call your name he
*   lets me be,*
I'm saying Lord when I come to die I want you to own me as a child.

The group disbanded in 1957.

Rosie Wallace and the Imperials

Philadelphia gave the gospel world a powerful group in Rosie Wallace and the Imperials. Wallace (b. 1932), the leader and pianist for the group, could sing in the traditional as well as the newer style of gospel with equal effect. "Reach out and Touch Him" and "Show Me the Way" were popular hits for the group.

Wallace was also a composer, writing most of her songs for her group. Among her most popular compositions are "Can't Turn around Now" and "Just to God Be True."

The Imperials

The Herman Stevens Singers

Herman Stevens (1928–70) is better known as one of the finest organists in gospel, serving as the gospel organist for Savoy Records. He was also the leader of a gospel group that he organized in 1952 with members Helen Bryant, Evelyn Archer, and Dorothy McLeod.

Right before her death, Dorothy McLeod (1927–61) was emerging as possible competition for Mahalia Jackson. A native of Florida, McLeod possessed a lighter

The Herman Stevens Singers

voice than Jackson's but enjoyed the same vocal qualities: evenness of tone, an extraordinary range allowing her to essay a bass quality in the bottom of her range without losing her soprano-like top voice, the ability to shout a house (she was a life-long member of COGIC), and the newly developed technique of "moaning like a true Baptist." In the late 1950s when she married Herbert Carson, a shouting baritone from North Carolina, he joined the Herman Stevens Singers, and the two were often featured in duets.

The Stevens Singers traveled little because Stevens was so active in the New York-Philadelphia-New Jersey area. The group became an opening act for traveling groups in New York and were celebrated for their renditions of "Peace in the Valley" and "Somebody Touched Me," which they recorded.

Professor Charles Taylor and the Gospel All Stars

While Raymond Rasberry adopted Alex Bradford's all-male piano-accompanied sound for his all-male singers, Charles Taylor inherited Bradford's performance flamboyance. Taylor (b. c. 1932), an Alabaman, arrived in New York in the early 1950s and affiliated with several Pentecostal churches in the capacity of soloist, pianist, and choir director. He was so interested in gospel that he absorbed everything that was happening in the field. Although Taylor was a talented and interesting performer, he was without a unique voice. His piano style was heavily based on Bradford's with Roberta Martin runs and chordal explosions and Bradford's penchant for dropping "bombs" (a very loud chord in the middle of an otherwise relatively quiet section). He trained his background singers in the Roberta Martin sharp attack, precise harmony, and slightly cultured timbre of the Baptist church, yet his lead was pure sanctified singing, complete with the high volume, explosive releases, and preaching style of delivery. The recordings of "On the Battlefield" and "New Born Soul" capture Taylor at the height of his style.

Other Piano-accompanied Groups

Several other piano-based groups were acclaimed during the last decade of the Golden Age. Two of the most popular were the Argo Singers and the Patterson Singers. While neither of these groups attained the stature of the Caravans or the Stars of Faith, they were solid gospel groups with the ability to stir a house during concerts. The Argo Singers had several successful recordings, including "He's Alright with Me." The Patterson Singers recorded on the Savoy label, producing such hits as "Throw out the Lifeline," "Going to Canaan," and "Christ Is Coming."

Professor Charles Taylor and the Gospel All Stars

The Highway QCs

Described as a farm team for the Soul Stirrers, the Highway QCs were organized in 1945. Their original membership consisted of Sam Cooke, Spencer Taylor, Lee Richardson, Creadell Copeland, and Charles Richardson. Original member Sam Cooke left the group in 1950 to join the Soul Stirrers and was replaced by Johnny Taylor, who at that time sounded very much like Cooke. In 1955 the group signed with Chicago's Vee-Jay Records and scored a success with their first release, "Somewhere to Lay My Head," with Taylor on the lead. In 1956 there were some personnel changes, and the group was dormant for a few years. In 1958, however, Overton Vertis Wright spent time as a lead with the group before he moved to the Sunset Travelers. Wright gave up gospel music for a career in secular music in 1964.

The QCs were heavily influenced by the Soul Stirrers, and their sound was a cross between the Soul Stirrers and the Swan Silvertones: a smooth, sweet style with an aggressive lead. Among their many popular recordings were "He Lifted My Burdens," "Do You Love Him?," and "Teach Me How to Pray." While the QCs were always a solid gospel group, they leaned toward popular music: their sound was smooth, with little of the grit associated with earlier quartets, and their stage manner was as close to a routine as possible without stepping across the invisible line between secular and sacred stage deportment. Their dress was ultrafashionable for their time, and they were one of the most popular gospel acts presented at the Apollo Theater.

The Skylarks, Violinaires, and Norfleet Brothers

By the mid-1950s it was evident that piano-accompanied gospel had replaced the purity of unaccompanied voices. Not only did all-male quartets travel with piano-accompanied groups, but they would also use the same accompanists for their own selections.

Only a small group of piano-accompanied quartets made their mark during the second decade of the Golden Age. Among them were the Skylarks. Organized in the late 1940s, the Skylarks were indistinguishable from the major quartets. They had powerful leaders, but not powerful enough to give the group real integrity, except in the thumping bass of Isaac "Dickie" Freeman, who later joined the Fairfield Four.

The Violinaires, on the other hand, created a big splash at their introduction into

Wilson Pickett singing pop later in his career

the mainstream of gospel. Organized in 1955 by Wilson Pickett (b. 1941), the Violinaires, despite having the smooth harmony of the Soul Stirrers and Dixie Hummingbirds, featured the hard lead of Pickett, who was emulating his idol, Julius Cheeks. After Pickett left the group in 1959 to become a soul singer, the group had several different lead singers but would not become a major force in gospel until the 1970s.

The Norfleet Brothers, composed of family members and friends, are a Chicago-based group that quickly earned a reputation as a solid gospel quartet that could easily stir up a house. The group has done little outside of Chicago and therefore has had little national influence.

Edna Gallmon Cooke

Edna Gallmon Cooke (1918–67) was born in Columbia, South Carolina. She studied music at Temple University and subsequently became a school teacher. In 1938 she heard Willie Mae Ford Smith sing gospel in Washington, D.C., and decided to adopt the style. She began singing in the area around Washington, D.C., and soon became known as the "Sweetheart of the Potomac," a title that remained with her throughout her career. She began recording in the early 1950s and by 1953 was a major gospel star, specializing in the song and sermonette. She performed most often with the support of a male quartet, beginning a song softly and subtly, then building in volume and drama as the song progressed.

Her most popular recordings, all made during the 1950s, include "Amen," "Evening Sun," and "Stop Gambler." In "Stop Gambler" Cooke recounts the story of the crucifixion of Christ and the gamble for his robe. She discusses the gamble in the contemporary parlance of a radio sports announcer and begins the countdown from the deuce to the ace like someone familiar with casinos:

> *I can see the first gambler as he throws down the deuce, the two spot—representing Paul and Silas bound in jail. They didn't do any wrong, God delivered them.*

> *The next gambler throws down the trey, the three spot—representing Shadrach, Meshach, and Abednego. God delivered them from a fiery furnace.*

> *Look at that next gambler, he is throwing down the four spot now—representing the four gospel writers, Matthew, Mark, Luke, and John.*

> *The next gambler is throwing down the five spot now—representing the fifth commandment: honor thy father and thy mother.*

> *The next one is throwing down the six spot—representing the six days God worked to create the earth.*

Cooke addresses each card in the deck with the same kind of biblical reference. By the time she arrived at the ace, representing the Father, Son, and Holy Ghost, her audiences would be standing and waving, clapping their hands, and generally acting as if they were at the sports event that she had created through her oration, which was always accompanied by soft organ music.

Jessy Dixon

Jessy Dixon was born in San Antonio, Texas, on March 12, 1938. He studied piano at St. Mary's College there with the aim of becoming a concert pianist. He first heard gospel music as a teenager through the recordings and concerts of Clara Ward and the Ward Singers and Dorothy Love Coates and the Original Gospel Harmonettes. Leaving college after two years, he served for a time as accompanist for Brother Joe May. In 1960 Dixon joined James Cleveland's Gospel Chimes. After five years with Cleveland, Dixon became director of the Thompson Community Singers, recording with them under the name of the Chicago Community Choir.

In the late 1960s he organized the Jessy Dixon Singers, modeling their sound and style on that of Cleveland and his group. Dixon provided a baritone lead, employing high falsetto in a repertory of call-and-response songs.

From his piano study, Dixon developed an interest in progressive harmony. In the early 1970s he left the Savoy label and moved to Light Records. There his style changed to that of contemporary gospel, in which the emphasis is on pure vocal sounds with melodies and harmonies borrowed from the popular music tradition and accompaniment is provided by electronic instruments. In June 1980 Dixon was selected to represent contemporary gospel at the Golden Jubilee Year Celebration of Gospel Music held in Chicago. His best-known compositions include "The Failure's Not in God," "Bring the Sun Out," and "Satisfied."

Joe Ligon and the Mighty Clouds of Joy

Willie Joe Ligon was born September 11, 1942, in Troy, Alabama. In 1959, while in high school in Los Angeles, he helped organize a male quartet, the Mighty Clouds of Joy. The original members were Ligon as lead, Elmore Franklin, Johnny Martin, and Richard Wallace; Paul Beasley joined in 1980. The group negotiated a recording contract with Peacock Records and by 1962 was one of the leading male gospel quartets. They began performing in the hard gospel style, singing loudly and rhythmically at the extremes of their vocal range, but later became one of the first groups to embrace the softer, contemporary gospel style. At the same time they employed a backup group of two guitarists, an organist, and a drummer, although their later recordings would include full orchestral accompaniment.

The group performs many traditional gospel songs, but in the 1970s they added "message" songs to their repertory—songs with lyrics that can be interpreted as either sacred or secular, for example, "You've Got a Friend." This made the group popular with multiracial and secular audiences. They have appeared with such artists as Earth, Wind, and Fire, the Rolling Stones, James Brown, Gladys Knight and the Pips, and Smokey Robinson and have performed in major concert halls throughout the country as well as on television.

Ligon's unique voice with its gritty timbre is capable of displaying many different colors and emotions; his range encompasses several octaves. His solo lead has earned the group two Grammy Awards.

OTHER SINGERS

A number of soloists made significant contributions to the development of gospel through difficult times. The ideal gospel sound in the late 1950s and early 1960s was that of a large group of singers led by an energetic and commanding soloist: the gospel choir. All the major soloists had begun to record with a backup group: Mahalia Jackson was with the Jack Halloran Singers, Brother Joe May sang with the Pilgrim Travelers, and Cleophus Robinson was recording with his church choir. The soloists who brought something new to gospel or were unique in their presentation of the old were able to survive the public's change in taste. Blind Harold Boggs (b. 1928) of Port Clinton, Ohio, and Singing Sammy Lewis (b. 1929) of Chicago both earned national reputations as singers before they entered the ministry.

Other soloists, while never attaining the status of a Mahalia Jackson, continued to offer the single voice that has been with gospel since the 1920s. Several of these singers gained new popularity after a period of dormancy, including the venerable R. L. Knowles; Brother John Sellers, who frequently performed with Mahalia Jackson; the Reverend Gary Davis, who continued to sing both gospel and blues; Gloria Griffin, who had been one of the leaders of the Roberta Martin Singers; Morgan Babb; Willie Morganfield; and Elizabeth Lands, who switched from gospel to rhythm and blues at the height of her gospel career. Chicago singers Myrtle Jackson and Myrtle Scott resurfaced, as did Molly Mae Gates, a longtime associate of Dorsey. An indication of the widespread acceptance of gospel was the organization of the Nashville-based BMC Choir, composed of Baptists, Methodists, and Catholics. Two young musicians who made a great impression on the gospel world through their singing, composing, and directing were Robert Fryson (1944–94) and Donald Vails (b. 1947). Pearl Williams Jones (1931–91) developed a cult following after the release of her recording of "Jesus Lover of My Soul," sung to the accompaniment of Bach's "Jesu, Joy of Man's Desiring."

FAMILY GROUPS

During the 1930s and 1940s, before television became a fixture in American homes, family singing sessions were a chief form of entertainment for many churchgoers. While most of the groups were community based, singing for their own church services and those of others, several of these family groups, parents and children, brothers and sisters, sisters alone, and brothers alone earned national reputations and became recording artists.

The Staple Singers

The Staple Singers are the only famous gospel group composed of a father and his children. The leader of the group is Roebuck "Pops" Staples of Winona, Mississippi, who with his wife, Oceola, moved to Chicago in 1935, bringing with them their one-year-old daughter Cleotha. In Chicago the couple had four more children: Pervis, Yvonne, Mavis, and Cynthia, all of whom eventually sang with their father as the Staple Singers. Often described as down-home gospel singers, the Staples' sound is

The Staple Singers

characterized by folk style and simple harmonies rendered in a country and western twang, supporting a lead by the tenor voice of Roebuck or the hard gospel voice and style of Mavis. With Roebuck's bluesy guitar, "Will the Circle Be Unbroken" and "Unclouded Day" were huge hits for these singers.

The Banks Brothers

The first gospel duet singing goes back to the beginning of the sanctified church when, in most cases, the preacher and his wife would hold "street meetings," singing to attract people and recruit new members. But the first modern male gospel duo was Jeff (b. 1927) and Charles (b. 1929) Banks. The Banks Brothers had the task of discovering the type of harmony, the kinds of songs, and the sort of style appropriate for two dark voices in gospel.

The Banks owe the development of their duo to Mary Johnson Davis, who organized her first group in the 1930s in Pittsburgh, Pennsylvania. The Banks Brothers became members of the Mary Johnson Davis Singers in 1947, although they began singing in their home church, the Christian Methodist Church (CME) in Pittsburgh, in 1943. Jeff was also the pianist for the group, and both brothers were song leaders. They remained with Davis until 1953, when they left the group to perform as a duo. Their first record, "I've Got a Witness," brought them into the national gospel scene.

The Banks Brothers' style involved one of the voices singing a harmony three tones above the melody in the other voice, using call-and-response technique, and occasionally singing in unison on the melody. These characteristic features would be adopted by other male duos, including the Boyer Brothers and the O'Neal Twins.

Both Banks brothers became ministers. Jeff became a bishop in COGIC and the pastor of Revival Temple Holiness Church of God in Christ, while Charles became the pastor of the Greater Harvest Baptist Church. Both churches are located in Newark, New Jersey. They continue to sing on occasion and celebrated their fiftieth anniversary of professional singing in 1994.

The Gay Sisters

Gospelizing standard Protestant hymns has been a part of the gospel movement since the Azusa Street Revival, but at no time was it more popular than in the 1950s. The Ward Singers produced a hit with "I Need Thee Every Hour"; the Caravans scored a hit with "Think of His Goodness to Me"; and Alex Bradford made his recording debut with a gospel-waltz version of "Everyday and Every Hour." None of these recordings could match the popularity of the gospelized version of the 1905 white Protestant hymn "God Will Take Care of You." The recording of this hymn introduced another group of family singers, the Gay Sisters.

Mildred (b. 1926), Evelyn (b. 1924), and Geraldine (b. 1931) were born to Jerry and Fannie Gay in Chicago. Fannie Gay and her children attended services at the Reverend Lucy Smith's All Nations Pentecostal Church. Inspired by the talent of "Little" Lucy, Evelyn and Mildred began singing as a duet, with Evelyn playing piano. Geraldine was an even more talented pianist than Evelyn (and as a youth Evelyn had accompanied Mahalia Jackson), and soon she played piano while Evelyn and Mildred sang. After Reverend Smith died, the Gay family moved its membership to the Church of God in Christ pastored by Elder William Roberts, where the three sisters became pianists and directors of music for the church. They concertized throughout the Midwest and made an annual trip to Memphis to sing at the Convocation of the Church of God in Christ.

In 1951 Evelyn and Mildred had their first session at Savoy Records (Geraldine had retired from the group). The first song sung during the session was also their first release, "God Will Take Care of You." With Mildred singing soprano and Evelyn singing and playing the piano, the sisters changed the hymn from the somber and lifeless performance usually given it to a rollicking 12/8 song of conviction and assurance. Particularly effective is the "high who" that Mildred inserts to introduce the last phrase. Evelyn's talent as a pianist was evidenced by her work on this recording, and the lyric soprano of Mildred was equal to that of Delois Barrett or Marion Williams. The Gay Sisters sang with Mahalia Jackson on Joe Bostic's annual Carnegie Hall concert bill in 1954 and made several tours throughout the United States in the 1950s and 1960s.

The Boyer Brothers

The Boyer Brothers, James Buchanan (b. 1934) and Horace Clarence Boyer (b. 1935), are two of eight children of the Reverend Climmie and Ethel Boyer of Winter Park, Florida. They received their education in the public schools of Winter Park and Eatonville and graduated from Bethune-Cookman College. The brothers were brought up in Faith Holy Temple Church of God in Christ, where their father was the pastor. Both played piano for services, and Horace directed the choir. They formed the Boyer Brothers when they were teenagers and sang throughout Florida.

When they were still in high school, they began recording on Excello Records, which was owned by Ernie's Record Mart of Nashville, one of the major distributors of gospel recordings in the 1950s. With Horace singing tenor and James singing baritone, the brothers sang two-part harmony on slow songs and used call and response on jubilee and shout songs. Singing in the sanctified style, they were adept at building tension through the use of the vamp. Among their popular recordings are "He Understands, He'll Say 'Well Done'"; "Step by Step"; and "Oh Lord, Be My Protector," composed by James.

"Step by Step," their first release, was their signature song and was performed with a mixture of harmony singing and call and response:

HARMONY
Step by step I'm nearing the kingdom
Step by step I'm going home.
Jesus will welcome me into His kingdom
Step by step around the throne.

I know this world is not my home
Horace: And I cannot
    James: I cannot
Horace: Make this journey
    James: this journey

HARMONY
Alone, Oh
Step by step I know Jesus will greet me
Welcome me home around the throne.

In the late 1960s the brothers returned to college for graduate study. Each holds a Ph.D. and teaches at the university level, James at Kansas State University and Horace at the University of Massachusetts–Amherst. Because of the distance, the Boyer Brothers have sung only occasionally since 1980.

The O'Neal Twins

Edgar (b. 1938) and Edward (1938–93), the O'Neal Twins, were the most successful gospel duo since Sister Rosetta Tharpe and Madame Marie Knight. The twins were born in East St. Louis, Illinois, and received their education in the public schools there. They were brought up in the COGIC and as teenagers came under the influence of Mother Willie Mae Ford Smith, who introduced them at one of her concerts and with whom they traveled for a time thereafter. They were also influenced by Mattie Moss Clark.

Edgar served as their pianist and arranger, while Edward was the song leader and announcer. Like the Banks Brothers and the Boyer Brothers, their style was one of close harmony, call and response, and occasional unison singing. The twins both possessed robust and attractive grainy baritone voices equipped with the timbre that was particularly effective in the hard gospel style.

Among their most popular recordings were "The Lord Is My Shepherd" and "I Have Decided to Follow Jesus." Their recording of "I'd Trade a Lifetime" placed them in the front ranks of gospel singers:

> *I sure would love to see loved ones*
> > ***who've gone on before,***
> *Shake hands with the elders,*
> > ***the twenty and the four;***
> *In that holy righteous place*
> > ***I'll see my Master's face,***
> *I'd trade a lifetime*
> > ***for just one day in paradise.***

The O'Neal Twins traveled widely and were one of the first gospel groups to appear at New York's Apollo Theater. Along with Thomas A. Dorsey, Sallie Martin, Mother Willie Mae Ford Smith, and the Barrett Singers, they were featured in the 1983 documentary film *Say Amen, Somebody*.

Cleophus Robinson and Josephine James

Cleophus Robinson (b. 1932) and his sister, Josephine James (b. 1934), were born in Canton, Mississippi and moved to Memphis as teenagers. Robinson attended

LeMoyne-Owen College for two years, then withdrew to pursue a career as a professional gospel singer. Robinson's early musical influences were Mahalia Jackson, from whom he adopted deliberate phrasing, and Brother Joe May, from whom he borrowed the technique of growling in the upper part of the tenor register. While Robinson recorded mostly as a soloist, he and James made several successful recordings including "Pray for Me" and "When I Cross Over."

The Consolers

Brother and Sister Pugh: The Consolers

Not since the days of Blind Mamie Forehand and A. C. Forehand has a husband and wife singing team generated as much enthusiasm as Sullivan Pugh and Iola Lewis Pugh of the Consolers. The youngest of four brothers and one sister, Pugh was born in 1925 in Morehaven, Florida. His mother, like hundreds of others, was lost in the massive hurricane that passed through Florida shortly after his birth. He, his sister, and youngest brother were adopted by James and Virginia Pugh and brought up in the south-west Florida coast town of Punta Gorda where he attended school. As an adult he moved to Miami to find work.

Iola Lewis (b. 1926), the third oldest of four daughters, was born in Cottonton, Alabama. When Lewis was three her mother died, and she was subsequently raised by her maternal grandmother. When Lewis was eleven, the family moved to Columbus, Georgia, where she completed high school. After attending Claflin College in Orangeburg, South Carolina, for a short period of time, Lewis moved to Miami. She met Pugh in 1949, and they were married in 1950. They began singing as the Consolers in 1953.

Pugh shared in the singing and was the composer for the Consolers. He wrote a number of highly successful songs on the fallibility and frailness of mankind: "May the Work I've Done Speak for Me," "I'm Waiting for My Child to Come Home," and "Thank God, They Are as Well as They Are." Delivered in the "old timey" style of the Angelic Gospel Singers and the country sincerity of the Staple Singers, the

Consolers' most popular song was based on an old African American church saying—Give me my flowers while I can smell them:

> Give me my flowers while I can see them
> So that I can see the beauty that they bring;
> Speak kind words to me while I can hear them
> So that I can feel the comfort that they bring.

"Give Me My Flowers" brought superstar fame to the Consolers and drew to a close the duet tradition of the Golden Age.

THE SECOND GOSPEL TRIUMVIRATE

As Thomas A. Dorsey, Sallie Martin, and Theodore R. Frye constituted that triumvirate of the 1930s that took gospel from dubious status to its place as the principal music of the African American church, the triumvirate in gospel during the 1960s moved gospel from being a music of the church to a music of the nation. James Cleveland, Edward Smith, and the Reverend Lawrence Roberts were the second triumverate of gospel. Like Dorsey, Cleveland had the talent; like Sallie Martin, Edward Smith possessed the business acumen to make money. And the Reverend Lawrence Roberts, a gospel record producer for Savoy Records, provided the conduit to the music-loving public.

James Cleveland

James Edward Cleveland (1931–91), gospel singer, pianist, composer, and conductor, was born in Chicago and began piano lessons at age five. By age eight he was a soloist in Thomas A. Dorsey's Junior Gospel Choir at the Pilgrim Baptist Church. At age fifteen he joined a local group, the Thorne Crusaders, with whom he remained for the next eight years. As a leader of this group, he strained to reach high notes and, in the absence of sound systems, sang louder than his vocal cords could accommodate. This vocal strain resulted in a throaty and gravelly quality that increased with the years. During his tenure with the Thornes, he began composing and by age sixteen had composed "Grace Is Sufficient," which was recorded by the Roberta Martin Singers and is now part of standard gospel repertoirc.

After leaving the Thornes, Cleveland served as pianist and arranger for Albertina

Walker's Caravans and recorded several sides with that group. He later joined other groups, including the Gospel Chimes and the Gospel All Stars, eventually organizing the James Cleveland Singers. In 1960 Cleveland joined with the Reverend Lawrence Roberts and his choir at the First Baptist Church in Nutley, New Jersey, to make a number of successful recordings, the first of which was "Peace, Be Still" (1963). Cleveland liked a treble sound and dispensed with the bass voice in the gospel choir. He also preferred the call-and-response delivery when singing in concert, and on all his choir recordings he played the role of the preacher to the choir's congregation. Further, he felt that gospel was in its element with a congregation and made all his choir recordings live.

During the 1950s and 1960s Cleveland was most prolific as a composer, writing more than five hundred songs. Many have become gospel standards, including "Oh Lord, Stand by Me," "He's Using Me," "Walk on by Faith," and "Lord, Help Me to Hold Out." He continued to compose into the 1980s and scored a huge success when the Mighty Clouds of Joy recorded his "I Get a Blessing Everyday."

The Cleveland style, which he employed and taught his singers, was half crooning, half preaching the verses, and then moving into snug refrains. His hard gospel technique of singing at the extremes of his register evoked a heavy contrast with the rich falsetto that he employed. He was particularly fond of the vamp in gospel music, over which he would extemporize variations. Like his model, Thomas A. Dorsey, he had the ability to write and sing in the everyday language of his audience, dealing with such subjects as paying rent, buying food, and heating the home in winter.

Cleveland's greatest contribution, again like Dorsey, was the organization of a gospel choir convention. In August 1968 he organized the Gospel Music Workshop of America (GMWA), an organization that had several hundred thousand members by the mid-1980s. Each large town had a chapter of the GMWA, and Cleveland would make periodic visits to chapters to teach new songs and techniques and to critique the work of the local choirs. An annual convention was held for one week, each year in a different location. Since many members of GMWA would choose this week for their vacation, attendance at these meetings was large. Each year's convention released a recording of the outstanding groups in attendance, with Cleveland leading one or two songs. One of his most successful recordings was with one of his protégés, Aretha Franklin, singing "Amazing Grace"; she had studied his style when he was the director of the Radio Choir at Detroit's Bethlehem Baptist Church, where her father was pastor.

Cleveland had many gold records and won three Grammy Awards, appeared at Carnegie Hall and many other prestigious performance venues around the United States, worked with Quincy Jones in the television production "Roots," and recorded the opera *Porgy and Bess* with Ray Charles and Cleo Lane. In 1980, along with Natalie Cole, he starred in the television special "In the Spirit," filmed in Northampton, England, for Granada Television (BBC). On August 12, 1981, Cleveland was awarded a star on the Hollywood Walk of Fame. In August 1983, accompanied by the Southern California Community Choir, Andrae and Sandra Crouch, and Shirley Caesar, Cleveland performed live in concert at the Sultan's Pool amphitheater in Jerusalem.

In November 1970 Cleveland had organized and become the pastor of the Cornerstone Institutional Baptist Church in Los Angeles with sixty charter members. When he died in February 1991, membership at the church totaled more than seven thousand.

Lawrence Roberts

The Reverend Lawrence Roberts was born in 1939 in Newark, New Jersey. He learned to play the piano at an early age, and by age fifteen he was the pianist for the junior choir at the Zion Hill Baptist Church in Newark. For the next ten years Roberts served as pianist for Newark gospel groups and organized his own group, the Gospel Chordettes, whose members were Bernadine Walls, Delores Best, Freida Roberts, Gertrude Deadwyler, and Margie Rains. In October 1954 he became a producer for Savoy Records and in that capacity supervised recordings for such groups as the Roberta Martin Singers, Dorothy Love Coates and the Original Gospel Harmonettes, the Five Blind Boys of Mississippi, the Gay Sisters, and the Ward Singers. He met James Cleveland in the late 1950s, and in 1960, at Cleveland's request, he began recording with Cleveland, backed by the choir of the First Baptist Church of Nutley, New Jersey, of which he had recently become pastor.

As a record producer always searching for new and different talent, Roberts attended Cleveland's GMWA convention each year and selected a choir to sign with

his label. Over the fifteen years of his association with Cleveland, he not only introduced many choirs into the national gospel scene but made Cleveland's workshop
the springboard to a recording career. He and Cleveland worked closely in establishing new gospel devices, such as variations on the standard vamp and polyphonic
call-and-response patterns.

Edward Smith

Edward M. Smith (1935–94) was born in Detroit, Michigan, attended Northwestern
High School, and graduated from Highland Park Junior College. His gospel career
began in 1962 as cofounder and business manager for the Harold Smith Majestics.
The owner of two florist shops, Smith developed a keen sense of business, which he
applied to his management of the Majestics and other gospel groups in Detroit.

Smith met Cleveland in the early 1960s and sang in several of his choirs during
Cleveland's stay in Detroit. When Cleveland organized the GMWA, he asked Smith
to act as its executive director, a position Smith held from 1975 until his death. It
was through Smith's management skills that the workshop became one of the most
successful financial ventures in gospel music.

GOSPEL ON BROADWAY

Religious dramas, complete with costumes, lights, scenery, and music, have
been part of African American church activities since the first quarter of this century.
Labeled by scholars as "recreational dramatics," the plays served several purposes:
fund raising, sacred entertainment, opportunities for actors and singers to display
their talents, and the introduction of new songs. William H. Wiggins, Jr., in a 1982
paper entitled "'From Auction Block to…Nativity': A Study of the Evolution of Black
Gospel Drama," noted that in 1937 *Heaven Bound* became the first of these church
dramas to be taken from its original church stage and performed on a professional
stage. (While Hall Johnson's *Run, Little Chillun* played on Broadway in 1933 and
used spirituals and folk songs for music—the usual music for these dramas—it was
not conceived nor presented as a church drama.)

Wiggins further noted that 1941 was the year that gospel musical made its debut:

> In 1941 W. Herbert Brewster, a Baptist minister from Memphis, Tennessee, had
> his religious drama, From Auction Block to Glory, *produced at the National*

Baptist Convention's annual meeting [in Memphis]. On the surface, there would not appear to be much to suggest that this would turn out to be a watershed event in Black American culture.... But Brewster's From Auction Block to Glory *broke...old dramatic molds. It was the first nationally staged black religious play that featured gospel songs written to be sung during that production.*

Brewster continued to write and stage gospel musicals and introduced several of his most popular songs within the drama. Among these were "Move on up a Little Higher," "How Far Am I from Canaan?" and "They Are They." In many instances church dramas were the only live theater many churchgoers saw since most traditional Protestant denominations frowned upon attending films and dramatic plays. These congregations adopted church dramas and inserted well-known gospel songs for music.

While Brewster moved the church drama from the church to the auditorium and composed gospel songs especially for the production, Langston Hughes (1902-1967), a prolific author and poet, moved the gospel song-play from small city theaters to the *great white way*. Hughes approached popular music composer Jobe Huntley in 1956 and asked him to write music for a play about a "store-front church and how it got started." As Hughes wrote scenes and song lyrics for the play he would pass them to Huntley who set them to music. The musical was completed in early 1957 and entitled *Tambourines to Glory, A Musical Melodrama*. Hughes pitched the play from early 1957 until March 1958 when he was notified that the Theater Guild would stage the play in summer stock in Westport, Connecticut. Among the actors and singers contracted for the summer stock performances were Hazel Scott, Nipsey Russell, John Sellars, Joseph Battles, Theresa Merritt, and, to provide an authentic gospel flavor, Clara Ward was cast as Birdie Lee. Eva Jessye conducted the choir and Sam Price led the orchestra.

The show opened in Westport on December 5, 1958 and ran through September 10, 1959. The opening night reviews were glowing, but despite the reviews and positive responses to audience questionnaires Hughes could not find a producer willing to gamble on a gospel musical for Broadway. Hoping that a producer would come forth in a few months, Hughes turned his attention to a gospel song-play celebrating the birth of Christ. Using dialogue, pantomime, dance, and song, Hughes fashioned *Black Nativity: A Gospel Song-Play* into a tapestry of African American religious and musical expressions. Fully aware of the rich legacy of Christmas Negro spirituals and Christmas gospel songs, Hughes chose well-known songs rather than new compositions for the production. The cast included gospel singer Alex Bradford and the Bradford Singers who were still riding high on "Too Close to Heaven"; Marion Williams and the Stars of Faith; the partially blind former concert singer Princess Stewart, with the entire production under the direction of Vinnette Carrol; and with dances staged by Louis Johnson. Although each of these groups and soloists sang separately, when they formed a chorus they turned New York's 41st Street Theater into a Pentecostal church. Among the well-known songs in the production were "Sweet Little Jesus Boy," "Mary, What You Gonna Name That Pretty Little Baby?" and "Children, Go Where I Send Thee." *Black Nativity* ran on Broadway for two years. After closing in New York the play had a successful run in London, toured throughout Europe, and filmed for television in Cannes, for which it received the Catholic Dove Award. Although the play has not returned to Broadway, it has become a Christmas staple in large cities throughout the United States, often involving casts of hundreds.

While *Black Nativity* ran in London Hughes turned his attention again to *Tambourines to Glory*. It was not until 1963, five years after its original summer stock production, that producers Joel Schenker, Hexter Productions and Sidney S. Baron agreed to take *Tambourines* to Broadway. Huntley wrote in his 1983 book *I Remember Langston Hughes*:

> When casting was completed, Louis Gossett and Hilda Harris were in the leading roles, Rosetta LeNoire played the mother, Clara Ward, Joseph Attles, and Anna English signed to play the roles they had created at Westport. Newcomers to the cast were Micki Grant and Robert Guillaume who played the young lovers. Lyn Hamilton played the Deaconess, Al Fann and Ruby Challenger were the policemen.

Vinnette Carrol directed for the second time and developed a first-rate production. The show opened on November 2, 1963, again to excellent reviews. To promote the play and ensure a continued big box office, Clara Ward and some of the singers from the show were scheduled to appear on the Ed Sullivan Show on Sunday night,

November 24. Jobe Huntley reported that he went to the theater late on Friday, November 22 and was sitting in a dressing room watching television when the news announced that President John F. Kennedy had been shot. In a dramatic show of respect all theaters on Broadway closed for the weekend, and Ms. Ward's appearance on the Ed Sullivan Show was canceled. *Tambourines to Glory* never regained momentum and closed after only twenty-six performances.

Black Nativity and *Tambourines to Glory* have not returned to Broadway but they inspired several gospel Broadway musicals and musicals that featured gospel songs. Of more importance is the continued influence of these two gospel musicals; they set the singing style for black Broadway musicals. Whether in *Purlie* (1970), *Don't Bother Me, I Can't Cope* (1972), *Raisin* (1973)—a musical version of *Raisin in the Sun*, *The Wiz* (1975), or *Dreamgirls* (1982), Broadway has been shouting to the gospel sound.

GOSPEL ABROAD

African American sacred music became the sensation of Europe in 1873 when the Fisk Jubilee Singers sang before Queen Victoria and other European royalty. A number of jubilee quartets went to Europe in the 1920s, and although Negro spirituals were featured in their concerts, the popular music of the period occupied the center of their repertoire. Gospel music as composed by Dorsey, Martin, Brewster, and Bradford did not reach Europe until 1953, when Mahalia Jackson toured Europe and made a sensational debut at Albert Hall in London.

The Golden Gate Quartet made their first tour of Europe in 1953 and although they had changed the Negro spiritual from sacred to popular music, spirituals were nonetheless included in their concerts. Likewise, J. Robert Bradley went to Europe in the 1960s to study and sing, but he divided his concerts between European art music, Negro spirituals, and the music of his mentor Lucie Campbell and other gospel composers of the National Baptist Convention.

Clara Ward and the Ward Singers made a much publicized tour of Europe in 1962, which culminated with a heavily attended concert in the Holy Land. In the same year Alex Bradford, Marion Williams, and Princess Stewart appeared in *Black Nativity* in several countries on the continent.

For the 1963 Spoleto Festival of Two Worlds, Gian-Carlo Menotti invited the Roberta Martin Singers, Madame Ernestine B. Washington, the Lorraine Ellison

Singers, the Twilight Gospel Singers, and Professor Albert Miller to perform. Presenting gospel in Italy suggested that gospel was no longer a ghetto music.

With their fondness for African American music in Europe, and especially gospel—a music so foreign to their culture—it was not surprising that Europeans accepted this music as another American innovation.

DESERTERS AND JOINERS

In the late 1950s, promoters of acts that appeared at Carnegie Hall, Radio City Music Hall, and Madison Square Garden approached gospel singers about appearances in those hallowed entertainment halls. Some promoters went further and described a utopia if gospel singers would only change their repertoire and performance attire—not their style—and become soul or popular music performers. Many were approached, but few accepted the offer. Ironically, those who accepted the invitation were some of the best performers in gospel.

Lou Rawls and the Pilgrim Travelers

Wynona Carr, for example, spent the last five years of her life performing in supper clubs and theaters where gospel was never mentioned. In addition to the love songs that she composed, she included such standard jazz repertoire as "Satin Doll" and "For All We Know." But Carr was not nearly as successful as Della Reese of the Meditation Singers who, with her 1954 release of "Don't You Know," moved from the choir loft to plush supper clubs and theaters.

Male *a cappella* quartets yielded a host of singers who switched to popular or soul music. The first singer during the last half of the Golden Age to make the switch was Sam Cooke, leader of the Soul Stirrers. His replacement in the Soul Stirrers, Johnnie Taylor, switched from gospel to soul music in the late 1950s, while Bobby Womack and the Womack Brothers quartet, who had sung gospel professionally for ten years, changed their name to the Valentines and sang soul music before Bobby left to become a single act. Lou Rawls sang with the Pilgrim Travelers from 1950 to 1960 when he left to begin a career as a nightclub singer. Wilson Pickett, who served a tenure with the Detroit-based Violinaires, left to join the rhythm and blues group the Falcons and eventually went on to a solo career. O. V. Wright scored a success with his pop recording of "Little Green Apples," after a tenure with the Spirit of Memphis. Brook Benton had learned his craft as a lead singer with the Bill Langford, and Joe Hinton left the Spirit of Memphis for the world of soul. Marie Knight, like her one-time partner Sister Rosetta Tharpe, recorded and performed popular music before returning to the church and becoming a minister. Imogene Green, the Pilgrim Travelers (under the name of the Travelers), and the Selah Jubilee Quartet (under the name of the Larks) all recorded secular music.

Conversely, a number of rhythm and blues and blues artists had "born-again" experiences and turned to gospel. Among these are Solomon Burke, Candi Staten, and Gatemouth Moore. Little Richard and Al Green both announced a born-again experience but that experience did not forbid their still singing secular music.

James Cleveland, the
crowned prince of gospel

Conclusion: I Looked Down the Line and I Wondered
1965 and Beyond

James Cleveland followed his 1963 hit "Peace, Be Still" with a string of successful recordings unlike any gospel artist before. He introduced choirs from around the nation in a series of recordings called "James Cleveland Presents," and by the end of the 1950s the choir, often with as many as 500 singers, had become the ideal sound in gospel. While Brother Joe May, Mahalia Jackson, Edna Gallmon Cooke, and other soloists were still in demand, gospel adopted a "more the merrier" attitude, and the gospel choir finally came into its own. The gospel audience grew by leaps and bounds, and it was not unusual for a gospel concert to garner an attendance of five to seven thousand; major record labels—before recording only white gospel singers and popular music artists—began contracting black gospel singers, and television beckoned gospel singers both current and past (Della Reese, Al Green, Little Richard). Major auditoriums, once hesitant to book gospel singers, sought out gospel packages for Sunday afternoons. Black gospel became big business, and artist fees, modest by any comparison only a few years earlier, rose astronomically. Cleveland, who by 1965 had earned the title "Crown Prince of Gospel," presided over gospel's new status in a princely fashion. And he should have.

He had inherited the mantle of singers who began their struggle for musical acceptance in store-front churches, dressed in threadbare robes, and singing to untuned upright pianos. These same performers' position elevated to presenting concerts in the Hollywood Bowl and Albert Hall, with limousine service to the stage door, large audiences, and fees that would satisfy rock stars. Equally important as the trappings was the development of the music and the style of performance. What began as experimentation in melody, harmony, and rhythm had evolved into a refined gospel song and style attractive enough to be performed at the inauguration of a president of the United States. But all was not well, for even though gospel was beloved in 1965, there was a faction within the group that was a decade or more younger than the leaders. This new generation wished not only for a modern sound in gospel but also more access to the popular music market. They wanted to drop choir robes and business suits and don the latest in casual fashions; they wanted to add synthesizers, drum machines, and other instruments from popular music, and they wanted a greater association with popular music performers. Popular songs were given religious words in order to attract a popular music market (Paul Anka's "My Way" became "His Way" and "I Had a Talk with My Man Last Night" became "I Had a Talk with God Last Night"), and gospel singers became the opening act for popular and blues singers. What once had been a genuine expression of ecstasy in responding to gospel soon became vocal and physical cliched responses to the music. In fact, gospel was bursting out of the world it had created.

It was at this time, 1969, that Edwin Hawkins rescued the uneasiness with "O Happy Day." Unfortunately "O Happy Day" had its largest sale among new gospel music lovers who wanted more of the same—and with few references to God, Christ, and heaven. Important to note is that the audience that clamored for more of the Hawkins gospel was not composed of anthropologists, sociologists, or ethnomusicologists who wanted to observe the music in its natural habitat. Instead it was made up of music and dance loving people who cared nothing for the gospel background or significance; the music just had to be catchy and rhythmic. A group of gospel singers were willing to comply with this demand but did not understand that in so doing, they presented music that did not necessarily further God's kingdom in the land. The next generation of gospel musicians would be challenged to bring back together the secular and religious sides of gospel. While there would always be singers who would attempt to carry on the legacy of Thomas A. Dorsey, Mahalia Jackson, and Roberta Martin—most notably Delois Barrett and the Barrett Singers, Vanessa Bell Armstrong, and Walter Hawkins—there would also be a cadre of singers who would fuse the Dorsey legacy with the music of jazz, rhythm and blues, and popular music. Chief among them would be the Winans, Take 6, Commissioned and BeBe and CeCe.

Like New Orleans traditional music (Dixieland), traditional gospel—the kind that Dorsey espoused—will survive as *one* type of gospel, for in the near future there will surely be many types of black gospel music. Like the blues, gospel will become part of the fabric of American music and will become synonymous with American music. It will be heard in elevators, over telephones, in department stores, movies, and commercials.

But while it is being used for advertising and dancing, it will also be used for meditation and worship. As the Reverend C. L. Franklin said, "Gospel music mends the broken heart, raises the bowed-down head, and gives hope to the weary traveler." Indeed, each time gospel serves such a function, it will surely create a "Happy Day."

BIBLIOGRAPHY

Allen, Ray. *Singing in the Spirit: African American Sacred Quartets in New York City*. Philadelphia: University of Pennsylvania Press, 1991.

Allen, William Francis, Charles Pickard Ware, and Lucy McKim Garrison. *Slave Songs of the United States*. New York: Freeport Press. (reprint; Books for Libraries Press, New York, 1971).

Anderson, R. and G. North. *Gospel Music Encyclopedia*. New York: Sterling Publishing, 1979.

Baker, Barbara Welsey. *Black Gospel Music Styles*, Ph.D. dissertation. Baltimore: University of Maryland, 1978.

Boyer, Horace Clarence. *An Analysis of Black Church Music with Examples Drawn from Rochester, New York*, Ph.D. dissertation. New York: Eastman School of Music (University of Rochester), 1973.

Boyer, Horace Clarence. *The Gospel Song: An Historical and Analytical Survey*, Master's thesis. New York: Eastman School of Music (University of Rochester), 1964.

Boyer, Horace Clarence, ed. *Lift Every Voice and Sing: An African American Hymnal*. New York: Church Hymnal Corporation, 1993.

Cobb, Charles. *A Theoretical Analysis of Black Quartet Music*, Master's thesis. Madison, WI: University of Wisconsin at Madison, 1974.

Cobbins, Otha B. *History of the Church of Christ (Holiness) U.S.A.* New York: Vantage Press, 1966.

Cone, James H. *The Spirituals and the Blues*. New York: Seabury Press, 1972.

Corum, Fred T. and A. Harper Sizelove, eds. *Like As of Fire: Newspapers from the Azusa Street World Wide Revival*. Washington, D.C.: Middle Atlantic Regional Press, 1985.

Davis, John P., ed. *The American Reference Book*. Englewood Cliffs, New Jersey: Prentice-Hall, Inc., 1966.

Dixon, Robert M. W. and John Godrich, comp. *Blues and Gospel Records, 1902-1942*. London: Storyville Publications and Co., 1963.

DuPree, Sherry Sherrod and Herbert C. DuPree. *African American Good News (Gospel) Music*. Washington, D.C.: Middle Atlantic Regional Press, 1993.

DuPree, Sherry Sherrod. *Biographical Dictionary of African American Holiness: Pentecostals, 1880-1990*. Washington, D.C.: Middle Atlantic Regional Press, 1989.

Goreau, Laurraine. *Just Mahalia, Baby*. Waco, Texas: Word Books, Publishers, 1975.

Harris, Michael W. *The Rise of Gospel Blues: The Music of Thomas Andrew Dorsey in the Urban Church*. New York: Oxford University Press, 1992.

Hayes, Cedric. *A Discography of Gospel Records, 1931-1971*. Copenhagen, Denmark: Knudson Music, 1973.

Heilbut, Anthony. *The Gospel Sound: Good News and Bad Times*. New York: Limelight Editions, 1985.

Hillsman, Joan. *The Progress of Gospel Music: From Spirituals to Contemporary Gospel*. New York: Vantage Press, 1983.

Hine, Darlene Clark. *Black Women in America: An Historical Encyclopedia*, Vols. 1 and 2. Brooklyn, New York: Carlson Publishing, Inc., 1993.

Hitchcock, H. Wiley and Stanley Sadie. *New Grove Dictionary of American Music*, Vol. II. New York: Grove's Dictionaries of Music, Inc., 1986.

Huntley, Jobe. *I Remember Langston Hughes*. New York: Huntley Press, 1983.

Jackson, Irene V. *Afro-American Gospel Music and Its Social Setting with Special Attention to Roberta Martin*, PhD. dissertation. Middletown, CT: Wesleyan University, 1974.

Jackson, Irene V., ed. *Afro-American Religious Music: A Bibliography and Catalogue of Gospel Music*. Westport, CT: Greenwood Press, 1979.

Jackson, Mahalia and Evan McLeod White. *Movin' on Up*. New York: Hawthorne Books, 1966.

Jones, Ralph H. *Charles Albert Tindley: Prince of Preachers*. Nashville: Abingdon Press, 1982.

Levine, Lawrence W. *Black Culture and Black Consciousness: Afro-American Folk Thought from Slavery to Freedom*. New York: Oxford University Press, 1977.

Lincoln, C. Eric and Lawrence H. Mamiya. *The Black Church in the African American Experience*. Durham, NC: Duke University Press, 1990.

Lornell, Kip. *Happy in the Service of the Lord: Afro-American Gospel Quartets in Memphis*. Urbana, IL: University of Illinois Press, 1988.

Lornell, Kip. *Virginia's Blues, Country, and Gospel Records 1902-1943: An Annotated Discography*. Lexington, KY: University of Kentucky Press, 1989.

M'Nemar, Richard. *The Kentucky Revival*. Cincinnati, OH: E. and E. Horsford, 1808.

Murray, Albert. *Stomping the Blues*. New York: Schirmer Books, 1976.

O'Daniel, Therman B. *Langston Hughes, Black Genius: A Critical Evaluation*. New York: William Morrow and Company, Inc., 1971.

Oliver, Paul. *Songsters and Saints: Vocal Traditions on Race Records*. New York: Cambridge University Press, 1984.

Paris, Arthur E. *Black Pentecostalism: Southern Religion in an Urban World*. Amherst, MA: University of Massachusetts Press, 1982.

Patterson, J. O., German Ross, and Julia Atkins Mason. *History of Formation of the Church of God in Christ with Excerpts from the Life and Works of Its Founder—Bishop C. H. Mason*. Memphis: Church of God in Christ Publishers, 1969.

Payne, Wardell J., ed. *Directory of African American Religious Bodies*. Washington, D.C.: Howard University Press, 1991.

Raichelson, Richard M. *Black Religious Folk Song: A Study in Generic and Social Change*, Ph.D. dissertation. Philadelphia: University of Pennsylvania, 1975.

Reagon, Bernice Johnson, ed. *We'll Understand It Better By and By: Pioneering African American Gospel Composers*. Washington, D.C.: Smithsonian Institution Press, 1993.

Roberts, Lawrence C. *The Gospel Truth*. Pittsburgh: Dorrance Publishing Company, Inc., 1993.

Rubman, Kerrill L. *From "Jubilee" to "Gospel" in Black Male Quartet Singing*, Master's thesis. Chapel Hill, NC: University of North Carolina at Chapel Hill, 1980.

Sherwood, William Henry. *Harp of Zion*. Petersburg, VA: Sherwood Orphan School, 1893.

Southern, Eileen. *Biographical Dictionary of Afro-American and African Musicians*. Westport, CT: Greenwood Press, 1982.

Southern, Eileen. *The Music of Black Americans: A History*. 2nd ed. New York: W. W. Norton & Company, Inc., 1983.

Southern, Eileen. *Readings in Black American Music*. New York: W. W. Norton & Company, Inc., 1971.

Spencer, Jon Michael. *Protest & Praise: Sacred Music of Black Religions*. Minneapolis, MN: Fortress Press, 1990.

Titon, Jeff Todd, ed. *Reverend C. L. Franklin—Give Me This Mountain—Life History and Selected Sermons*. Urbana and Chicago, IL: University of Illinois Press, 1989.

Townsend, Willa, ed. *Gospel Pearls*. Nashville: Sunday School Publishing Board, 1921.

Tyler, Mary Ann Lancaster. *The Music of Charles Henry Pace and Its Relationship to the Afro-American Church Experience*, Ph.D. dissertation. Pittsburgh: University of Pittsburgh, 1980.

Walker, Wyatt T. *Somebody's Calling My Name: Black Sacred Music and Social Change*. Valley Forge, PA: Judson Press, 1979.

Warner, Jay. *The Billboard Book of Singing Groups—A History 1940-1990*. New York: Watson-Guptill Publications, 1990.

INDEX

SONGS

"All Alone," 176
"All Night, All Day," 219
"Amazing Grace," 61, 87, 130, 248
"Amen," 238
"Back to Dust," 112
"Battle Hymn of the Republic," 42
"Beams of Heaven," 28
"Birmingham Boys," 98
"Blessed Assurance," 180, 219
"Bring the Sun Out," 239
"Can't Turn around Now," 233
"Children, Go Where I Send Thee," 252
"Christ Is All," 75
"Christ Is Coming," 235
"Come Holy Spirit," 210
"Come, Ye Disconsolate," 117
"Daniel in the Lion's Den," 159, 160
"Dear Lord, Look Down upon Me," 113, 122
"Death Is Riding through the Land," 40
"Denomination Blues," 39
"Dig a Little Deeper in God's Love," 76, 173
"Do You Love Him," 236
"Does Jesus Care," 161, 162
"Don't Drive Your Children Away," 133
"Don't Drive Your Mama Away," 222
"Don't Forget the Family Prayer," 77
"Don't You Know," 255
"Even a Child Can Open the Gate," 144
"Even Me," 87
"Evening Sun," 238
"Every Day and Every Hour," 78, 228, 243
"Everybody Get Your Business Right," 40
"Everybody Ought to Love His Soul," 96
"Eyes Hath Not Seen," 76, 93, 207
"Ezekiel Saw the Wheel," 11
"Faded Roses," 222
"Failure's Not in God," 239
"Faith Can Move Mountains," 141
"Farther Along," 171
"15 Rounds with Jesus," 130
"For All We Know," 255
"Get Away Jordan," 215
"Get Right with God," 115
"Give Me My Flowers," 247
"Glory to the New Born King," 112

"God Be with You Till We Meet Again," 183
"God Be with You," 183, 206, 210
"God Is So Good to Me," 208
"God Is Still on the Throne," 68
"God Rode in a Wind Storm," 115
"God Shall Wipe All Tears Away," 73, 88
"God Will Take Care of You," 243
"God's Goin' to Separate the Wheat from the Tare," 73, 88
"God's Little Birds," 179
"God's Power Changes Things," 65
"Going to Canaan," 235
"Grace Is Sufficient," 247
"Great Day," 81
"Grow Closer," 208
"Hallelujah, It's Done," 221
"Hand Me Down My Silver Trumpet, Gabriel," 83
"Handwriting on the Wall," 39
"He Knows How Much We Can Bear," 68
"He Knows My Heart," 89
"He Lifted My Burdens," 236
"He Sits High and Looks Low," 225
"He Took My Sins Away," 98
"He Understands, He'll Say 'Well Done'," 92, 115, 139, 181, 244
"He'll Wash You Whiter Than Snow," 64, 207, 228
"He's a Friend of Mine," 206
"He's All I Need," 78
"He's Alright with Me," 235
"He's Got Better Things for You," 40
"He's My Lord," 101
"He's Using Me," 248
"Heavenly Sunshine," 144, 145
"Hide Me in Thy Bosom," 155
"His Way," 258
"Holy Ghost Singing," 16
"Holy Spirit Surely Is My Comforter," 118
"Honey in the Rock," 39
"How Far Am I from Canaan," 251
"How Much I Owe," 101, 178
"I Believe in Thee," 225
"I Call Him Jesus, My Rock," 80–81
"I Can Put My Trust in Jesus," 92
"I Can See Everybody's Mother, but I Can't See Mine," 183, 202
"I Can Tell the World About This," 66
"I Claim Jesus First and Last," 64
"I Come to the Garden Alone," 162
"I Do, Don't You," 59
"I Get a Blessing Everyday," 248

"I Had a Talk with God Last Night," 258
"I Have Decided to Follow Jesus," 245
"I Heard the Preaching of the Elders," 33
"I Know the Lord Will Make a Way, Oh Yes, He Will," 69, 70, 171
"I Need Thee Every Hour," 117, 242
"I Never Heard of a City Like the New Jerusalem," 141
"I Shall Wear a Crown," 38
"I Thank You, Lord," 163
"I Trust Him on My Journey All the Way," 151
"I Want a Double Portion of God's Love," 208
"I Want Jesus to Walk around My Bedside," 96, 164
"I Want to Rest," 89
"I Wish My Mother Was on That Train," 39
"I Won't Be Back No More," 225
"I Won't Let Go," 215
"I Won't Sell Out," 228
"I'd Trade a Lifetime," 245
"I'll Be a Servant for the Lord," 75
"I'll Never Let Go His Hand," 79
"I'll Tell It Wherever I Go," 64
"I'm a Soldier in the Army of the Lord," 23, 24
"I'm Bound for Canaan Land," 100, 138
"I'm Bound for Higher Ground," 78
"I'm Going to Die with the Staff in My Hand," 70, 76, 77
"I'm Going to Leave You in the Hands of the Lord," 201
"I'm Going to Tell God All about It," 89, 200
"I'm Going to Wait Until My Change Comes," 89
"I'm Going to Walk That Milky White Way," 65
"I'm Happy in the Service of the Lord," 146
"I'm Happy with Jesus Alone," 21, 22, 43
"I'm in the Battlefield for My Lord," 25
"I'm Just Waiting on the Lord," 68
"I'm Leaning and Depending on the Lord," 141
"I'm Not Tired Yet," 222
"I'm Sealed," 214
"I'm Sending My Timber up to Heaven," 73
"I'm So Glad Jesus Lifted Me," 183

"I'm Waiting for My Child to Come Home," 246
"I'm Willing to Run," 200
"I've Been Running for Jesus a Long Time," 222
"I've Got a Witness," 242
"I've Got the River of Jordan to Cross," 138
"I've Had My Chance," 179
"If I Don't Get There," 43, 59–60
"If We Never Needed the Lord Before..." 183
"If You Just Keep Still," 135
"If You See My Savior," 99
"In My Home over There," 87, 181
"In My Savior's Care," 179
"In the Morning When I Rise," 115
"In the Morning," 113
"In the Sweet By and By," 16
"In the Upper Room," 91, 214
"It Don't Cost Very Much," 64
"It's My Desire to Do Thy Will," 81
"Jesu, Joy of Man's Desiring," 240
"Jesus Gave Me Water," 140, 174, 198
"Jesus Is Always There," 128
"Jesus Is the Only One," 103
"Jesus Lover of My Soul," 240
"Jesus Met the Woman at the Well," 174
"Jesus on the Main Line, Tell Him What You Want," 154
"Jesus Only," 21
"Jesus Steps Right in When I Need Him Most," 76, 116
"Jesus Will Answer Prayer," 122
"Jesus, When Troubles Burden Me Down," 112
"Jesus," 107, 166, 174
"Johnny and Jesus," 224
"Jonah," 44
"Joshua Fit the Battle of Jericho," 11
"Joy Bells Ringing in My Soul," 103
"Just a Closer Walk with Thee," 75
"Just a Little Talk with Jesus," 150, 151, 152
"Just Look for Me in Heaven," 206
"Just over the Hill," 91, 141
"Just to God Be True," 233
"Keep Me Every Day," 88
"King Jesus Will Roll All Burdens Away," 76
"Lead Me, Guide Me," 208–9
"Leave It There," 28, 43
"Let It Breathe on Me," 65
"Let Jesus Fix It for You," 28
"Let Us All Go Back to the Old Landmark," 143
"Let Us Sing Praise," 210
"Let's Go Out to the Program," 123
"Let's Talk about Jesus," 172, 179
"Little Boy," 25

"Little Green Apples," 255
"Little Weather-Beaten White-washed Church," 45
"Living on Mother's Prayers," 202
"Lonesome Road," 155
"Lord Jesus," 147
"Lord, Come See About Me," 122
"Lord, Don't Move the Mountain," 208, 223
"Lord, Help Me to Hold Out," 129, 248
"Lord, I've Tried," 70, 144
"Lord, Lord, Lord," 228
"Lordy, Won't You Come by Here," 161
"Mary, Don't You Weep," 177–78, 223
"Mary, What You Gonna Name That Pretty Little Baby," 252
"May the Work I've Done Speak for Me," 246
"Milky White Way," 171
"Mother Bowed," 174
"Move on up a Little Higher," 65, 89–90, 110, 141, 143, 144, 214, 251
"Must Jesus Bear the Cross Alone," 61
"My Life Is in His Hands," 146
"My Man and I," 155
"My Soul Is a Witness for My Lord," 37
"My Troubles Are So Hard to Bear," 180
"Neerer to Thee," 198
"Negro Gospel and Religious Festival," 168
"Never Grow Old," 130
"New Born Soul," 235
"No Charge," 222
"No Coward Soldier," 225
"No Tears in Heaven," 229
"Nothing Between," 28
"Now Lord," 79–80
"O Happy Day," 5, 209, 258
"Oh Lord, Be My Protector," 244
"Oh Lord, Is It I," 72
"Oh Lord, Stand by Me," 248
"Oh, My Lord," 88
" Old Account Was Settled," 72
"Old Ship of Zion," 72
"On the Battlefield," 235
"Only a Look," 68
"Only What You Do for Christ Will Last," 229
"Operator, Operator," 131
"Our Father," 201
"Our God Is Able," 107, 141, 143, 144
"Own Me as a Child," 232
"Packing Up," 232
"Peace Be Still," 248, 257

"Peace in the Valley," 234
"Please Be Patient with Me," 220
"Pray for Me," 246
"Prayer Changes Things," 71
"Precious Is He," 103
"Precious Lord," 89
"Reach out and Touch Him," 233
"Rock Me," 155
"Rock My Soul in the Bosom of Abraham," 11
"Salvation Is Free," 127
"Satin Doll," 255
"Satisfied," 239
"Save Hallelujah," 127
"Saved Till the Day of Redemption," 72
"Savior Don't Pass Me By," 132
"Search Me, Lord," 122, 137, 166
"Sending up My Timber up to Heaven," 65
"Shadrack, Meshack, and Abendigo," 45
"Shake a Hand," 165
"Shine for Jesus," 42
"Should I Ever Love Again," 131
"Show Me the Way," 233
"Signed and Sealed with His Blood," 144
"Soldiers in the Army," 223
"Somebody Bigger Than You and I," 79, 225
"Somebody Save Me," 181
"Somebody Touched Me," 182, 234
"Something within Me," 132
"Somewhere to Lay My Head," 204, 236
"Southbound Train," 98
"Sow Righteous Seeds," 101
"Stand by Me," 28, 42, 57, 70, 171
"Standing Here Wondering Which Way to Go," 232
"Standing on the Highway," 100
"Step by Step," 244
"Stop Gambler," 238
"Strange Things Happening Every Day," 156, 157
"Surely God Is Able," 107-08, 110
"Sweeping through the City," 222
"Sweet Little Jesus Boy," 252
"Sweet, Sweet Spirit," 208
"Take My Hand, Precious Lord," 61, 76, 91, 139, 224
"Take Your Burden to the Lord," 39
"Tales from Harlem," 168
"Teach Me How to Pray," 236
"Telephone to Glory," 40
"Testify," 25
"Thank God, They Are as Well as They Are," 246
"Thank You, Jesus," 174
"That's All," 155
"That's Enough," 215

"That's Heaven to Me," 198
"The Ball Game," 130
"The Boy and the Kite," 224
"The Church Is Moving On," 26, 27
"The Denied Mother," 224
"The First Noël," 115
"The Last Mile of the Way," 204–5
"The Lord Is My Shepherd," 245
"The Lord's Prayer," 183
"The Old Lady's House," 224
"There Is a Fountain Filled with Blood," 130
"There's Gonna Be Joy," 178
"There's Not a Friend Like the Lonely Jesus," 112
"These Are They," 91, 118
"Think of His Goodness in You," 219
"Think of His Goodness to Me," 243
"This Same Jesus," 181
"Throw out the Lifeline," 235
"Thy Servant's Prayer, Amen," 93
"Tight Like That," 59
"To Me He's So Wonderful," 103
"To Whom Shall I Turn," 225
"Today," 164
"Too Close to Heaven," 115, 220, 228, 252
"Touch Me, Lord Jesus," 112, 113
"Tree of Level," 150
"Try Jesus, He Satisfies," 68
"Twelve Gates to the City," 115
"Unclouded Day," 242
"Up above My Head," 158
"Walk Around," 97, 164
"Walk in the Light," 118
"Walk on by Faith," 248
"We Are Climbing Jacob's Ladder," 11
"We'll Soon Be Done with Troubles and Trials," 152
"We'll Understand It Better By and By," 28–29, 43
"We're Crossing over One by One," 229
"We've Come This Far by Faith," 210–11
"What a Friend We Have in Jesus," 160, 196
"What Are They Doing in Heaven," 28, 45, 173
"What Could I Do if It Wasn't for the Lord," 183
"When God Dips His Love in My Heart," 151
"When He Calls," 178
"When He Spoke," 208
"When I Cross Over," 246
"When I Lost My Mother," 202
"When I've Done the Best I Can," 181

"When My Saviour Calls Me Home," 112
"Where Shall I Be When the First Trumpet Sounds," 21
"Why I Like-a Roosevelt," 44
"Why Should I Worry," 72
"Will Jesus Be Waiting," 200
"Will the Circle Be Unbroken," 242
"Wouldn't Mind Dying if Dying Was All," 39
"Yes, God Is Real," 75
"Yes, Lord," 23
"Yield Not to Temptation," 206
"You Can't Beat God Giving," 208
"You Can't Hurry God," 215, 218
"You Must Be Born Again," 215
"You Send Me," 196

SUBJECTS

a cappella, 36, 47, 48
Abrams, Lawrence, 200
activity singer, 121
Adams, Fay, 165, *167*
Adrewettes, 223
African Methodist Episcopal, 82
Akers, Doris, 92, 208
Alexander, J. W., 131, 173, 198–99, 214
Allen, Bill "Hoss," 53
Allen, Estelle, 88
Allen, George N., 61
Allen, Ray, 153
Allen, William Frances, 12
Allison, Margaret, 111–13, 119
alter call, 13
AME, *see* African Methodist Episcopal
American Federation of Musicians, 51
American Negro Spirituals, 9
Anderson, James, 178
Anderson, Queen Candice, 89, 107, 143–44
Anderson, Robert, 67, 70–72, 92, 205
Andrews, Inez, 222–23
Angelic Gospel Singers, 112–13
Apollo Theater, 190–91, 245
Apostolic Faith Gospel Mission, 15
Argo Singers, 235
Armstrong, Bertha, *58*
Armstrong, Joe, 171
Armstrong, Vanessa Bell, 24, 259
Assemblies of God, 16
Attles, Joseph, 252
Ausbrooks, Dave, 33
Azusa Street Movement, *see* Azusa Street Revival
Azusa Street Revival, 12–13, 15, 20
   closed, 205
   favored music, 47
   Mason, Charles, 22

new music, 16
racism, 15
rise of gospel, 103
simple refrains, 62
Smith, Lucy, 78
Babb brothers, 178
Babb, Morgan, 240
Bailey, Bishop, 123
Bainbridge Street Methodist Church, 28
band, gospel, 184–85
Banks Brothers, 24, 118, 242
Banks, Lucie, 118
Bannister, Ethel Davenport, 180
Baptist Church, 8, 14, 19
   gospel, 43
   and Smith, Willie Mae Ford, 134
   split, 20
   Sunday concerts, 47
Baptist Training Union (BTU), 139
Barber, Keith, 173
Barnes, Larry, 132
Barnett, Vernon, W., 31
Barnwell, Charlie, 178
Baronets, 203
Barrett Singers, 259
Barrett, Delois, 67, 70, 117, 259
Bass, Martha, 134, 138
battle of song, 121
Battle, John H., 148
Battles, Joseph, 251
Beal, Charlie, 99
Beale, Beatrice, 81
Beamon, Gladys, 79
Beasley, Paul, 239
BeBe and CeCe, 259
Bells of Joy, 179
Benton, Brook, 255
Berman, Bess, 89
Best, Delores, 249
Bethlehem Baptist Church, 124, 130, 133
Bible Way Church of Our Lord Jesus Christ of the Apostolic Faith, 26
Birmingham Jubilee Singers, 33, 98, 99
Bishop Wallace, 156
Black American Music: A History, 12
Black Nativity, 228, 232, 252, 253
Blackwell, Bumps, 199
Bledsoe, "Jet," 146, 147
Blind Boys of Alabama, the Five, 201–2
Blind Boys of Mississippi, the Five, 199–201, *200*
blind gospel singers, 38–40
Blue Jay Singers, the Famous, 33, 98–101, 146
blues, 194–95
BMC Choir, 240

Bobo, Willie, 121, *122*
Boddie, Reverend Louis, 79
Boddie, Sylvia, 79
Boggs, Harold, 240
Bolden, Alfred, 134
Bossard, Henry, 176
Bostic, Joe, 50, *89*, 168
Boush, William, 34
Bowles Music House, 66, 73
Bowles, Lillian, 65, 73
Boyer Brothers, 24, 243–44
Bradford Specials, *227*, 228, 252
Bradford, Alex, 64, 78, 226–29, *227*, 234, 252, 253
Bradley, J. Robert, 144–45, 206, 253
Bram, Emily, 180
Branham, Reverend John L., 181
Brendon, James, 228
Brewer, Cora Juanita, *see* Cora Martin
Brewster Ensemble, 107
Brewster Theological Clinic, 141
Brewster, W. Herbert, 107, 151, 140–43, 250–51, 218
Bridges, Charles, 33, 98, 99
Broadnax, William, 146, 147
Broadway, 250–53
Brother Paul, 52
Brown, Beatrice, 61
Brown, James, 193
Brownlee, Archie, 199–201, *200*, 204
Bryant, Jimmie, 132, 133
Bryant, Sammie, 133
Bunn, Allen, 164
Burke, Solomon, 255
Burns, Ed, 156
Burruss, Connie and Becky, 165
Butter Beans and Susie, 58
Butts, Magnolia Lewis, 60, 65–66, 70, 78
Caesar Singers, 222
Caesar, Shirley, 117, 220–22, 223
Cafe Society, 45, 47, 157
California School of Gospel, 205–11
call and response, 12, 17, 90
Camp Meeting Revival, 8, 9
Campbell, Catherine, 79
Campbell, Charles, 228
Campbell, Lucie E., 42, 44, 115, 138–40, 144–45
Caravans, 146, 191, 218–25, *219*
Carnegie Hall, 44, 46, 156, 168
Carr Singers, 131
Carr, Wynona, 130–32, 229, 255
Carrethers, Harold L., 148
Carrethers, Reverend J. R., 147
Carrethers, Rufus, 148
Carriers, 121
Carrol, Vinnette, 229, 252
Carroll, Howard, 203
Carson, Herbert, 234

Cavalier Singers, *see* Silver Leaf Quartet
Challenger, Ruby, 252
Charles, Ray, 192–93, 249
Cheeks, Reverend Julius "June," 203–5
Chicago Pilgrim Baptist Church, 60
Chicago, 57–103
    publishing houses, 102
    quartet singing, 93–95
    women gospel singers, 100
Childs, Alvin A., 101
Choir of First Church of Deliverance in Chicago, 183
choir, gospel, 181–84
chop jubilees, 119
Church of Christ (Holiness), 20, 21
Church of God in Christ, 21, 23
    Convocation Choir, 127
    director of, 5
    gospel singers from, 24
    and Mason, Charles, 22, 24
    women, 40
Church of Our Lord Jesus Christ of the Apostolic Faith, 25
CIO Singers, 52
Clara Ward House of Music, 111
Clara Ward Specials, 111, 230
Clark Sisters, 126
Clark, Elbernita "Twinkie," 126, 127
Clark, Mattie Moss, 125–27
Clarke, Kenny, 156
Cleveland, James, 125, 128, 225, 247–49
    and Andrews, Inez, 222
    Carnegie Hall, 168
    crowned prince of gospel, *256*, 257–58
    and Franklin, Aretha, 130
    and Roberts, Lawrence, 249–50
    and Smith, Edward M., 250
    and Smith, Harold, 129
Clinkscale, J. T., 199, 200
CME, *see* Colored Methodist Episcopal Church
Coates, Carl, 204
Coates, Dorothy Love, 117, 212–18, *213*, *214*, *215*
Cobb, Arnett, 89
Cobb, C. H., 102
Cobb, Reverend Clarence H., 63, 74
Coldten, Melvin, 164
Cole, Bernice, 113
Cole, Nat "King," 192–93
Colored Methodist Episcopal Church, 45
concert fees, 56
concerts, 51, 187
Connor, William "Pete," 176
Consolers, 246–47
Cooke, Dale, *see* Sam Cooke

Cooke, Edna Gallmon, 237–38, 257
Cooke, Sam, 98, *186*, 195–99, 236, 255
Cooper, Vivian, 158
Copeland, Creadell, 236
copyrights, 89
Cornerstone Institutional Baptist Church, 249
Cotton Blossom Singers, 200
couplets and quatrains, 109–10
Cowans, Henry, 156
Crain, Silas Roy, 95–96
Crawford, William "Pee Wee," 178
Crenshaw, Reverend Robert, 146
Crouch, Andrae, 24, 37
Crouch, Samuel M., Jr., 36
crying in the wilderness, 11
culture, African American, 194
Dabney, Elizabeth, 104
Dabney, Thomas, 104
Daniels Singers, 165–66
Daniels, Billy, 89
Daniels, Jackie, 165–66
Daniels, Nellie Grace, 218
Daniels, Sarah, 92
Darling, James, 100, 146, 147
Dave Weston Singers, 211
Davies, Reverend Samuel, 7
Davis Sisters, 114–17, *116*
Davis, Alfreda, 114
Davis, Audrey, 114
Davis, Carl, 178
Davis, E. Clifford, 118
Davis, James, 119
Davis, Mary Johnson, 117–18, 242
Davis, Reverend Gary, 240
Davis, Ruth "Baby Sister," *114–17*
Davis, Thelma, 114, 117
Davis, Virginia, 80
de Graca, Bishop Marcelino Manoel, *see* Sweet Daddy Grace
Deadwyler, Gertrude, 249
Deas, E. C., 42
Dennis, Archie, *67*
Derricks, Cleavant, 150–52
Detroit, 123–34
Detroiters, *see* Evangelist Singers
Dickinson, Viola Bates, 81
disk jockeys, 52
Dixie Humingbirds, *46*, 118-23, *120*, *122*
    and the Angelic Gospel Singers, 113, 122
    Apollo, 191
    Cafe Society, 47
    formed, 35
    Newport Jazz Festival, 122
    and Simon, Paul, 122
    television, 122
Dixon, Jessy, 238–39
Doane, William Howard, 16

Dolomite Jubilee Singers, 33
Dominoes, 191–92
Don't Bother Me, I Can't Cope,
    228, 253
Dorothy Love Coates Singers, 218
Dorsey, Thomas A., 43, 44,
    57–62, *58*
    Baptist, 87
    California, 205
    and Cleveland, James, 248
    father of gospel, 195
    and Frye, Theodore R., 64–65
    and Jackson, Mahalia, 87
    and Martin, Roberta, 66
    and Martin, Sallie, 62–64
    and Morris, Kenneth, 72
    ridiculed, 82
    and Smith, Willie Mae Ford,
        135, 136
    and the Soul Stirrers, 97
    and the Ward Singers, 104
Dot Akers and Her Swingsters, 208
Douglas, "Memphis" Minnie, 154
Dranes, Arizona, 36–38, 50, 162
Dreamgirls, 253
Drinkard Singers, 133
Dublin, Curtis, 115
Ebenezer Baptist Church, 64, 66, 72
Echoes of Eden Choir, 182–83, 206,
    207, 210
Edmondson, William, 153
"Ed Sullivan Show," 91
Edwards, Jonathan, 6
Edwards, Odessa Glasgow, 214
81 Theater, 58
Elkins, James Lewis, 207
Emmanual Church of God in Christ,
    37
English, Anna, 252
Ensley Jubilee Singers, 33
Ernie's Record Mart of Nashville,
    53, 113, 244
Europe, 45, 253–54
Evangelist Singers, 133
Evans, Clay, 103
Evans, Jennie, 14–15
Evans, John, 132
Excell, Edwin O., 59
Ezion Methodist Episcopal Church,
    27–28
Fairfield Four, 35, 113, 147–50
Falcons, 255
Falls, Mildred, 90, 91
falsetto, 34, 175
family groups, 241–47
Fancy, Sister Cally, 40
Fann, Al, 252
Farley, J. J., 97, 202
Farrow, Reverend Mrs. Lucy F., 13
Fellowship Baptist Church, 103
Fields, Johnny, 201
Fields, Kansas, 156

First Church of Deliverance, 74,
    102, 211
Fisher, Fletcher, 32
Fisk Jubilee Quartet, 30, 33, 153,
    163, 253
Five Royales, 192
Flying Clouds, 132
folk music, African American,
    193–95
Folk, Bessie, 67
Ford Sisters, 135
Ford, Anna Broy Crockett, 123–24
Ford, Esther, 230
Ford, Herman James, 180–81
Ford, Joseph, 200
Forehand, A. C., 39
Forehand, Blind Mamie, 39, 50
Foster Singers, 31–33
Foster, Paul, 98
Foster, R. C., 31, 32, 34
Fountain, Clarence, 201–2
Four Harmony Kings, 175
Francis, James "Blind," 89, 165,
    166
Franklin, Aretha, 111, 124, 125,
    129–30, 193, 249
Franklin, Elmore, 239
Franklin, Reverend C. L., 124–25,
    127, 259
Frazier, Thurston, 209–10
Freeman, Art, 89
Freeman, Isaac "Dickie," 149–50,
    176, 236
Friendly Five, 96
From Auction Block to Glory, 141,
    250–51
"From Spirituals to Swing," 44, 46,
    156
Frye, Theodore R. 57, 60, 61, 64–65
Fryson, Robert, 240
Garden of Prayer Church of God in
    Christ, 104
Gates, Molly Mae, 240
Gay Sisters, 243
Gay, Dettie, 58
Gay, Evelyn, 87, 243
Gay, Geraldine, 243
Gay, Mildred, 87, 243
George, Casietta, 146, 225
Georgia Peach, 47, 89, *159–61*
get on board, 17
Gholson, Clara Hudman, *see* the
    Georgia Peach
Gholston, Reverend T. T., 160
Gibson, Louis, 228
Gipson, Barney, 119
Golden Gate Quartet, 44–45
    Carnegie Hall, 47
    Europe, 253
    and the Five Blind Boys of
        Alabama, 201
    inspiration for, 35, 153

    radio, 52, 171
    and the Selah Jubilee Singers,
        165, *166*
    style, 34
Golden Stars, 146
Good Will Singers, 145, 206
Goodpasteur, Ralph, 101–3, 183
Goodson, Albert A., 210
Gospel All Stars, 234, *235*
gospel beat, 38
gospel blues, 69–70
Gospel Caravan, 71
Gospel Chimes, 239
gospel choir, 49
Gospel Chordettes, 249
Gospel Harmoneers, *see* the
    Original Gospel Harmonettes
Gospel Music Workshop of
    America, 129, 248, 249, 250
Gospel Pearls, 41–44, 59, 82, 97
gospel,
    abroad, 253–54
    audiences, 189
    beginnings, 26
    big business, 257
    California, 205
    Chicago, 57–103
    entitled, 42, 43
    expansion, 187–88
    first composer of, 28
    folk music, 193–95
    Houston, 172
    jazz, 193
    new generation, 47, 50
    New York, 152–69
    peak, 82
    Pentecostalism, 19–20
    piano, 50, 212
    soul music, 192
    spreads around the nation,
        169
    style, 40, 43, 49
    text of songs, 50
    white composers of, 16
Gospel, Spiritual, and Folk Musical
    Festival, 169
Gossett, Louis, 252
GP, see Gospel Pearls
Grace, Sweet Daddy, 185
Gracey, George, 148
Grant, Golius, 32
Grant, Micki, 252
Graves, Blind Roosevelt, 39
Great Awakening, 6
Great Depression, 29
Great Migration, 26
Greater Harvest Baptist Church,
    79, 92
Greater Salem Baptist Church, 86
Green, Al, 255, 257
Green, Imogene, 117, 225, 255
Green, Oliver, 133

Griffin, Anna Quick, 165
Griffin, Bessie, 219, 220
Griffin, Gloria, *67*, 240
growl, 40
Guillaume, Robert, 252
Hall, Carl, 229
Halloran, Jack, 91
Hamilton, Lyn, 252
Hamler, Lon "Big Fat," 33
Hammond, John, 44, 46, 168
Hampton, Lionel, 58
Handly, Levi, 169
Happy Land Singers, *see* the Blind
    Boys of Albama
hard gospel, 117
Harmonizing Four, 34, *35*, 158,
    169–71
Harold Smith Majestics, 250
Harp of Zion, 26, 27
Harper, Billy, 228
Harris, A. C., 146
Harris, Crip, 164
Harris, Hilda, 252
Harris, Rebert H., 95–98, 175,
    197, 200
Hawkins, Edwin, 5, 24, 258
Hawkins, Walter, 24, 259
Haywood, Garfield Thomas, 25
Heaven Bound, 250
Heavenly Gospel Singers, 121
Heidt, Horace, 133
Henry, William, 203
Herman Stevens Singers, *234*
Herndon, James, 225
Heywood, Eddie, 58
Highway QCs, 103, 196, 236
Hines Good Will Singers, 210
Hines, J. Earle, 101, 145, 168,
    182–83, 206, 209, 210
Hinton, Joe, 255
Holiness church, 13–14
Holiness convention, 20
Hollingsworth, James "Jimmie," 99
Holy Temple Church of God in
    Christ, 104
"Hootenanny," 190
Hoover, Odie, 145
Hopkins, Ora Lee, 218
Houston, 172
Houston, Cissy, 133
Houston, Whitney, 133
Howard, Josephine, 225
Hughes, Langston, 251–52
Huntley, Jobe, 251, 252–53
Hymns and Spiritual Songs, 6
Imperials, *233*
inaugurations, 45, 88, 91
Interdenominational Chorus, 207
International Music Department at
    COGIC, 126
International Sweethearts of
    Rhythm, 200

Isaac, Reverend E. W. D., 145
Issac, E. W. D., Sr., 42
Jackson Harmoneers, 200
Jackson Studio of Music, 77
Jackson, Emma L., 76–77
Jackson, Jonathan, 228
Jackson, Mahalia, *48*, 82–91, *84*,
    85, *86*, *89*
    beautician, 88
    and Bradford, Alex, 227
    and Bradley, J. Robert 145
    Carnegie Hall, 168, 188, 189
    and Dorsey, Thomas A. , 87
    "Ed Sullivan Show," 91
    funeral, 145
    and Griffin, Bessie, 220
    influences upon, 85
    international fame, 91
    and King, Martin Luther Jr.,
       91
    and May, Joe , 137
     Newport Jazz Festival, 91,
       189
    popular music, 91
    radio, 89, 90, 91
    recordings, 88, 89
    and Reese, Della, 128
    Sanctified church, 83
    television, 188
Jackson, Myrtle, 240
"James Cleveland Presents," 257
James Cleveland Singers, 248
James, Josephine, 245–46
Jamison, Charlie, 33
jazz, 193
Jefferson County, 31, 33, 34, 98
Jessy Dixon Singers, 239
Jessye, Eva, 251
Jeter, Claude, *175–78*
Jeter, J. A., 20
Johnson Brothers, 86
Johnson, Bernice, 118
Johnson, Blind Willie, 39
Johnson, Bunk, 47
Johnson, James Weldon, 9, 30
Johnson, Joe, 173–74
Johnson, Joseph, 171–72
Johnson, Louis, 176, 252
Johnson, Reverend C. J., 159
Johnson, Sister Bessie, 40
Johnson, Thomas "Goat," 169
Johnson, William "Bunk," 162, 163
Johnson, Willie, 44, 50
Joiner, Ben, 203
Jones, "Prophet," 133
Jones, Charles Price, 20–22, 43
Jones, Deacon, 52
Jones, Jimmy, 170–71, 176, 178
Jones, Ozro Thurston, 103, 119
Jones, Pearl Williams, 26, 240
Jones, Ralph, 90
Jones, Richard M., 37

Jones, Ruth, *see* Dinah Washington
jubilees, *see also* quartet, 119
Keels, James, 171
Kelly, Otha M., 152
Kelsey, Samuel, 25
Kendricks, Professor, 87
Kenneth Morris Jazz Band, 73
Key, Leo "Lot," 33
King, Martin Luther Jr., 64, 91, 129
Kings of Harmony, 185
Knight, Marie, 158–59, 255
Knowles, R. L., 240
Kolb, Vera Conner, 214
Kramer, Worth, 182
Ku Klux Klan, 14, 29
Lands, Elizabeth, 240
Lane, Cleo, 249
Langford, Willie, 44, 164
Larks, *see* the Selah Jubilee Quartet
Lawrence, James, 67
Lawson, Robert Clarence, 25
LeBeau, Walter, 96
Lee, James, 89, 91
Lemon, Louise, 86
LeNoire, Rosetta, 252
Lewis, James, 178
Lewis, Sam, 200
Lewis, Willie Frank, 150
Lightener, Gwendolyn Cooper,
    182–83, 210
Ligon, Willie Joe, 239–40
lining out, 7
Little Richard, 192, 255, 257
Lockhart Singers, 232–33
Lockhart, Esther, 232
Lomax, John, 97
Lorraine Ellison Singers, 253
Love, Dorothy McGriff, *see* Dorothy
    Love Coates
Love, Willie, 33, 150
Lucius "Lucky" Millinder jazz
    orchestra, 155
Lucy Smith Singers, 79
Lux Singers, 103
mail order industry, 53
Majestics, 128–29
Malone, Early, 146
Manhattan Conservatory of Music,
    72
Martin and Morris Music, Inc., 63,
    66, 74, 92
Martin Singers, 71
Martin, Cora, 92, 93
Martin, Johnny, 239
Martin, Roberta, 60, 63, 66–69, *67*,
    79, 227
Martin, Sallie, 57, *58*, 62–64
    Azusa Street Revival, 62
    and Bradford, Alex, 228
    California, 205
    daughter, 207

and King, Martin Luther Jr., 64
Nigeria, 64
Sallie Martin Singers, 92–93
and Smith, Willie Mae Ford, 136
and the Ward Singers, 104
Martin-Frye Quartet, *see* Roberta Martin Singers
Martin-Moore, Cora, 207
Mary J. Small Singers, 118
Mary Johnson Davis Gospel Singers, 118
Mason, Charles Harrison, 20, 22–24, 36, 57, 138
Mason, Mary, 123
May, Brother Joe, 131, 134, 136–38, 257
McCary, Samuel, 147–50
McDonald, Louise, 225
McDowell, Josephine, 112
McGriff Singers, 217–18
McKenny, Roasalie, 89
McKissick, Norsalus, 67, 72
McKissick, Sarah, 79
McLeod, Dorothy, 234
McPhatter, Clyde, 191
McPherson, Aimee Semple, 93
McPherson, Ellis, 34
McQueen, Norman, 32
Meditation Singers, 127–28
Memphis, 145
Merritt, Theresa, 251
message songs, 239
Methodist Church, 8, 14, 19
Methodist Episcopal Church, 27
Metropolitan Community Church Gospel Chorus, 65
Meyers, Johnny, 88
Midnight Musicals at COGIC, 125, 126
Mighty Clouds of Joy, 239
Millender, Lucky, 47
Miller Singers, 166
Miller, Alfred, 163, 165, 166, 168
Miller, Mildred Madison, 212, 215
Miller, Professor Albert, 254
Mills Brothers, 44
minors, 119
Mitchell Christian Singers, 47
Mitchell, Lillian, 128
Moore, Gatemouth, 255
Morganfield, Willie, 240
Morris, Ella Mae, 112
Morris, Kenneth, 63, 72–76, 92, 93
mother songs, 201, 202, 224
Mount Calvary Work of Faith Church, 222
Mount Pilgrim Baptist Church, 95
Mount Zion Fire Baptized Holiness Church, 114, 119

Movin' On Up, 83
moving to the music, *see also* shouting, 9, 18, 19
Mt. Helm Baptist Church, 20
Mumford, Gene, 164
Musical Department for COGIC, 124
Myers, Johnny, 86
Myles, John, 176
Naional Quartet Association, 98
National Baptist Convention Publishing Board, 26, 43
National Baptist Convention, 42, 82
Bradley, J. Robert, 144
Campbell, Lucie E., 139, 140
Chicago, 57
Davis, Mary, 118
Dixie Humingbirds, 121
Dorsey, Thomas A., 59
gospel support, 43
Hines, J. Earle, 206
Jackson, Emma L., 76
Jackson, Mahalia, 88, 91
loses importance, 125
May, Joe, 137
Smith, Willie Mae Ford, 135
St. Louis, 134
Ward Trio, 105
National Baptist Music Convention, 65
National Camp Meeting Association for the Promotion of Holiness, 13
National Convention of Gospel Choirs and Choruses, Inc., *see* NCGCC
NCGCC, 61, 65
Negro Spirituals, Volume Two of American, 150
New Pleasant Grove Singers, 96
New York Gospel Organ Guild, 168–69
New York, 152–69
Newberry, Willie Mae Brooks, 214
Newport Jazz Festival, 91, 122, 136, 188
nightclubs, 189
Nix, Reverend W. M., 59
Noble, Gene, 53
Norfleet Brothers, 237
Norwood Singers, 224
Norwood, Dorothy, 223–25
Nubin, Katie Bell, 154, 155
Nubin, Rosetta, *see* Sister Rosetta Tharpe
Nugrape Twins, 40
O'Neal Twins, 24, 245
Oakley Memorial Church of God in Christ, 111
Oedipus, 202
Oliver, Paul, 41

oom-ma-lank-a-lank-a-lank, 95, 165
Opportunity Baptist Church, 207
organists, 221
Original Gospel Harmonettes, 107, 191, 212–18, *213, 214, 215*
Orioles and Sonny Til, 192
Owens, Fred, 119
Owens, Henry, 44
Owens, Paul, 176–77, 203
Pace Jubilee Singers, 57
Pace Music House, 73
Pace, Charles Henry, 57, 73
Page, Emmett Morey, 36
Parham, Charles, 13, 15–16
Parham, Kitty, 111, *230, 232*
Parker, Hattie, 57
Parks, Barney, 119
Parks, Reverend B. L., 203–4
Parnell, Clarence, 99
Patterson Singers, 235
Pentecostal/Holiness, 15
across the country, 103
Angelic Gospel Singers, 112
Baptist and Methodists, 41
blind singers, 38
concerts, 47
dress, 19
gospel band, 184
greetings, 19
influenced, 25
isolated behavior, 19
popularity, 18
shout songs, 24
white cogregations, 16
Perkins, Reverend Percell, 200
Person, Carrie Booker, 43
Peters, Arthur Atlas, 211
Peters, Lowell, 153
Petrillo, James C., 51
Philadelphia, 103–123
Phillips, Washington, 38, 50
pianists, 216
piano-accompanied gospel, 36, 47, 49–50, 68, 118–19, 195, 212–40
Picard, Herbert "Pee Wee," 133
Pickett, Wilson, *237, 255*
Pilgrim Baptist Church Junior Gospel Choir, 247
Pilgrim Travelers, 173–74, 193, *254, 255*
planting, 36–37
Pleasant, Earl A., 207
Pleasant, W. S., 20
Plymouth Rock Baptist Church, 83, 85
Price, Evelyn, 165
Price, "Sammie" Blythe, 156, 251
promotion, 56, 254
Protective Harmoneers, 226
publishing houses, 102

Pugh, Sullivan and Iola, 246–67
Purlie, 253
quartet, 29–35, 36, 204
    appearance, 94
    Chicago, 93–95
    Detroit, 132
    Europe, 253
    female, 135, 145
    "Hootenanny," 190
    Jefferson County, 31
    Memphis, 145
    New York, 153
    piano-accompanied, 195, 212
    secular stars, 255
    soloist-oriented, 94–95
    style, 179
    universities, 29
race records, 41, 44
Radio City Music Hall, 47, 159
Radio Four, 178
radio stations, 52–53
radio, 44, 45, 47, 52–53
    Bostic, Joe, 168
    Fairfield Four, 148
    first quartet, 153
    "Hootenanny," 190
    Jackson, Mahalia, 89, 90, 91
    Original Gospel Harmonettes, 214
    Philadelphia, 123
    Soul Stirrers, 97
    Swan Silvertones, 176
    Trumpeteers, 171
Rainey, Gertrude "Ma," 58, 85
Rains, Margie, 249
Raisin, 253
raising, *see* lining out
Randy's Record Shop, 53
Rasberry Singers, 229
Rasberry, Raymond, 229
Ravens, 192
Ravizee Singers, 33, 34
Rawles, Lou, *254*, 255
reading music, 63
record companies, 41, 123
recordings, 51–54, 257
recreational dramatics, 250
Reddick, Clyde, 44
Reed, Robert, 146
Reese, Della, 111, 127–28, 255, 257
Refuge Church of Our Lord Jesus
    Christ of the Apostolic Faith, 25
Reid, LeDella, 103
Renfro, Sister Jessie Mae, 179
reprise, immediate, 110
Revival Movement, *see* Camp
    Meeting Revival
revival, 12
rhthm and blues, 51, 191–92
rhythm section, 50
Rice, D. C., 25

Richardson, Charles, 236
Richardson, Lee, 236
Richardson, Reverend W. L., 149
Richbourg, John "John R," 53
ring shout, 9
Robert Anderson's Good Shepherd
    Music House, 72
Roberta Martin School of Music, 68
Roberta Martin Singers, 66–68, *67*,
    78, 168, 205, 218, 253
Roberts, Freida, 249
Roberts, Lawrence, 247
Roberts, Reverend Lawrence,
    249–50
Roberts, William, 57, 152
Robinson, Cleophus, 245–46
Robinson, R. B., 196
Rogers, Willie, 196
Rosette Gospel Singers, 158
Royal Gospel Singers, 217
Ruffner, Elmer, 145
Rufus, James, 33
Run, Little Chillun, 250
Rundless, Earnestine, 127
Rundless, Edward R., 96
Rupe, Art, 228
Russell Steet Usher Board Four, *see*
    the Flying Clouds
Russell, Nipsey, 251
Ruth, Thurmon, 152, 163–65
Sallie Martin Colored Ladies
    Quartet, 93
Sallie Martin Singers, 64, 92–93,
    112
Sanctified Singers, 40
Sanders, Sister Sallie, 40
Sankey, Ira David, 16
scams, 54, 56
Scott, George, 201
Scott, Hazel, 251
Scruggs, Anna, *see* Anna Tuell
Scruggs, Fay, *see* Fay Adams
Second Great Awakening, *see* Camp
    Meeting Revival
secular style gospel, 158
Selah Jubilee Singers, 152, 163–65,
    164, 255
Sellers, John, 240, 251
Sensational Nightingales, *203–5*
sentimentals, 119
sermonette, 100
Settle, Reverend Glenn T., 181
Seymour, William Joseph, 13, 14,
    15
Shelby, Thomas, 133, 145, 205, 206
Sherrill, Ed, 33
Sherwood, William Henry, 26
Shird, Lucille, 112
Shirley Caesar Outreach Ministries,
    222
shout music, 24, 25
shouting, 9, 15, 19, 41, 43, 94

Silver Leaf Quartet, 33, 34
Simmons, Dorothy, 92, 209
Simmons, Horace, 132
Simmons-Akers Duo, 92
Simmons-Akers Singers, 208
Simms, Charles, 145
Simon, Paul, 122
Simpkins, Robert, 169
Sky Pilot Choir, 208
Skylarks, 236
Slave Songs of the United States,
    9, 12
slaves, 6–7, 9–10, 77
Small, Reverend B. J., 118
Smallwood Singers, 207
Smallwood, Eugene Douglas, 207
Smith, "Little" Lucy, 78–79
Smith, Bessie, 85
Smith, Edward M., 250
Smith, Eugene, *67*, 69, 70
Smith, Harold Eugene, 128–29
Smith, Homer, 153
Smith, Julia Mae, 92
Smith, Lonnie, 170
Smith, Melvin, 34
Smith, Reverend Lucy, 78
Smith, Wille Mae Ford, 63,
    134–36, *135*
Sons of Thunder, 185
Songbirds of the South, 225
Songsters and Saints, 41
soul music, 192
Soul Revivers, 103
Soul Stirrers, 52, 95–98, 100,
    195–99, *197*
Sounds of the South, 185
Southern Junior Girls, 146
Southern, Eileen, 12
Southernaires, 45, 52, 153
Sowing in Tears, Reaping in Joy, 143
speaking in tongues, 13, 14, 15
Spirit of Memphis, 101, 146–47
Spiritual Echoes, 111, 112
spiritual, 9, 12, 17, 47
Spirituals Triumphant, Old and New,
    26
Spoleto Festival of Two Worlds,
    69, 253–54
St. Louis, 134–38
St. Paul Baptist Church Choir, 181
Stallworth, Elmer, 132
Staple Singers, *241–42*
stardom, 110
Starks, Evelyn, 212
Stars of Faith, 111, *230–32*, 252
Staten, Candi 255
Steadman, Frances, 111, 232
Steele, Silas, 99–101, 146–47
Stevens, Herman, 165, 234
Stewart, Calvin, 172
Stewart, Princess, 133, 252, 253
Stewart, Walter, 123

Storey, Charlie, 152
street meetings, 37, 242
Sumler, Sally, 40
Sunset Harmonizers, 158
Sunset Jubilee Singers, 165
Swan Silvertones, 52, *175–78*
Swanee Quintet, 178
swing lead, 97
Tabernacle Baptist Church, 124
Taggart, Joe, 39, 50
Take Six, 65, 259
Tambourines to Glory, 251–53
Tampa Red, 58, 59
Taylor, Billy, 156
Taylor, Johnnie, 98, 196, 236, 255
Taylor, Professor Charles, 234, *235*
Taylor, Raphael, 176
Taylor, Richard, 174
Taylor, Melinda, 40
Taylor, Spencer, 236
television, 122, 190, 257
Temple Church of God in Christ, 25
Tennessee, 138–51
Terrel, Forrest, 146
Terrell, Sister O. M., 179
Terry, Neely, 13
Tharpe, Sister Rosetta, *85*, 153–59
    and Carr, Wynona, 130
    COGIC, 24
    and Harmonizing Four, 170
    jazz, 47
    recordings, 88
    secular, 255
    and Terrell, Sister O. M., 179
Thatch, William, 34
The Apostolic Faith, *15*, 16
Theater Owners Booking Associa-
    tion, 58
Thomas, Bob, 132
Thomas, Olice, 201
Thompson, Beachy, 122
Thorne Crusaders, 247
Three Sons of Thunder, 207, 211
Thurston, Oralee, 78
Tidewater quartet movement, 34
Tindley Gospel Singers, 43
Tindley Seven, *see* Tindley Gospel
    Singers
Tindley Temple Methodist
    Episcopal Church, 43
Tindley, Charles Albert, 27–28, 43,
    44, 70, 118
TOBA, *see* Theater Owners Booking
    Association
Toney, Jay Stone, 153
Townsend, Willa A., 42
travel, 54–57
Travelers, *see* the Pilgrim Travelers
Traylor, Velma Bozman, 201
Trumpeteers, the CBS, 171–72
Tucker, Ira, 121, *122*
Tuell, Anna, 165, *167*

Turnage, Raleigh, 171
Turner, Kylo, 173, 174
"TV Gospel Time," 190
Twilight Gospel Singers, 254
under the spirit, 17, 18
Union, Joe, 132
United House of Prayer for All
    People, Church on the Rock
    of the Apostolic Faith, Inc.,
    184–85
United Methodist Church, 27
Utica Jubilee Quartet, 153
Vails, Donald, 240
Valentines, *see* the Womack
    Brothers
vamp, 110, 141–42
Verdell, Jacqui, 117
Victory Baptist Church, 211
Violinaires, 236
Voices of Hope Choir, 210
"Voices of Victory," 211
Waddy, Henrietta, 105, 111, 230,
    231
Wade, Theo, 146
Walker, Albertina, 71, 218–20, *219*
Walker, James, 122
Walker, Madame Edyth, 145
Wallace, Joseph "JoJo," 204
Wallace, Richard, 239
Wallace, Rosie, 233
Walls, Bernadine, 249
Ward Singers, *4*, 104–111, *104,
    106, 109*
    Apollo, 191
    and Davis, Virginia, 80
    Europe, 253
    influenced Little Richard, 192
    Newport Jazz Festival, 188–89
Ward Trio, 105
Ward, Billy, 191–92
Ward, Clara, *4*, 104–5, 107, 108,
    109, 110–11
    and Franklin, Aretha, 129
    piano, 119
    stage, 251, 252
    and Williams, Marion, 230
Ward, Gertrude, *104*, 105, 118
Ward, Willarene, 104, 105
Warwick, Dionne, 133
Warwick, Mancel, 133
Washington, Delores, 225
Washington, Dinah, 89, 92, 93, 104
Washington, Ernestine B., 47, *85*,
    161–63, 253
Washington, Rev. Frederick D.,
    162, 163
Washington, Rufus, 178
Waters, Ethel, 33
Waters, Marie, 128
Watson, John Fanning, 8,9
Watson, Romance, 67
Watts, Isaac, 6

Webb, Willie, 67, 70, 78
Weber, Ozella, 78
Wendell Phillips High School,
    66, 196
Wesley, John, 6
Weston, Dave Carl, 211
Whispering Serenaders, 58
Whitaker, Jesse, 173
Whitefield, George, 6
Whittaker, Hudson, *see* Tampa Red
Wildcats Jazz Band, 58
Williams, "Gospel Joe," 169–71
Williams, Charles, 123
Williams, Eddie, 225
Williams, J. Mayo "Ink," 88
Williams, L. K., 42
Williams, Leroy, 33
Williams, Louis, 123
Williams, Marion,
    Europe, 253
    stage, 252
    Stars of Faith, 111, 229–32,
        230, 231
    Ward Singers, *4*, 105, 107,
        108, 117
Williams, Melva, 92
Williams, Riley Felman, 36–37
Williams, Ronnie, 50
Williams, Smallwood Edmond, 25
Willie Webb Singers, 227
Willingham, Reuben W., 178
Wilson, Jackie, 192
Wilson, Mattie, *58*
Wilson, Orlando, 44
Winans, 259
Windom, A. B., 134, 138
Wings of Healing Gospel Choir, 210
Wings Over Jordan Choir, 52, 75,
    131, 171
"Wings Over Jordan," 181
Wise Singers, 66
Wise, Bertha, 67
Wiz, the, 253
Womack Brothers, 255
Womack, Bobby, 98, 255
Womack, Solomon, 175–76
Women's International Convention
    of the COGIC, 124
women, 100, 103, 114, 118, 154
Woodard, Lloyd, 200
Work, John W. III, 148
working out, *see* planting
Wright, Arthur, 146
Wright, Overton Vertis, 236, 255
Yancey, Elyse, 218
Yes, Lord!, 23
Youth Choir of the Metropolitan
    Community, 65
Zion St. John Jubilee Singers, 169